D1826030

Disrupting Hierarchy in Education

Students and Teachers Collaborating for Social Change

EDITED BY

Hakim Mohandas Amani Williams
Hana Huskić
Christina M. Noto

Foreword by Antonia Darder
Afterword by Monisha Bajaj

TEACHERS COLLEGE PRESS

TEACHERS COLLEGE | COLUMBIA UNIVERSITY
NEW YORK AND LONDON

Published by Teachers College Press,® 1234 Amsterdam Avenue, New York, NY 10027

Copyright © 2024 by Hakim Mohandas Amani Williams, Hana Huskić, and Christina M. Noto

Front cover image: Anna Atkins (1799–1871) and Anne Dixon (1799–1864), *Papaver rhoeas*, from a presentation album to Henry Dixon, 1861, cyanotype. Private collection, courtesy of Hans P. Kraus Jr., New York.

All rights reserved. No part of this publication may be reproduced or transmitted in any form or by any means, electronic or mechanical, including photocopy, or any information storage and retrieval system, without permission from the publisher. For reprint permission and other subsidiary rights requests, please contact Teachers College Press, Rights Dept.: tcpressrights@tc.columbia.edu

Library of Congress Cataloging-in-Publication Data is available at loc.gov

ISBN 978-0-8077-6976-8 (paper)
ISBN 978-0-8077-6977-5 (hardcover)
ISBN 978-0-8077-8242-2 (ebook)

Printed on acid-free paper
Manufactured in the United States of America

Hakim: Dedicated to Nora Simmons, Celia Williams, Dr. Marlon Collins, and the ancestors who watch over me

Hana: Dedicated to my teachers in Kakanj, Mostar, and Gettysburg

Christina: Dedicated to my first teachers, Glen Noto and Mary Velez (parents), and my first student, Maria Noto (sister), all of whom are now my learning partners

Contents

PART II: INSTITUTIONALIZING SOCIAL CHANGE: SKILLS AND PROGRAM DEVELOPMENT

PART III: REFLEXIVITY AND CONSCIENTIZATION FOR SOCIAL CHANGE

Foreword

Decolonizing Hierarchy as a Revolutionary Act

> For the master's tools will never dismantle the master's house. They may allow us temporarily to beat him at his own game, but they will never enable us to bring about genuine change.
>
> —Audre Lorde (1983)

Disrupting Hierarchy reminds me of Audre Lorde's poignant words to feminist scholars and activists at the Institute for the Humanities Conference in 1979. Forty-four years later, similar questions about social change and the perpetuation of what seem to be recalcitrant structures of human oppression continue to perplex our struggles for liberation. What is compelling about this edited volume by Hana Huskić, Christina M. Noto, and Hakim Mohandas Amani Williams is that it seriously attempts to grapple, pedagogically and politically, with the concept of hierarchy and its traumatic consequences on our educational system and the larger society, beyond simply advancing social critiques. Instead, contributors earnestly wrestle to reveal ways of disrupting hierarchical thinking and practices *at the root*—essential to building revolutionary consciousness, mobilization, and organization "for the defense of rights [and] for laying claim to justice" (Freire, 1976, p. 40).

This is vitally important, for without embodying a grounded decolonizing praxis to overcome wretched binaries, unjust meritocracy, and elitist foundations of education, the necessary level of resistance and revolutionary transformation required for substantive social change is impossible; leaving us to participate endlessly in an exercise of moving the furniture, from here to there, but leaving the basic structure of the room unchanged. This, of course, was Audre Lorde's major concern—as long as we remain trapped in an abyssal epistemological prison, responsible for social inequalities and exclusions in the first place, transforming society will remain an impossible affair. For veteran educators and activists in the struggle for liberation, who are watching with much frustration at our past gains in educational, labor, and women's rights being undone by the proponents of dehumanizing neoliberal policies, *Disrupting Hierarchy* is a much-appreciated endeavor that reignites radical hope.

> You have to act as if it were possible to radically transform the world and do it all the time.

> —Angela Davis (2014)

Angela Davis's words echo the passion and spirit that the editors of *Disrupting Hierarchy* bring to their readers. Beyond the rhetoric of social change, they call for transformative action—action with the capacity to rupture the tyranny of hierarchy in schools and society. Yet they recognize that the process of disrupting hierarchy, albeit a formidable act, can often be uncertain, messy, and uncomfortable. Thus, such a worthy political intent requires us to labor courageously and forthrightly within classrooms and communities to build a liberatory praxis anchored in a vision of the world we seek to create together. True to this revolutionary intent, the chapters in this book signal a powerful decolonializing praxis to dismantle the debilitating relationships and practices of education that disrespect our differences and diminish our humanity.

Paulo Freire's spirit is indeed at the heart of the decolonizing vision for disrupting hierarchy presented in this volume. Dynamic approaches are presented that can prepare teachers and students for critical engagement with conditions that betray the promise of democratic life. Here, teachers and students labor together to make and remake knowledge, engendering new forms of knowing previously denied, invisibilized, negated, or unimagined. In contrast, contributors articulate a humanizing praxis, where the interdependence and value of all life remain central to our political struggle for a more loving and just world. Reminiscent of Freire's pedagogy of love, *Disrupting Hierarchy* speaks eloquently to forms of dialogue that can support the formation of critically empowered, historical subjects—human beings who are able and ready to decolonize hierarchy as a revolutionary act.

—Antonia Darder

REFERENCES

Freire, P. (1976). *Pedagogy of the oppressed*. Seabury Press.
Freire, P. (1998). *Pedagogy of freedom: Ethics, democracy and civic courage* (M. Ramos, Trans.). Rowman & Littlefield.
Lorde, A. (1983). The master's tools will never dismantle the master's house. In C. Moraga & G. Anzaldua (Eds.), *This bridge called my back: Writings by radical women of color*. Kitchen Table Press.

Acknowledgments

This project is, in large part, made possible by the generosity and kindness of many people. Please forgive us if we have inadvertently forgotten to list someone; the omission, however, does not in any way diminish their contributions or our appreciation.

First, thank you, authors, for your patience with this incredibly complex process with over 60 voices. Special thanks to (in alphabetical order): Liya Aklilu, Imran Ali, Matthew H. Amster, Camilla Arias, Bill Ayers, Monisha Bajaj, Grace Bamford, Jennifer Bloomquist, Kathryn Brautigam, Tonni-Ann Brodber, Milo cat, Adam Cordle, Antonia Darder, Kerima Delibašić, Elizabeth Dokas, Quincy Ellis, Mary Elmquist, Amy Young Evrard, former students in Hakim's Education for Social Change classes, Leslie François, Brooke Harris Garad, Rozina Gilani, Suzanne Gockowski, Maria Hantzopoulos, Dževdet and Sanida Huskić, Ekrem Huskić, Ismeta Huskić, Daniel Jones, tavis d. jules, Andrew Kadi, John Katunich, Austyn Knox, Venissa Ledesma, McKinley Melton, Lindora Myers, Kim Khánh Nguyễn Nalpas, Glen Noto, Maria Noto, Ellen Nye, Antonevia Ocho-Coultes, Julian Oddman, Emina Pjanić, Greg Robertson, Liz Rose, Denise Shaffer, Roozbeh Shirazi, Monica Solis, Emily Sprangler, Tabitha St. Bernard Jacobs, Brent Talbot, Ana Vashakmadze, Mary Velez, Janelle Wertzberger, Emily Wielk, Celia Williams, Jamali Williams, Amina Ame Zaimović, and Zeena Zakharia.

Artwork by Kathryn Brautigam

Modeling Prefigurative Praxes

Disruption for Social Change

Christina M. Noto, Hana Huskić,
and Hakim Mohandas Amani Williams

To disrupt: to break apart; to throw into disorder; to interrupt the normal course or unity of; to successfully challenge by using an innovation

—Merriam-Webster Dictionary, n.d.

"Authority is hierarchy's inseparable handmaiden."

—Leavitt, 2003

"The revolutionary educator . . . must engage with students in a quest for mutual humanization . . . to achieve this, they must be partners of the students."

—Freire, 2000, p. 75

"Knowledge alone will not effect change."

—Davis & Harrison, 2013, p. 83

"Decoloniality is a positive disruptor."

—Schockman et al., 2019, p. 6

"A decolonial approach . . . must fundamentally involve dismantling."

—Patel, 2016, p. 90

We are *not* waiting for tomorrow! All that we have tangibly before us is the here and now, and maximize it we shall! Hakim invited Hana and Christina (two of his former students) to coedit a book about the stories of students and teachers who disrupted hierarchy by collaborating on social change projects. Without thinking twice, they said yes. The yes was so immediate because we were all drawn to the idea of compiling a collection of positive praxes. We are also not satisfied with just critiquing all that is awry with education or just writing about interventions either. This book, and the process of co-constructing it, *is* our praxis as intervention; it is our own humble way of co-making the road by walking (Horton & Freire, 1990), that as we disrupt, we also build anew. However, disrupting hierarchy and building anew are practices not often intentionally and adequately taught/ modeled in schools. Instead, too many of us are socialized within punitive, competitive systems in which we see people and nature as usable and disposable. We cannot build equitable, revolutionary futures if students and teachers inhabit an imbalanced, toxic, oppressed–oppressor relationship.

Additionally, we are disturbed, but not surprised, by the persistence of varied hierarchies, colonial power structures, the arrogant minimizing of culturally different (i.e., non-Western) ways of being and knowing, and the plunder of our planet at all costs. These systemic ills render trauma that distorts social relations (Mishler, 1994). However, we are also aware that hierarchies (and the other named problems) do not exist everywhere, nor are they inevitable.

Many societies and social systems do possess hierarchies (Diefenbach, 2013). While there are some seeming benefits to hierarchies, such as being effective for large, complex tasks and addressing our desires for order and security, there are serious downsides; as authoritarian structures/systems of power and control, they can be exploitative and oppressive and can create fear, inflexibility, corruption, and conflict (Diefenbach & Todnem By, 2012; Leavitt, 2003; see Williams, 2016).

We therefore proceed with compassionate and joyful urgency; that is, we balance our work with deep care for self, each other, and the Earth while centering joy in collaborative creation, so that we retain stamina for when revolutionary tomorrows dawn. The critical urgency with which we work is premised on Vandana Shiva's exhortation that we have a "moral duty to not cooperate with exploitative and undemocratic processes that destroy the Earth and rob us of our humanity and our freedoms" (2018, p. 1; also see Mignolo's [2011] decolonial work, which urges us to delink from apparatuses of oppression).

We do acknowledge that this book project builds on a long lineage of critical work in education. Humans have long been disrupting hierarchies; we create structures and discourses whose logics then take on lives of their own, necessitating counterhegemonic interventions (i.e., critiquing or dismantling dominant power structures and relations). One example is early educational functionalism (i.e., the view that education should culturally socialize us and prepare us for specific societal roles), which reached its height in the Industrial Revolution. However, we still live in its long shadow because critical education (i.e., education that raises our consciousness toward liberation for all) is far from the norm in most schools, globally. Disrupting hierarchy to create just futures—as ethos and ethic, and as strategy and technique—(in education and beyond) continues to be imperative because the unsustainable accompaniments of human domination, deprivation, and dehumanization are clear: empire building, neofascism, civil wars, economic greed, hollowed-out democracy, and ecological crises.

Together, we set out to disrupt hierarchy via an Education for Social Change course (that Hakim offers every year), in which we read Paulo Freire's *Pedagogy of the Oppressed (PotO)* and became inspired by "Freire's constant and unstoppable ethics of solidarity and unrepentant utopianism" (McLaren, 2000, p. 13). In this book, co-authors describe some of the major themes from *PotO* that scaffold their projects:

- Banking education: A model of education where students are treated as receptacles of knowledge from the teacher and are expected to uncritically reproduce said knowledge.
- Problem posing education: The inverse of banking education; a collaborative model in which teacher and student, in critical dialogue, are coinvestigators of the world to then transform it.
- Non-neutrality: There is no such thing as neutrality in education (content and form); education either is an instrument that fosters conformity to the present system or it serves as a practice of freedom.
- Students' knowledge and experiential bases are valid, and therefore the teacher is also a student, and the student is also a teacher.
- Iteration: Using critical feedback to further experiment, revise and refine, and course correct.
- Praxis: A form of iteration in which the feedback loop of critical reflection and critical action is created by the student and teacher working together to change the world.
- Conscientization: The emergent and constantly deepening consciousness about the social, political, and economic conditions of the world, as the student and teacher co-strive toward co-liberation (Freire, 2000).
- Decoloniality: Decentering Western, colonialist, and imperialist hierarchies, and recognizing alternative ways of knowing and being in the world (n.b., Freire does not use this term explicitly in *PotO*, but the work itself is considered to be decolonial).

We gather these concepts in our book to demonstrate *how* disrupting hierarchies can be pursued by students and teachers.

However, we do not wish to uncritically idolize Freire or *PotO*. In fact, we have several critiques of (or related to) *PotO*, which is delightful because multilayered critique signals that his work is provocatively stimulating. Some of our critiques, among others, are the following:

- While critical dialogue is valuable, there are limits to it in terms of social change, especially in circumstances where there is stark power imbalance between parties in conflict.

- The oppressed–oppressor binary is not sufficiently nuanced because someone could inhabit both categories simultaneously based on their multiple and overlapping identities.
- Ironically, much of this work is dedicated to inspiring social change, but a significant portion is inaccessible because of the jargon.
- At times, this work is far too abstract and inadequate for practitioners who want usable tools.
- Freire centers class but seems to ignore or not engage as directly with other "isms," such as racism and sexism.

Nevertheless, despite these critiques, our aim in this book is to celebrate the revolutionary values that we believe can and should be continuously challenged, transformed, and customized for varied contexts. *PotO* is indeed quite idealistic, but aspirations can sometimes shift mindsets and practices. In this book, we feature projects that echo critical hope by merging this idealism with pragmatism. By operationalizing some Freirean concepts, the projects here demonstrate that possibility is not mere fantasy but an embodiment of (albeit flawed) human striving. In other words, Freirean concepts are not a perfectly defined blueprint but a set of generative values.

Compiling *Disrupting Hierarchy* models solidarity between two former students and their professor, who, through vulnerability, power sharing, and reciprocity, became learning partners in the classroom and beyond (Cook-Sather et al., 2014). We, and many of the coauthors, use the term "learning partners" as a stand-in for the Freirean terms "teacher–student" and "student–teacher," and to evoke an active disruption and dismantling of that too-often strict, hierarchical distance between "teacher" and "student." Each chapter is cowritten by "teacher(s)" and "student(s)," a purposeful act that is a form of disrupting hierarchy within the academy and the publishing world. In fact, most of the chapters are cowritten by multiple persons, resulting in a total of 64 participants in this book project. We conceptualize these learning partnerships *as* praxis and as a mutually symbiotic relationship between teaching and learning.

Therefore, this "strategic radicalism" (Yang, 2009, p. 455)—this intentional co-disruption—centers liberatory praxis as both means and ends. Our unapologetic utopianism informs the prefigurative praxis that we (Hakim, Hana, and Christina) are modeling as coeditors and co-curators of this intellectual and exhibition space for others who are using disruption and dismantling of hierarchies toward social change as a decolonial tool.

By prefigurative praxis, we mean that we embody, in the here and now, the synergy between reflection and action to enact elements of a future world that is more equitable, sustainable, and just (Boggs, 1977; Freire, 2000). Prefiguration is about enacting today—the best way we can—the world we envision for tomorrow; it is about our methodology for revolution and social change mirroring our visions of a better world. We, the coeditors and chapter coauthors, intentionally disrupt the traditional meanings of "student," "teacher," "classroom," "teaching," "learning," and "knowledge production." To model this kind of praxis—disrupting hierarchy via learning partnership—in academic and publishing arenas is decolonial social change in and of itself.

There is much theorization about Freirean praxis but few examples of *how* to do it with students and teachers as learning partners. A model for critical praxis as fleshed out by Gilbert and Marine (2021) is a useful framework. They suggest that critical reflection involves asking critical questions, reframing assumptions (i.e., questioning longstanding practices), and envisioning a better world, while critical action involves challenging dominant narratives, disrupting power dynamics, and resisting neoliberal forces (i.e., recognizing that the hierarchical and commodified aspects of education often dominate decision-making processes). This project represents and documents attempts at disrupting hierarchical logics, practices, and structures within education that constrain teachers and students within mutually exclusive categories; a constraint that prevents equitable student–teacher pursuits of collaboration, disruptions of the status quo, and social change–anchored coliberation.

Many of the chapters also address the complexities and challenges of dismantling hierarchy. The emergent narratives convey both the incredible courage and discomfort in the process of disrupting, whether the disruption is ongoing or discrete. The chapters therefore represent varied approaches to social change: Some are about folx working within institutional confines where they contest and stretch the boundaries of their respective contexts, and others are about creating new spaces and processes that exert pressure on the status quo. These chapters are in conversation with each other to nuance the either/or debate about the efficacy of working within or outside of institutions and systems (Horton & Freire, 1990).

We, as coeditors, issued a call for book abstracts focused on the theme of learning partners who disrupt hierarchy to collaboratively work on a social change project, and we received over 40 submissions. Selected chapters had to be cowritten by the "teacher(s)" and "student(s)"; it is too often the case that the "teachers" publish the documentation of the amazing projects they have done with their "students," but we wanted the chapters to reflect disrupting of hierarchy in terms of learning partners co-documenting the work that they had co-constructed.

Coauthors in the book are diverse: undergraduate and graduate students, youth advocates, professors, artists, curators, founders and leaders of NGOs, elementary school teachers, and one medical doctor. Some of these coauthors were under 10 years old or were in high school when they worked on these social change projects, and a number of them are from the Global South. With this abundance of ideas and perspectives, you will encounter different writing styles and formats; we relish and embrace this diversity, because we do not wish to reinforce particular hierarchies of knowledge production and articulations. For example, parts of some chapters are written in the first person or as a conversation, choices that are often not privileged in traditional academic writing/contexts. As you read each chapter, we invite you to enter the world of the coauthors, instead of approaching their work solely through your lens; this invitation, of course, need not be divorced from robust critical engagement.

The far-ranging topics with which the coauthors engage are community education, public writing, using media for popular education, adolescent and youth development, climate change education, peace and justice leadership development, revolutionary nonviolence, literacy teacher education, citizenship education, the development of Latin American Studies, palliative care, reflections on identity and subjectivity, anti-racism education, trauma-informed pedagogy, wellness, and art curation.

We sorted the selected chapters into three domains that we think are important to collaborative social change projects among learning partners:

- Engaging Different Publics for Social Change
- Institutionalizing Social Change: Skills and Program Development
- Reflexivity and Conscientization for Social Change

The first domain demonstrates how learning partners can create and implement projects that center public intellectualism and community engagement. We recognize that there is a spectrum of public spheres, and although some overlap, many of them have their own mores, goals, and audiences. The four chapters in this domain include learning partners in

- South Africa, collaboratively writing op-eds to amplify the voices of working-class youth;
- New York City, cocreating a radio show and newsletter about the legacy of the Black Panthers;
- a climate change and education course in Maryland, joining efforts to preserve a university campus forest from proposed development; and
- Brazil, using educommunication to reach millions of other teachers and students.

The second domain demonstrates how to create more structure and skills-/capacity-building for social change efforts so that their impact is neither short-lived nor easily diluted. Institutionalizing does not necessarily mean a physical institution or space but refers to creating more structure and capacity (whether it be legal, cultural, economic, etc.) that lends itself to longevity. The six chapters in this domain include learning partners in

- Pennsylvania, designing national projects to develop undergraduate student peace and justice leadership;

- the midwestern United States, starting an anti-racist network of multicultural scholars at a university;
- Texas, fostering research inquiries between preservice teachers and their elementary students on community-related issues;
- New York City, using people-centered curatorial practices to create a wellness studio for artists;
- Minnesota, leveraging skills from a university course to craft open access resources and plan a conference for youth development professionals; and
- Utah, storytelling/*platicando* about rebel studies that center Latine[1] identity.

The third domain demonstrates the kind of intra- and interpersonal critical reflection that is necessary to sustain social change work. Reflexivity (in critical pedagogy) refers to an intentional and constant reflection on one's actions, their impetus and impact; conscientization refers to a deepening analysis, understanding, and transformation of one's social reality via critical reflection and action (Freire, 2000). The two chapters in this domain include learning partners in

- South Africa, interrogating how identity and subjectivity impacted their PhD supervision relationship; and
- England, advocating for trauma-informed education in peace studies (and beyond).

The book ends with a chapter coauthored by the three coeditors in which we use the rhizome as metaphor to articulate a justice-grounded leadership model based on revolutionary relationships and solidarities among learning partners. A rhizome is a stem structure that grows horizontally underground and generates different stems in unpredictable directions; Deleuze and Guattari (1987) critique the hierarchical nature of Western rationality and linearity, in contrast to rhizomatic alternatives. We contend that modeling, scaling, and institutionalizing community-based iterative processes are key to resisting these kinds of critical projects, presented in this book, from being co-opted or diluted.

We hope that these chapters, in parts or as a whole, will speak broadly to multiple audiences: high school and college/university students; educators of all stripes; education consultants; leaders in public, private, and nonformal educational settings; teacher educators; community activists; scientists; artists; and scholars of critical pedagogy and peace education.

Each chapter ends with a few discussion questions and/or activities that might be generative for readers. We also invite readers to lead and/or join further engagement via our website: www.DisruptingHierarchy.com (under the *Praxis Forum* tab); this is our small contribution to facilitating what Sivanandan (1990) calls "communities of resistance."

Abujbara et al. (2018) contend that "[g]rassroots movements . . . are responding with astounding courage and creativity, even in the face of unspeakable violence. But to actually win, these social movements need ways to share, analyze, and learn from one another" (p. 5). In this spirit, we convened this project so that many can learn from the experimentations of other learning partners. We hope that this book, and the rich collaborations documented, encourage learning partners the world over to pursue their own beautifully audacious projects for social change.

DISCUSSION QUESTIONS/ACTIVITIES

1. Are there any social change projects you have pursued with and/or in community that have then been co-opted or diluted? If so, how did your community respond?
2. How do you coenvision bold new futures, and how do you prioritize different parts of your action plan, knowing that bold new futures, if they are to be sustained, will not be created overnight? What specific steps from a practical and theoretical lens can you take?
3. The feedback loop that emerges from the synergy between critical action + critical reflection is praxis. In your experience, what have been some obstacles to cementing this feedback loop, and what have you done to address them?
4. Because a decolonial approach must involve dismantling, how do we prepare ourselves for the possibly resultant disorientation and destabilization?
5. The three domains that we used for dividing up the chapters are not exhaustive. Apart from Engaging Different Publics for Social Change, Institutionalizing Social Change: Skills and Program Development, and Reflexivity and Conscientization for Social Change, what other domains do you think are pertinent to social change?

NOTE

1. In this book you will see both Latine or Latinx spellings; authors choose which term they prefer since there is not any settled consensus on either of these terms.

REFERENCES

Abujbara, J., Boyd, A., Mitchell, D., & Taminato, M. (2018). Introduction. In J. Abujbara, A. Boyd, D. Mitchell, & M. Taminato (Eds.), *Beautiful rising: Creative resistance from the Global South* (pp. 5–9). OR Books.

Boggs, C. (1977). Marxism, prefigurative communism and the problem of workers' control. *Radical America, 11*(6), 99–122. Retrieved from https://library.brown .edu/pdfs/1125404123276662.pdf

Cook-Sather, A., Bovill, C., & Felten, P. (2014). *Engaging students as partners in learning and teaching: A guide for faculty.* Jossey-Bass.

Davis, T., & Harrison L. (2013). *Advancing social justice: Tools, pedagogies, and strategies to transform your campus.* Jossey-Bass.

Deleuze, G., & Guattari, F. (1987). *A thousand plateaus: Capitalism and schizophrenia.* University of Minnesota Press.

Diefenbach, T. (2013). *Hierarchy and organisation: Toward a general theory of hierarchical social systems.* Routledge.

Diefenbach, T., & Todnem By, R. (2012). Bureaucracy and hierarchy—What else!? In T. Diefenbach & R. Todnem By (Eds.), *Reinventing hierarchy and bureaucracy: From the bureau to network organizations* (pp. 1–30). Emerald Group.

Freire, P. (2000). *Pedagogy of the oppressed* (M. Ramos, Trans.). Continuum.

Gilbert, C., & Marine, S. (2021). Conclusion: Social justice in action: A model for critical praxis. In S. Marine & C. Gilbert (Eds.), *Critical praxis in student affairs: Social justice in action* (pp. 196–213). Stylus.

Horton, M., & Freire, P. (1990). *We make the road by walking: Conversations on education and social change* (B. Bell, J. Gaventa, & J. Peters, Eds.). Temple University Press.

Leavitt, H. (2003). Why hierarchies thrive. *Harvard Business Review.* Retrieved from https://hbr.org/2003/03/why-hierarchies-thrive

McLaren, P. (2000). Paulo Freire's pedagogy of possibility. In S. Steiner, H. M. Krank, P. McLaren & R. Bahrut (Eds.), *Freirean pedagogy, praxis, and possibilities* (pp. 1–22). Routledge.

Mignolo, W. (2011). *The darker side of Western modernity: Global futures, decolonial options.* Duke University Press.

Mishler, E. (1994). Foreword. In A. Aron, & S. Corne (Eds.), *Writings for a liberation psychology by Ignacio Martín-Baró* (pp. vi–xiv). Harvard University Press.

Patel, L. (2016). *Decolonizing educational research: From ownership to answerability.* Routledge.

Schockman, H. E., Hernández, V., & Boitano, A. (2019). Introduction: On peace, reconciliation and social justice. In E. Schockman, V. Hernández, & A. Boitano (Eds.), *Peace, reconciliation, and social justice leadership in the 21st century: The role of leaders and followers* (pp. 1–10). Emerald.

Shiva, V. (2018). Foreword: The planetary satyagraha. In J. Abujbara, A. Boyd, D. Mitchell, & M. Taminato (Eds.), *Beautiful rising: Creative resistance from the Global South* (pp. 1–4). OR Books.

Sivanandan, A. (1990). *Communities of resistance: Writings on Black struggles for socialism.* Verso Books.

Williams, H. M. A. (2016). A neocolonial warp of outmoded hierarchies, curricula and disciplinary technologies in Trinidad's educational system. *Critical Studies in Education, 60*(1), 93–112. Retrieved from https://doi.org/10.1080/17508487 .2016.1237982

Yang, K. W. (2009). For and against: The school-education dialectic in social justice. In W. C. Ayers, T. Quinn, & D. Stovall (Eds.), *Handbook of social justice in education* (pp. 455–465). Routledge.

Part I

ENGAGING DIFFERENT PUBLICS FOR SOCIAL CHANGE

CHAPTER 1

"Our Ideas Were Welcomed"

Disrupting the Teacher/Student Binary in a Collaborative Writing Project With High School Students in South Africa

Ashley Visagie, Helene Rousseau, Taahirah Hoosain,
Imaan Adams, Jason Cloete, and Thea Mennas

This chapter reports on the experiences of youth and adult coauthors in collaborative writing activities, organized by Bottomup, an organization involved in political education and youth work in Cape Town, South Africa. Focal points discussed include how young people from marginalized communities interrupt the status quo by inserting their (counter-)stories into the public sphere and mainstream news, how teacher–student hierarchical relations may be disrupted in the process and production of cowritten texts, and the challenges that must be navigated in attempting to do so. We begin by introducing the context of the Cape Flats in order to render this writing intelligible to an international audience.

> I'm that mass marcher and tyre burner
> Minimal wage sub-economic earner
> I'm that doctor, lawyer and politician in the ghetto
> Wait a minute . . . Most of them have moved out though
> —Emile YX?

Emile YX? represents a generation of hip-hop artists hailing from the Cape Flats. His lyrics above allude to the histories of colonialism, apartheid, and dispossession that are inscribed in the bodies of youth, the way in which young people have been part of resistance movements, as well as the intensifying class stratification in the Cape Flats in contemporary South Africa (SA).

The Cape Flats is a subeconomic area to which many people classified as "Colored" under apartheid were relocated through the forced removals of the 1950s Group Areas Act. So-called "Colored" neighborhoods were co-located with factories and separated from wealthier suburbs by highways, canals, railways, and industrial buffer zones. Nearly 30 years after the first democratic election in 1994, the spatial divides in the city persist; while formerly White areas have become racially mixed, middle-class neighborhoods, the township and ghettos, like the Cape Flats, remain spaces in which Black working-class and poor families are concentrated (Crankshaw, 2012).

In terms of schooling and education, the deracialization of schools, which began in the early 1990s, resulted in limited mobility for a fraction of families who could afford to remove their children from under-resourced Cape Flats schools and send them to formerly White suburban schools.

The result of deracialization has similarly intensified class divides in South African schools, and while schools have become more racially integrated, they have done so in different ways. Formerly White schools are now the most racially diverse schools in the country but continue to exclude poor families through high fees (Gruijters et al., n.d.). Formerly Black schools have also diversified but continue to serve mainly Black families as students move from one township or ghetto to another in the hope of finding a better school. Immigrant youth, mainly from Southern African Development Community nations (a regional bloc focused on economic development), are also seeking a more sustainable future in South Africa and, generally, find access to schools in the urban townships and ghettos.

While the Cape Flats is often portrayed in popular media as a wasteland or gangland, it was in fact a site of political struggle and a hotbed of student resistance and politics, which came to a peak in the 1980s when students hosted mass rallies, participated in political awareness programs, and ceremonially "reopened" schools that had been temporarily closed during the 1985 state of emergency. The government had declared this state of emergency because of an upsurge in violent and nonviolent resistance to apartheid, and because schools were being used as sites to organize student resistance (Bundy, 1987).

Out of these radical student organizations and their student representative councils came the ideas for deepening democracy through the inclusion of students within school governance structures. In the postapartheid period, however, legislation now exists to legitimize student involvement by mandating representative councils of learners (RCLs) while also constraining student participation and depoliticizing the role of student leadership (see Mathebula, 2017). For example, the provincial gazette concerning RCLs (Western Cape Government, 2014) states that only two students have voting rights in school decisions on the School Governing Body (SGB). This implies that students may raise their concerns but may be effectively ignored because they are an insignificant voting bloc. The government gazette also states that before an RCL's constitution is established, it must be approved by the governing body. This limits the scope and foci of what RCL groups do in schools. Consequently, this means that the RCL is often treated as a vassal body within school governance.

In addition to the structural conditions that result in a material lack and the discursive construction of the ideal student in policy frameworks that limit engagements, many students on the Cape Flats also face significant challenges at home and in religious communities where obedience and respect are conflated (Murris, 2012); students who challenge adults on any matter tend to be viewed as disrespectful or troublemakers. When students choose to act, they may be accused of being "brainwashed" or used by other adults. In short, the oppression youth face is intersectional and systemic and hampers equal participation in school and society.

Within this context, we, the coauthors, engaged as co-constructors in knowledge production, attempting to interrupt dominant narratives about students and schools on the Cape Flats. The insertion of student voices into mainstream newspapers reflects the liberatory, hierarchy-disrupting practices discussed in this chapter, and while empowerment does result from this, we also confront the challenges involved in the process of collaborative writing itself. We discuss writing as a disruptive "praxis" and why it matters in contexts where young people are silenced and where being heard so frequently requires what Mark Hunter (2019) describes as "White tone" (i.e., Whiteness as embodied by stereotypically White characteristics, linguistic repertoires, and cultural arbitraries that carry prestige in South Africa's racialized market of schooling).

Bottomup, a grassroots organization based in Cape Town, South Africa, and started in November 2007, works with high school students from the Cape Flats. Bottomup is concerned with the way the schooling system serves to reproduce race and class inequalities in South Africa. The organization engages with high school student leaders like the youth coauthors of this chapter. Bottomup facilitates various programs for high school students to develop skill sets (e.g., critical visual literacies through creative expressions and critical literacies through reading, writing, and communicating for social change) that allow them to advocate for issues important to them.

The projects highlighted in this chapter are the Writing for Justice club and the Student Assembly. The Writing for Justice club works with students who want to use their voice through writing, and the Student Assembly offers space for young people to meet, discuss issues, and work together to effect change. All of Bottomup's projects begin with helping participants develop a *critical* sociological imagination (i.e., an awareness of power imbalances in society and how they affect us), to analyze problems more deeply, and to avoid a deficit mindset. We use critical participatory methodologies, anchored in critical social theory and inspired by the work of Paulo Freire, Augusto Boal, bell hooks, and other critical pedagogues.

Together, we identify issues and engage in dialogue to understand the root causes. For example, a problem identification may begin with the symptoms (e.g., disruption in the classroom), but through dialogue, we investigate systemic contributing factors such as overcrowded classrooms, lack of teachers, shortages of textbooks, general under-resourcing, and student alienation. A crucial part of this process also involves identifying what needs to change (e.g., better funding for schools? hiring more teachers?). Participants then propose a course of action that includes how to address the problem and what strategies of advocacy and activism they want to use. Through this work, we begin to disrupt the teacher–student binary by working in ways that center students' voices and place value on their ideas and opinions.

CONCEPTUALIZING SOCIAL RELATIONS IN EDUCATION

As co-participants engaged in self-reflective critique, we recruit the conceptual tools of Freire (problem-posing, humanizing pedagogy), Fraser (participatory parity), and Biesta (subject–subject relations) to analyze the writing group's experience:

> Teachers and students (leadership and people), co-intent on reality, are both Subjects, not only in the task of unveiling that reality, and thereby coming to know it critically, but in the task of re-creating that knowledge. (Freire, 2000, p. 69)

A central concern in Freire's body of work, which is contrasted with "banking" education, is a humanizing and problem-posing pedagogy: teachers and students relating to each other as subjects, co-constructing knowledge, and cocreating the world (Freire, 2000).

Freire's terms—"teacher–student" and "student–teacher"—are an attempt to overcome binary categories and to recognize how both have knowledge and experiences to offer. For Freire, reframing educational encounters stems from understanding that liberation of oppressed and marginalized people depends on their conscious action or "limit-acts" in the world to transform oppressive conditions or "limit-situations" (Freire, 2000, p. 97).

Such critical consciousness, Freire believes, is possible through the collective investigation of generative themes and cannot be bestowed on others through manipulation and propaganda. In the writing group, we come together as concerned citizens reflecting on inequalities and social injustices and use our writing to "speak back" or to "speak truth to power." We remain conscious that within the group we also had to wrestle against the ways in which traditional relations between participant teachers and students, or adult "facilitators" and youth "participants," tend to shape (and be shaped by) spaces for thinking against the grain.

The practical challenges, for example, include how adults manage their mobilization of specialized disciplinary knowledge in ways that benefit the process without controlling it. For participants, often a challenge in a radical space involves allowing oneself to speak freely, whereas in other spaces such expression is hampered. For example, in a classroom setting, students often are required to regurgitate information without needing to critically evaluate the subject content or having the ability to express their opinions. In traditional classroom settings, students are often marginalized due to assumptions about age, life experience, and assessment practices that promote "teaching to the test." These, and many others, are contributing factors that limit students from being more expressive and confident.

Drawing on Nancy Fraser et al.'s (2004) framework that conceptualizes social justice issues along three domains—namely, problems of re/distribution (economy), issues of recognition (identity), and issues of representation (participation and democracy)—we discuss the disadvantageous ways in which students on the Cape Flats are positioned within the field of power (the political sphere).

First, youth from the Cape Flats are located at the lower end of the economy in a nation that has some of the most class inequality (Sulla et al., 2022). Second, the historical legacies of colonialism and apartheid persist through contemporary issues of coloniality in which markers such as a strong command of a particular variety of English, and the mannerisms and bodily deportment that accompany this, are still considered to be "capitals" (Bourdieu, 1986) rather than cultural arbitraries. Finally, social class locations and race identities are co-constituted and translate into a situation where voices "from below" are marginalized. Race is no longer explicitly coded into the law and policy, but it remains difficult to be heard without having or acquiring the capitals (economic, social, and cultural) to make one's voice heard.

The newspaper thus represents a sphere of cultural production in which these inequalities are acutely expressed, often requiring a tone and register much more easily acquired in schools serving White and middle-class families. This reality presented a challenge to the writing group as we attempted to breach the barrier of getting published in mainstream newspapers; we would also have to confront the ways in which the mode of writing would inadvertently structure relations in the writing group.

Lastly, we recruit Gert Biesta's (2016) mobilization of Buber's "I and thou" or subject-to-subject relations, recognizing that truly democratic educational experiences are manifested in the meeting of both teacher and student as human beings capable of thinking for themselves. Where Freire critiques the banking mode of education, Biesta cautions against the "learnification" (Biesta, 2019) of education that places students at the center and turns the teacher into an object or merely a "facilitator" of a learning experience. We take Freire's and Biesta's views not in conflict with each other but as complementary views that encourage teachers and students to bring their full selves, knowledge, and experience into learning and to meet as coinvestigators in exploring the world.

In the section that follows, we introduce the projects that inform our discussion and reflect on these collaborative writing and advocacy projects with the benefit of the conceptual tools that we have presented. The collaborative writing projects referred to in this chapter include three examples: (1) an independent newspaper opinion piece written by three grade 12 participants and a PhD student; (2) a collaborative piece produced within a student club called "Writing for Justice"; and (3) the Student Assembly, an initiative of youth participants to form an interschool forum of student representatives.

THEORIZING OUR EXPERIENCES

Writing Together as "Praxis"

Leveraging Freire's notion of critical praxis, we view the activity of collaborative writing as praxis in which we reflect together on social injustices and, through the act of writing, insert our voices into the public sphere in an attempt to interrupt dominant discourses about students from the Cape Flats.

Emile YX?, cited in the opening of this chapter, was part of a hip-hop crew who fought the apartheid regime with words, arts, and cultural production. Similarly today, we recognize that for young people from the Cape Flats, to write can be a form of activism, especially within the context of a school system that is underfunded and inadequately equipped. The progressive reduction in spending on education dispossesses students of meaningful educational opportunities, where apartheid has already dispossessed their families through acts like the Industrial Conciliation Act of 1956 (a "color bar" in the workplace) and the Group Areas Act of 1950 (segregation of land and immovable property).

To write from the "bottom" of this system is to reject a logic that excludes marginalized voices as we demand to be part of the conversation. Yet, even though we see value in interrupting mainstream channels, we must also acknowledge and engage with the challenges and constraints of doing so while attempting to stay true to our principles.

Writing Together as an Unsettling Practice

The act of "students" and "teachers" writing *together* interrupts binaries by positioning students as coproducers of knowledge. A common experience in the conventional classroom for the student collaborators within this project is experiencing teacher–student relations as hierarchical and unidirectional. Contrasting experiences at school and in the writing groups, students expressed feelings of being respected or of being considered as capable beings when their ideas are welcomed and when they are expected to contribute. Very pertinently, the writing initiatives we present all engage with "real-world" problems that students identified, relate to, and care about. Equally important, the writing is for publication rather than assessment; in treating their products as having value beyond an assigned grade, this experience allows them to identify as writers rather than learners.

Of course, developing critical capacities and being encouraged to speak up also has the effect of unsettling the conventional classroom when students return with the self-knowledge that they are capable of both resisting certain power structures and binaries, and organizing to push for change that would enable all learners to be treated fairly.

When we highlight these contrasts, we do not do so with a deficit view of teachers at working-class schools. Rather, we consider how the conditions and contexts in which schooling takes place (the overcrowded classrooms, ailing infrastructure, lack of resources, and assessment regimes not discussed here) constrain pedagogical practices.

EXPERIENCES FROM THREE COLLABORATIVE WRITING ACTIVITIES

"The Matric Exams Are Unfair!" (Topic From a Writing Activity Organized via WhatsApp and Zoom)

At the height of the pandemic in 2020, schools shut down for long periods of time, yet grade 12 students in their final year of high school were put under tremendous pressure to prepare for the "matric exam" (a national senior certificate exit exam that determines access to higher education), despite having been out of school for an extended period of time and having missed substantial portions of work. This was most severe for students in working-class schools (the majority of South African schools) who did not have access to online learning and whose schools, even on reopening, could not continue with the regular program because their facilities were inadequate to meet the COVID-19 protocols, in contrast to fee-collecting schools where programs were minimally interrupted. The Stats SA Report on the impact of the pandemic on learning (https://www.statssa.gov.za/?p=15197) suggests that only 11.7% of South African schools were able to offer remote learning. We decided to write a newspaper article about the experience.

Taahirah (youth coauthor, age 19) offers a reflection:

When the start of the exams approached, we were able to see how the concept of banking education was deployed. That year it felt like the desire to have dialogue about the work was heavily frowned upon because of intensified pressure on teachers to finish the syllabus. It was particularly concerning to us as students who were already in positions that required us to be exceptional to beat the odds. At some point, the department was pushing for schools to return to normal during a time when vaccinations were not available, and people (teachers specifically) were dying. We recognized that the government was pushing for things to return to normal to "save the economy" but the poor would be disadvantaged no matter what. The economy needed schools to open up because they serve as child-care for parents who need to work in positions that were seen as essential services, positions that are severely underpaid. This also made us question the different purposes of schooling.

Not only did we want to raise awareness on the matter, but we also wanted people to hear the perspective of those most affected. We were appealing to the wider community to hear us and stand in solidarity with our situation.

We wrote that, because of school disruptions, we were not adequately prepared for exams. We were tested on content that was never taught to us, and because of space and staffing, we had to attend school on a rotational basis. We were also forced to write "mock exams" (school-administered) and National Senior Certificate (final school exit exams) within a two-month period.

The schools we attended are poorly positioned because of state funding structures. We wanted to write from this lens so that people could begin to understand the ways in which racialized capitalism works. For us, our futures were on the line, as universities in South Africa select students on the basis of the final Grade 12 results.

The writing process for the op-ed ("The Matric Exams Are Unfair!") took place at a time when there were hard lockdowns enforced and we had to work together digitally via mobile phones. The writing process was mediated through video calls, WhatsApp, and Google Docs. The matter was urgent, since the Department of Basic Education's decision-making about whether to administer the exam or not was happening quickly; this did not leave us with enough time for deep dialogue, and furthermore our online discussions as writers were made difficult by network connectivity problems. Collaboration was challenging in these circumstances, but we persisted.

In the Classroom (A Writing Activity Where Students Met to Write Together)

The second writing activity, initiated by Bottomup's Writing for Justice club, consisted of 15 high school students and two facilitators from Botttomup. The purpose of this group is for high schoolers to learn how to write for publication in both creative and critical ways and analyze relevant social issues.

In our first meeting, participants and facilitators discussed issues that have an impact on public schooling. Many issues were raised, but it became apparent that the conflicts that happen within our respective classrooms that restrict learning and teaching were deeply felt and widely shared in the group. In our second group meeting, we began to think sociologically and considered the systemic factors perpetuating these conflicts. The public policies that we discussed included the inexpedient poverty quintile funding system, which aims to distribute more funds to poorer schools but that in practice redistributes only a small portion of education funds in an equitable manner (20%) and does not extend to teacher post-provisioning (i.e., the assignment of teachers to schools, which is calculated the same way for all schools despite socioeconomic status).

We also debated the Growth, Employment, and Redistribution model of 1996, which registered a commitment to austerity, marketization, and privatization by the post-apartheid ruling party, the African National Congress. The underfunding and understaffing of our schools that resulted from these policies were understood to undoubtedly contribute to the disempowerment and demoralization of teachers as well as students. These discussions culminated in the news opinion piece we wrote together, "We Need to Fight for Public Policies That Will End the Bad Education Plaguing Our Schools" (Writing for Justice, 2021).

Imaan (youth co-author, age 17) reflects:

> We certainly had more freedom in the writing club regarding what opinions we were allowed to share compared to how we share opinions at school. For some of our students this meant that even when given the opportunity to express ourselves, we feel apprehensive because of how we are treated at school (where asking questions may appear disruptive). It is uncommon for high school students to discuss and be exposed to theory and policy in this way, and we felt important and included when facilitators brought this knowledge to the table enabling us to speak and act with new information to address our concerns.
>
> Often, students are subjected to a curriculum and pedagogies that are detached from their lived experiences. They are dehumanized and objectified as they are not seen as part of the "real world" until they have graduated and left school.

Activities like that of the writing club, where high school students can share their experiences and participate in the public sphere, disrupt this idea of "the real world," as this dissemination *is* participation in the real world.

Collaborating in this way was eye-opening and insightful to hear and learn about others' experiences in schools and communities across the metro. As adults and students, it was enlightening to delve into and explore the root causes of the issues using tools such as power analysis (which considers who is involved or affected by an issue, and who benefits or is disadvantaged) and the wheel of power and privilege (which highlights how different people may be affected by systems and structures in society). This enabled us to target issues in a way that acknowledges systemic failure and shortcomings that exacerbate school inequalities rather than adopting deficit views about teachers and students.

Discriminatory School Uniform Practices (A Writing Activity Organized out of a Student Activist "Working Group")

The third writing activity occurred in 2021; it focused on the discriminatory practices of school uniform policies. The newspaper article was co-written by two adult facilitators and three youth participants of Bottomup. The three participants recently finished high school and were establishing the Student Assembly with and for high schoolers (from various high schools in Cape Town that Bottomup has been working with) with the purpose of providing a space to reflect and act on issues important to high schoolers.

The Student Assembly identified discriminatory school uniform policies as an issue about which they would like to raise awareness. The problem is especially felt by girls of color whose hair is frequently targeted in school codes of conduct. Additionally, school codes often do not allow girls to wear trousers, instead requiring them to present as "girls" through uniformed school dresses or skirts.

Participants collected school uniform policies from Cape Town schools by visiting school websites, contacting schools via email or telephone, and asking their peers to obtain copies of the uniform policies. Participants and facilitators then collated the information and brainstormed ways to raise awareness about discriminatory uniform practices. We felt that many people were unaware of what was happening in schools, so we decided to write an article and submit it for publication in a widely read newspaper.

To initiate this, we started working on a statement regarding the issue of school uniforms and tried to understand why and how particular uniform policies are racist, sexist, undemocratic, classist, and discriminatory in terms of religious and gender differences. This work became the basis of our article (The Student Assembly, 2021) and was discussed in depth with the wider student community through group meeting dialogues and a WhatsApp forum. As writers together, the participants articulated what was happening at the schools through their own lived experiences, and the facilitators, as educationists, brought theoretical insight to the issues through their academic knowledge in both the philosophy and sociology of education.

The writing was done collaboratively through conversation, writing, reading aloud, and editing. Both young people and adults moved between the roles of teacher and student, which, generally, is not a common practice in the high school education space. This type of work is not usually expected of young people by adults, and their opinion on matters is not valued. Creating a space for this was liberating.

The newspaper article was published (in print and online) in the *Cape Argus*. The response to it was substantial, receiving roughly 150 comments when it was shared on the newspaper's social media feed. Some comments were negative and reflected the dominant discourse around the issues participants raised.

Snippets of comments from the *Cape Argus* (2021) Facebook page where the article was shared:

- All this ho ha over a lot of crap. Please just teach the learners to read and write then some manners. . . . And respect for their elders.
- This is identity politics. If you do not like a particular school's policies, enroll your kid in another . . . or send them to a school who has no uniform.
- The victim mentality will never end with some.
- Today, society wants no rules, no God . . . and look at the state of schools . . . undisciplined kids, violence, no respect. If you don't like rules, stay at home and educate your kids yourself.

Other viewers, however, defended the points we presented, which made us feel validated and heard:

- The cost of uniforms is ridiculous when people are battling to pay school fees. Simple grey pants and a golf shirt is comfortable and cool.
- What century are we in? The fact that girls are still forced to wear dresses in schools is ludicrous IMO [in my opinion]. The fact that learners with a certain hair type are demonised. . . . The rules are archaic. It's time for change!
- There should be a standard set of items in a uniform. Learners should be able to choose items from the range without attention paid to whether they're male or female. Hair rules should also take into account different types of hair.

If nothing else, we felt good that readers believed it was important enough to discuss the issue. We also think that when people engage, room for the conversation spreads wider.

The process of writing together was empowering, because, for the writers "fresh out of school," discriminatory school policies and practices are still felt deeply. We believe that writing raises critical consciousness of the general public and can foster empathy from others. On the flip side, one can also be hurt and angered when people belittle students' lived experiences and label them as troublemakers or social justice warriors. Control of student voices and bodies is entrenched within society, and even though we find ourselves taking small steps to disrupt this, much more work is needed for students to be taken seriously.

LESSONS AND CHALLENGES

Trust, Courage, and Mutual Respect

We learned from our experiences that the process of collaboration must begin with mutual respect and trust. For the adults involved, this means allowing participants to speak from their experiences as a starting point that guides investigation; in a sense, working from the known to the unknown. But in practice it means consciously trying to lead with the questions first rather than rushing to answers.

Reading sociology, for example, helps develop a set of tools to recognize what is not easily seen, but the task of the facilitator is not to simply represent a completed analysis but to help participants grasp the concepts themselves by conducting their own analysis and determining their own conclusions. In a system that attempts to mark and stigmatize young people, this allows them to be courageous in speaking up. This is no easy task, and it means risking ourselves (e.g., potential victimization by others who do not agree with us), but as Audrey Lorde (1978/1996) put it: "When we speak we are afraid our words will not be heard or welcomed. But when we are silent, we are still afraid. So it is better to speak" (p. 37).

In the context of the Student Assembly, for example, speaking up on issues like gender-biased uniform policies, discriminatory language policies, or corporal punishment often means making yourself visible as you confront power. Yet the risk of young people not speaking up is that the system continues to perpetuate itself and that our younger siblings and community members continue to endure the injustices.

Young people and teachers in the 1980s, and throughout apartheid, found the courage to build roadblocks to stop an inhumane system, and it is up to us to find that same courage today. Speaking up is indeed disruptive— to speak up is to add an alternative, and sometimes counter-hegemonic perspective, into the public arena. Lastly, to enter the public sphere is to show up as a subject (as an "I") and to interrupt the positioning of students as "objects" to be spoken about.

What Is "Publishable"? And on Which Platform?

There are also some challenges to acknowledge and recognize potentially limiting factors that result from the ways in which the chosen medium structures the activity of writing. For example, writing in popular news outlets that are aimed at a middle-class readership often means writing in English or Afrikaans and in a particular tone and register that are considered to be "publishable" in the mainstream. The ways in which young people express themselves in daily life on the Cape Flats and the code-switching evident, for example, in the lyrics shared at the start of the chapter, are not always welcomed in the mainstream.

In an art form like poetry or song, greater license is afforded for artists to express themselves in the way they speak, but less so in a news article or in academic writing (although a group of researchers at the University of the Western Cape and activists are working to normalize Kaaps [a stigmatized South African language] through the production of the first Trilingual Dictionary of Kaaps; see http://dwkaaps.co.za/). Working-class youth from the Cape Flats often make double the effort that middle-class youth have to: to abstract their experiences and then to convey them in ways that can be heard in arenas of dominant power.

Distributive Injustices in Education and Schooling

There is a lot working against the equal participation of working-class youth in society, and engaging systems of power frequently requires the mobilization of capital not easily acquired in poorly funded schools.

Schools in working-class communities of the Cape Flats are attenuated places that undermine democratic participation through structural injustice. Broken buildings and poor infrastructure are not just inconvenient or unfortunate but also mean that working-class youth do not always have access to specialized spaces of learning where they may be inducted into the various bodies of knowledge that school offers. For example, the lack of school libraries is an assault on the intellectual nurturing of working-class youth, and overcrowded classrooms and the general lack of resources work together to produce situations in which working-class students are forced to endure broken rhythms of teaching and learning. These injustices are not accidental. They are consistent with longstanding patterns of race and class inequities and inadequacies in schooling orchestrated under racial capitalism, which provided the engine for colonialism and apartheid, and which was not abandoned in the post-1994 South Africa.

Gathering Together

When time is limited, practical challenges are also present in collaborative activist work. Time constraints hinder deep engagements. Getting together (literally) to find time and travel across the city also requires the mobilization of resources. Members of the Student Assembly go to school in the Metro South Education District but are spread across the city. These practical challenges, together with the dictates of news outlets seeking fresh stories on current affairs and operating on short news cycles, often truncate the time for production; in some ways, this goes against what we believe is optimal for critical education.

We are reminded when we engage the word and the world, and confront the injustices our families endure, that there is also an affective dimension to the work that cannot be "managed" but rather invites us to hold safe space for each other. Taahirah (youth co-author, age 19) says:

> The challenge I experienced was putting all thoughts and emotions in words and on a page. It's one thing to read works like Freire and understand what it says. The moment you connect the dots and see how it connects with our reality and society, I become overwhelmed and feel hopeless. However, I feel a great joy, because critically I have awakened and feel the drive to further engage with topics like this.

CONCLUSION

In this chapter, we have argued about the importance of writing as a form of activism that interrupts dominant narratives. We argued how especially valuable this can be for youth who experience structural, institutional, and symbolic violence in the context of deeply unequal social arrangements.

We have also foregrounded how collaborative work provides an opportunity to unsettle teacher–student binaries. In the "protected" context of writing clubs and student organizations, these spaces boost students' confidence as they assert themselves and demand to be engaged as full humans within the context of schools that are typically hierarchical and where critical questions are not always welcomed. For democratic experiences like the ones in the writing club to be normalized or to become embedded within the day-to-day life of schools, however, fundamental changes are necessary. The unequal social and schooling arrangements in South Africa (resulting from historical and contemporary injustices), together with the intensification of teachers' work that is driven by a global education reform agenda, produce a situation in which antidemocracy thrives and in which teachers and students become like cogs in the machine as they struggle to make it through the day.

DISCUSSION QUESTIONS/ACTIVITIES

1. Think about the quote from Audre Lorde used in this chapter. Why do you think it is sometimes difficult for young people to speak up against injustices they face? And what do you think society loses out on when young people do not speak up?
2. Can you identify a popular or mainstream media platform, local to where you are, in which youth perspectives are not adequately represented? What are some ideas you might have of how to change this?

REFERENCES

Biesta, G. (2016). The rediscovery of teaching: On robot vacuum cleaners, non-egological education and the limits of the hermeneutical world view. *Educational Philosophy and Theory*, 48(4), 374–392. https://doi.org/10.1080/00131857.2015.1041442

Biesta, G. (2019). Should teaching be re(dis)covered? Introduction to a symposium. *Studies in Philosophy and Education*, 38(5), 549–553.

Bourdieu, P. (1986). The forms of capital. In J. Richardson (Ed.), *Handbook of theory and research of the sociology of education* (pp. 241–258). Greenwood.

Bundy, C. (1987). Street sociology and pavement politics: Aspects of youth and student resistance in Cape Town, 1985. *Journal of Southern African Studies*, 13(3), 303–330. Retrieved from http://www.jstor.org/stable/2636385

Cape Argus. (2021). *Home* [Facebook page]. Facebook. Retrieved September 6, 2023, from https://www.facebook.com/page/177281015730581/search/?q=uniform%20policies%20deeply%20political

Crankshaw, O. (2012). Deindustrialization, professionalization and racial inequality in Cape Town. *Urban Affairs Review*, 48(6), 836–862.

Fraser, N., Dahl, H. M., Stoltz, P., & Willig, R. (2004). Recognition, redistribution and representation in capitalist global society: An interview with Nancy Fraser. *Acta Sociologica*, 47(4), 374–382. Retrieved from http://www.jstor.org/stable/4195051

Freire, P. (2000). *Pedagogy of the oppressed*. 30th anniversary edition. Continuum.

Gruijters, R. J., Elbers, B., & Reddy, V. (n.d.). *Opportunity hoarding and elite reproduction: School segregation in post-apartheid South Africa*. https://osf.io/2z6qa/download

Hunter, M. (2019). *Race for education: Gender, White tone, and schooling in South Africa*. Cambridge University Press.

Lorde, A. (1996). From "A litany for survival." *BOMB*, 56, 34–37. Retrieved from http://www.jstor.org/stable/40425851

Mathebula, T. (2017). From "boy-government" and "student-government" to "learner-government": The best of both worlds? *Africa Education Review*, 15, 1–15. https://doi.org/10.1080/18146627.2016.1224576

Murris, K. (2012). Student teachers investigating the morality of corporal punishment in South Africa. *Ethics and Education*, 7, 45–58. https://doi.org/10.1080/17449642.2012.672030

The Student Assembly. (2021, October 20). *School uniform policies deeply political and undemocratic*. iol.co.za. Retrieved April 30, 2023, from https://www.iol.co.za/capeargus/opinion/school-uniform-policies-deeply-political-and-undemocratic-be6c4387-14cc-4c8b-9660-bccf7b53be02

Sulla, V., Zikhali, P., & Cuevas, P. F. (2022). *Inequality in Southern Africa: An assessment of the Southern African Customs Union*. World Bank Group. Retrieved from http://documents.worldbank.org/curated/en/099125303072236903/P1649270c02a1f06b0a3ae02e57eadd7a82

Western Cape Government (WCG). (2014). Provincial Gazette Extraordinary 7317.

Writing for Justice. (2021, May 31). OP-ED: We need to fight for public policies that will end the bad education plaguing our schools. *Daily Maverick*. Retrieved from https://www.dailymaverick.co.za/article/2021-05-31-we-need-to-fight-for-public-policies-that-will-end-the-bad-education-plaguing-our-schools/

The Black Panthers, Multicultural Peace Education, and Power Sharing in a New York City Alternative High School

Krista Ambats and Matt Meyer

The process of learning—for both teachers and students—underwent major transformations in the public high schools of New York City (NYC) throughout the 1990s and early 2000s. As the largest public school system in the United States, NYC was both a leader in experimenting with growing privatization and a point of resistance to this (and other kinds of) neoliberal changes. In this context, an almost immediate positive connection was struck between radical educator Matt Meyer and activist student Krista Ambats, and this chapter is the story of our collaborative work to transform our classroom and a single, small school of 50 students and a dozen staff. At the time, Meyer was a veteran social studies teacher tasked by the NYC superintendent with leading multicultural peace education reforms for NYC's specialized district known as the Alternative High Schools and Programs (AHSP); Ambats was a recent transfer to Meyer's classroom. Aware of similarities in our overall sociopolitical approach to history and social change, a commitment to peace and nonviolence, an admiration for the legacy of the Black Power movements of the 1960s and the Black Panthers, and a rebellious streak that had previously led each of us to "break hierarchies" in our personal lives, we quickly became attracted to the idea of classroom transformation.

The classroom project this essay spotlights—the creation of a 2-hour, student-produced radio show on Black Panther history and contemporary peace issues—was based on a process of power sharing between students and staff, breaking hierarchies in traditional secondary school and teacher–student relationships. In this chapter, our narrative presents a contextual understanding of the NYC school system, alternative schools, and the Black Panther legacy along with a recounting of the classroom Panther project we co-led and our post-project analysis and hopes to summarize how our successes and challenges might be built on into the future.

Over a decade later, we now reflect on the successes we had becoming learning partners and ultimately (years after Krista's graduation) lifelong friends. We also examine the institutional challenges we faced. Even as our work took place in a context generally open to social change and Freirean approaches, we were still pleased with the short-term positive influences our project had on the school and district in showcasing new relationships based on youth-centered and empowering practices. Over the long term, however, our work and the overall work of the district failed to create lasting citywide change in the face of the national drive toward privatization and standardization of top-down schooling.

THE SCHOOLS CONTEXT

The advent of "peace education" as a distinct and popularly identified discipline in 1973 occurred amidst the global high tide of resistance movements for Black Power and Black liberation, and an end to war, especially the U.S. imperialist war in Southeast Asia. Growing social change campaigns led by women, workers, Indigenous peoples, LGBTQ+ folx, and many others swept across the world, and in particular in the Americas these campaigns and movements were accompanied by educational innovations (Haavelsrud & Reardon, 2022). Given the era and the radical political–educational transformations, conversations about schooling and society sometimes included challenges to the very nature of power itself, including the power dynamics in a given class, community center, or gathering place (Dyson, 2014).

The foundation of NYC Alternative High Schools' growth came amid a period of progressive possibilities (1990–1994), during the one term of Mayor David Dinkins, NYC's only top official of African descent until the 2021 election of former police officer Eric Adams. Dinkins's mayoralty was marked by many controversies, including splits between Black and Latine communities and turmoil over LGBTQ+ rights and AIDS initiatives, but few were perceived as divisive or threatening as the multicultural education policies of Dinkins's appointed board of education (BoE) chancellor, Harlem-born, Puerto Rican educator Joseph Fernandez (Hymowitz, 1993).

Fernandez's most remembered contribution was the introduction of a citywide, pre-K through high school series of year-by-year multicultural curricula. This "rainbow curriculum" was designed to foster tolerance, sensitivity, and safety for all students, and included overall school-based management and shared decision-making at all administrative levels. Despite far-reaching transformational plans that included some visionary justice-based, conflict-solving, methodologically substantiated reforms, the rainbow plans collapsed when right-wing newspaper tabloids in NYC published a single page out of tens of thousands, spotlighting a book on a suggested reading list for early childhood educators. The book, *Heather Has*

Two Mommies, was a lesbian-and-gay-friendly picture book that told the story of a student whose two parents were both women. Over a year of active controversy about the book's inclusion on the rainbow reading list ultimately led to Fernandez's removal as chancellor.

THE PERSONAL CONTEXT

In 1993, with offices and a mini-library in midtown Manhattan, Matt Meyer was educational director of the alternative high school that was housed in the St. Luke's/Roosevelt Hospital's Department of Child and Adolescent Psychiatry. Many bright and hard-working students who needed short-term, outpatient counseling support spent a short portion of their high school careers at the St. Luke's/Roosevelt Alternative School.

Prior to her transfer to the school-within-the-hospital, Krista Ambats was a successful student at Hunter College High School, often ranked as the top public high school in the United States (Brody, 2019). Attached to the City University of New York's Hunter College, it was not a traditional part of the NYC public school system nor a part of the alternative network, though many progressive educators in NYC knew that some of the brightest and most activist-oriented students came from Hunter. As an artist and writer with an interest in history, Krista had eclectic roots and interests: Her mom was a top professional juggler and dad the inventor of the mood ring.

Together, we were quickly drawn to our own and one another's critiques of the institutions surrounding us. In particular, we were both disturbed by the racialized, gendered, ageist, and class-based ways in which schools and students (and in some cases teachers and administrators) were identified as "good" or "bad" and tracked (largely unofficially and covertly) into areas of future work that were limiting for some (especially poor and working-class young women of color) and more open and freer for others (especially perceived middle-class, middle-aged men of Euro-American descent).

We were both drawn to a peace action–oriented view of multiculturalism that served as the framework for Meyer's job and for our school-based work together. The fact that St. Luke's school had all small classes of under 15 students each, and focused on student-based needs rather than various psychological or cognitive labels, provided us with a relatively supportive and comfortable space to develop our personal/political/pedagogical relationship. Krista was sharply self-aware of her intelligence and skills and felt enabled to speak up and speak out. Matt was in a relative position of power within the school system (tenured, a local director, and citywide Office of Multicultural Education official), but was also committed to giving up and/or sharing some of that power. However, we were also very aware of the class, race, gender, and age differences between us in that Krista is a biracial African American young woman and Matt is an older White man. Our radical beliefs and work were in part based on Freirean principles. We were aware, for example, that Freire and Cape Verdean linguist Donaldo Macedo wrote extensively about how critical pedagogy could not be separated from or dichotomized against economic and/or sociocultural processes (Freire & Macedo, 1987). In our practical conversations, this meant for us that our relational, classroom, and institutional experiments had to be empowering for everyone involved.

SCHOOL AND SOCIETY: SOCIAL CHANGE, SOCIAL DYNAMICS, AND US

As we got to know one another and worked together as student and teacher within a U.S. history course, our political and personal connections as activist-organizers and rebels began to come out as part of regular classroom (and out of classroom) dialogues and exploration. One class trip stands out: As a means of connecting local and national history, 10 students walked through and engaged with significant places and people in the NYC Lower East Side. We spoke with a leading Nuyorican Episcopal priest about housing rights and squatters' movements. Students also came prepared to interview a World War II pacifist conscientious objector who served time in prison for refusing to fight.

When it came time for the last stop at the historic rock club CBGB, many students were ready to go home since it was already past the time when the typical school day ended. Krista was very interested in checking it out, and Matt, who was aware of the location but did not have contacts there, was game to continue. The two of us stumbled on the founder and owner of the place, who invited us into the otherwise closed venue where many famous musicians got their start. We don't remember how we introduced or explained ourselves, but we improvised an unplanned interview by asking questions that we were curious about. From that point on, the positive connection between the two of us was cemented, and we emerged with the clear expectation that we could do more, and have fun in the process, through planned collaborations.

The Lower East Side encounters, which took place during the 2005–2006 school year, were part of the first semester of us getting to know one another. Although a teacher in a traditional classroom holds certain power, the expectation in *this* classroom was to question and challenge authority. Respect did not equate to agreement, blind acceptance, or repeating the teacher's or textbook's perspective. The power dynamics between the two of us, then, followed this principle. We were friendly and had aligned interests and goals but noted to one another that "becoming friends" in any significant sense would both complicate our existing student–teacher relationship and compromise our ability to "professionally" interact with and positively affect our colleagues. While maintaining some traditional lines of student–teacher differentiation, we still publicly challenged the idea that one of us was entitled to all the power and decision-making initiative. Our alliance was based on wanting to create a good project for the entire class and school that transformed the power dynamic between teacher and students (Illich, 1971). Though it might have seemed to some like a fine line at the time, being clear that we were friendly but not "friends" during that time was important for us and helped many students in the class consider Matt a potential friend or mentor following graduation. The special connection and deep friendship between us blossomed more fully and intentionally later.

In this same period, a number of events concerning current and former political prisoners who had been leaders of the Black Panther Party (BPP) and other Black liberation movements began to make headlines across the city. We then began to openly discuss, research, negotiate, and ultimately implement a major project that would bring together many of our student and staff alternative school peers. We learned about Teen Talk Radio (TTR), a NYC Department of Education initiative that was connected to the Alternative Schools district. The Teen Talk staff offered annual semester-long training programs designed to take around a dozen students out of the classroom once a week to work in a professional radio studio managed and maintained by the Department of Education. They correctly assumed that most teachers did not have professional radio production experience either, so their approach was to teach both teachers and students. In the beginning of the fall 2006 semester, our 2nd year working together, we started to develop a plan to incorporate the Teen Talk training and radio work, our past experiences of interviewing historical figures, and our vision of breaking hierarchies, such that the student–teacher dynamics would be blurred, and a collaborative project would be created that benefited and educated the entire school community. Though based in one classroom, our single-issue newsletter, our reports, workshops held at citywide conferences, and the broadcast itself all reached thousands of students, staff people, and members of the general public.

The spring 2007 project was a 2-hour, student-produced TTR show called *The Black Panther Party: Its History and Relevance Today* and was designed by the two of us and produced by a dozen students from our history class in cooperation with the AHSP, WNYE-FM, and WBAI Pacifica Radio.

THE BLACK PANTHERS, PEACE EDUCATION, AND OUR PROJECT

As our plans developed and our research began, we were greatly aided by the 2005 HBO documentary *Bastards of the Party* (Sloan, 2005), which looked at the connections between the Black Panthers and modern gangs. The entire class watched it together, pausing frequently to gain a collective understanding. We also investigated who we would interview, how we could teach one another needed background information, and what readings would be most useful. Matt's prior relationships with members of the NY Panther 21 (see Kioni-sadiki & Meyer, 2017) helped us access a number of Panther leaders. If the two of us, along with those from the Black community, could provide some historical background, we could rely on the staff at TTR to help us with the radio production. The TTR staff equalized the student–teacher hierarchy between all of us since we (Matt and his students) all became their students. We learned about and interviewed the Panthers who agreed to talk with us on air in TTR's studio.

Our 2007 project also benefited from the headline-making court proceedings of the San Francisco Eight (SF8), who were eight Panthers indicted for an alleged crime in 1971. Like the many Panthers before them, the defendants vehemently claimed a frame-up, arguing that evidence was old and unreliable. The trial was held in California even though two members were serving long sentences in upstate New York and considered themselves political prisoners.

We felt that general discussions about the Panthers, and the *Bastards* film and SF8 trials in particular, were part of an overall challenge within urban communities to address the public's perceptions of terms such as "violence" and "peace." With this came a narrative of "Martin-Luther-King-was-peaceful-and-good/Malcolm-X-was-violent-and-bad," which we rejected. Following Dr. King's assertion defining peace not as the absence of violence but as the presence of justice and viewing much of the Black Panther legacy as part of a long history of unarmed (though not explicitly pacifist) positive community development, we see our work as part of deepening an overall peace education curriculum that was especially familiar to Matt in these years. From this viewpoint, Rev. Dr. Martin Luther King Jr. and Minister Malcolm X were not so far off from one another at the end of their lives (Cone, 2012), and their lessons were profoundly relevant for building peaceful, power-equitable classrooms, schools, and communities (Meyer, 2016).

The two of us along with a dozen students in the TTR developed radio production skills, learned about contemporary Panther legacies and politics, conducted interviews for our background and public written and audio products, and modeled a dynamic student–teacher collaborative project in one busy semester. With Krista and Matt serving as unofficial but very active co-coordinators alongside students in the class, we endeavored to interview whomever we could about how past events connected to current policies and politics, including the politics of state violence, peace, and the role of contemporary conflict resolution practices in making our communities safer and more empowered places (Pari & Shor, 1999). Though the radio show was our grand finale, the one-shot newsletter was a means to publicize our project to the entire school district. We distributed hundreds of copies to friends, peers, and contacts throughout NYC.

We learned that NYC Council member Charles Barron, an original member of the NY Black Panthers, was holding a press conference at the City College of New York (CUNY) because the administration had removed a student organization's sign that supported a Panther leader and replaced it with their own. We arranged a class trip to the press conference to interview Barron. The councilman criticized the CUNY officials for attempting to block students from hanging their sign and not recognizing the students' right to free speech. In a dramatic close to the event, Barron took down the administration's sign and replaced it with a makeshift sign with the students' preferred names.

Krista recalls the inspiration of being part of the small, college-based event and wrote at the time:

> Though I wasn't one of the students, we had agreed in advance to interview City Councilmember Barron if that became possible. It was amazing just watching as the scene unfolded. Barron was a passionate speaker in general, and before an audience made up mainly of CUNY students who were active with the club, he was fiery. It felt more like a direct action than a press conference, especially at the end when this sign with the Panther and Young Lords' leaders' names was physically pasted over the college's official sign. That Barron, an elected official, was doing this added an extra emphasis on the idea that institutions could be confronted and challenged. (Zweig & Meyer, 2007)

After writing up our experiences at City College and reflections on the HBO film and readings, we used this information for our first meeting at Teen Talk. With a soundproof room, professional microphones, and other equipment relevant to an active station, we were introduced to one of the technical producers who would record us. Although they assisted in the taping, we had to develop the content. One of our group members, student Shamar Sowell, agreed to write a rap/PSA based on his love of composing.

Shamar's poem "Legacy," which was aired, describes his reflections on our work:

Huey P. Newton, Bobby Seale and George Jackson
I look up to them now because they stood up as a Nation
Led by demonstrations, to stop all the racism.

As a member of a gang, I've been patiently waiting,
Debating about what's right and wrong
Trying to stay Strong!

But as I look up to the BLA and the BPP
I know as a young man that police brutality
Is still going on in our community!

Cruelty is not the answer—See:
There's other ways that you could fight
For a way to survive, try to stay alive
Say what we've got to say by using our Voice
Instead of violence, stand together—Don't be silent!

It's about doing what is right:
Giving back to the community
And being together
A Black Nation in Unity!

Matt remembers working with Shamar and the feelings in the group as a whole after Shamar successfully recorded the public service announcement (PSA):

> As the teacher in the group, Shamar invited me to look over and edit his poem before taping. Shamar knew that I was impressed with his lyricism, and the whole class knew that I wanted to be as hands-off as possible with their work, especially while we were in the radio studio. . . . [During the taping] at first, there was a nervous/silly mood. We were all experiencing something new, and though we felt certain that what we were doing was important, Shamar especially found it difficult not to laugh upon hearing his voice played back. After a few takes, we all settled down to a more serious mood, recognizing that making a "perfect" recording which sounded just the way we wanted it was going to take some focus and time. After a little over an hour, Shamar and the producer completed [the recording] . . . and we had our first completed, two-minute segment of what would ultimately become our two-hour program. (Zweig & Meyer, 2007)

The completion of the PSAs made us feel ready to move toward our big day of interviews, which were taped at the studio and mixed with previous interviews. During this process we had the opportunity to work with and interview additional Black Panthers.

Finally, one of the imprisoned members of SF8, Herman Bell, was having a hearing at the courthouse, only a 2-hour drive from NYC. Seeing this as a not-to-be-missed opportunity, Krista and Matt decided to attend the hearing and try to visit. The two of us joined one other community member, who was not affiliated with the school or the project but supportive of the Panthers, to drive to the hearing and to go through the sometimes humiliating and lengthy security process of getting admitted into the prison's visiting room. Krista still remembers the many times she had to go through the metal detectors before finally realizing that there was a small wire in her bra, which then had to be removed before entering the prison. Much of that was forgotten as soon as Herman Bell stood before us, a tall man with a beaming smile and warm teddy-bear embraces. At the time, Krista wrote in our student-run newsletter:

> I have never been to court before. In fact, I don't think I even knew anyone who was in prison before meeting Black Panther Herman Bell. Herman was brought upstairs [to the courtroom], hands and feet shackled, and we all silently waved to him and he raised his fist in return. It was a weird experience for me to suddenly feel kinship with someone five feet away who I'd never met before. . . .
>
> Bob Boyle, Herman's attorney, made the case for why he shouldn't be moved to California to join the other members of the SF8, for a whole new trial on a whole new set of charges. Maybe 10 minutes went by before the whole thing was over. Ten minutes, one man, seven heavily armed guards. I felt as if the priorities of the court were misplaced. . . .
>
> I went to go visit Bell in prison after the hearing. He asked questions about our personal lives, how our friends were, and about the news of the day—the situation in Darfur. He asked what I was doing in school. It was as if we were old friends meeting at our favorite coffee shop, except for the setting. I was so taken by his charm and cheer, he hardly seemed like someone who had spent more than half of his life in prison. And seeing him locked up in such a horrible place like some kind of animal was truly heartbreaking to me. . . .
>
> What kind of system did I live in where innocent people, beautiful people, are tortured into confessing to crimes they didn't commit? I feared for Herman and I feared for the rest of the San Francisco Eight who were suffering a similar fate. Having to leave him behind there in that horrible place was possibly the most morally difficult thing I was ever forced to do. If justice is so blind, then how come there was never a day in my life when I felt more aware of the color of my skin than on the day I went to court and prison? (Krista Ambats's excerpt from student-run newsletter, Zweig & Meyer, 2007)

Of course, we talked about our experiences on the ride home. Our conversations ranged from our thoughts of Herman, feelings about the speed of the hearing, to personal discomforts with the prison and outrage seeing him in shackles during the hearing. The ridiculous idea that Herman was a physical threat underscored the ways in which the legacy of the Panthers' work toward self-empowerment and community self-defense was seen as a threat to the U.S. status quo. But the silent moments between us in the car—older White teacher and younger Black student—were as poignant and bonding as all the words we could muster. Up close against the power of the state, our own power dynamics seemed easier to negotiate, and more urgent to transform than ever. Almost all the officers transporting Herman were White, and Herman stood tall as a proud Black man. Where actual power came from and how best to utilize it seemed like part of the lesson for us personally and not just part of some previous history or classroom lesson plan. Despite the shackles, Herman was fighting for greater freedoms for

Black, African, and peoples everywhere. We shared a palpable feeling that working for justice and peace, even when one is not winning at any given moment, builds power and shifts power dynamics even behind prison walls.

Once back in the classroom and the radio studio, we spent hours chatting about meeting an original member of the Black Panthers, what it would be like to interview him in the studio, and how the power dynamics between the two of us, and between us and him, could be mediated such that our relationships would be strengthened as our knowledge of his life and perspectives increased. When the day came for us to record in the studio, we had a detailed agenda of who would be there and who would be interviewing whom. We had arranged times for several Panthers and activists to meet us in the studio, received a handwritten letter sent to us by one Panther political prisoner still behind bars, and had call-in times with family members of famous hip-hop artist Tupac Shakur, who was raised by Black Panther parents and community members.

Producing the show was hard but exhilarating work; we overcame challenges with a spirit of collaboration and did whatever we needed to accomplish a task. The TTR studio had a series of technical problems and was unusable for the planned day of recording, so we called contacts and switched to Pacifica Radio's NYC public broadcast station WBAI, which had done a lot of programming on the Panthers and whose employees were more than happy to assist us. We communicated with guests to ensure their timely arrival so students could interview a few guests at a time. At no point was a teacher directing all the action nor a student following directions. Everyone had distinct tasks for the entire day, which ensured our collaborative work together. The radio producers did all the technical work and facilitated our collective group process. By the day of the taping, we had developed the camaraderie and trust that spotlighted the importance of our work and superseded any past teacher–student hierarchies. Our 2-hour show, gently edited by the TTR and WBAI producers under our basic oversight, aired publicly in May and June 2007.

CONCLUSION: WHAT THE PANTHERS AND YOUTH EMPOWERMENT HAVE TO DO WITH 21ST-CENTURY PEDAGOGY

A cottage industry of books, articles, and forums chronicling the legacies of the Black Panther Party make clear that the Party was ahead of its time in terms of both ideas of radical power transformation and the popular presentation of those ideas (Boyd, 2015). The often selfless ways in which they found power in giving back to and defending their communities mirrored the vulnerability and selflessness that the two of us tried to allow for throughout our relationship and especially in building this project. We sought to share with our colleagues all that we learned about power, peace and justice, and the historical role of the Panthers. The basis of our relationship and work, however radical it may seem, was rooted in principles that we still both believe are central to teaching, even if hierarchies are not explicitly disrupted: mutual respect, learning from and with each other, and genuine interest in one another's perspectives. We still believe and discuss that ending oppression is not simply rooted in struggles for institutional power shifts but also in interpersonal connections based on respectful relationships. Mutual respect can and must be afforded across age, race, gender, class, and other traditional power lines for social change.

The popular rallying cry of the Black Panthers was "Power to the People." This essay chronicles a particular project spotlighting the NY Panthers and the radical power shifts they tried to ensure. The project was conducted in the spaces created by NYC's Alternative High Schools and Programs, a single district that at one time brought together more students, educators, and community leaders in experiments at power-sharing pedagogies than anywhere else in the United States (Raywid & Schmerler, 2003).

The Panthers are not currently an active organization, but new generations continue to learn from their experiences as they address tomorrow's struggles. All charges against the members of the San Francisco Eight were eventually dropped, and Herman Bell, as well as the other incarcerated member of the Eight, are now out of prison. The Alternative Schools and Programs still exist in some form, now commonly referred to as "District 79," but the liberatory educational visions of its founding days are long gone from its mission. While our radio project felt small in comparison to the larger forces of change centered on the Black liberation movement and the federal efforts to monetize public education, we highlighted one school district, and the possibilities open if we are willing to rethink and rebuild along more egalitarian lines. Our cohort, the school, district-wide peers, and our project were unable to institutionally sustain the new work models. Other social change organizers face similar institutional challenges. How can we strengthen localized, grassroots initiatives so that they last and gain influence beyond the initial circle of those directly involved?

The two of us, now older, and with fewer power differences between us than when we first met, remain committed to a radical transformation of a society with oppressive power dynamics based on race, class, gender, age, and other arbitrary factors. Though separated now by a continent, several time zones, and busy lives, we still share stories about our human rights work; we still seek to inform and challenge one another to make the world and ourselves better and stronger. We are proud of what we accomplished but painfully aware of all that we couldn't do to make the world or even our communities substantially safer and more just. We still aren't satisfied, and in our different spaces we still intend to struggle. Ongoing struggle is, after all, a central part of what "Power to the People" has always been about.

DISCUSSION QUESTIONS/ACTIVITIES

1. Based on the curriculum used in your school or community, how are the Black Panthers and their legacy discussed? How do they fit into our general understanding of the Civil Rights Movement and Black Lives Matter movement today? Consider reading some parts of the references below (especially kioni-sadiki & Meyer; and Boyd) for further reflection.
2. Reflect on and discuss how race, class, and gender influence and complicate our attempts to break hierarchies between students and teachers. Are there benefits or positive things to be gained from examining and confronting these challenges together, holistically?
3. How, in your experiences, does work for peace/conflict resolution, justice/unity in diversity, and power sharing relate? This chapter has used terms less common in their fields (e.g., "multicultural peace education"). Based on your work and readings, do you find these melding of terms and concepts to be helpful or confusing, and why?

REFERENCES

Boyd, H. (2015). *Black Panthers for beginners*. For Beginners.

Brody, L. (2019, June 1). This selective New York school has found a formula for diversity. *Wall Street Journal*. Retrieved September 10, 2023, from https://www.wsj.com/articles/this-selective-new-york-school-has-found-a-formula-for-diversity-11559394000

Cone, J. (2012). *Martin and Malcolm and America: A dream or a nightmare?* Orbis Books.

Dyson, O. L. (2014). *The Black Panther Party and transformative pedagogy: Place-based education in Philadelphia*. Lexington Books.

Freire, P., & Macedo, D. (1987). *Literacy: Reading the word and the world*. Bergin & Garvey.

Haavelsrud, M., & Reardon, B. (2022, September 21–December 22). *IPRA-PEC: Projecting a next phase: Reflections on its roots, processes and purposes*. Global Campaign for Peace Education. Retrieved September 10, 2023, from https://www.peace-ed-campaign.org/ipra-pec-projecting-a-next-phase/

Hymowitz, K. (1993, Spring). The futile crusade: The rise and fall of Joe Fernandez. *City-Journal Magazine*, Manhattan Institute for Policy Research. Retrieved September 10, 2023, from https://www.city-journal.org/html/futile-crusade-12652.html.

Illich, I. (1971). *Deschooling society*. Harper and Row.

Kioni-sadiki, D., & Meyer, M. (Eds.). (2017). *Look for me in the whirlwind: From the Panther 21 to 21st-century revolutions*. PM Press.

Meyer, M. (2016). We have not been moved: Black Lives Matter, racism in the peace movement, and the future of solidarity. *Fellowship Magazine*, 80(1–10).

Pari, C., & Shor, I. (1999). *Critical literacy in action: Writing words, changing world / A tribute to the teachings of Paulo Freire.* Heinemann.

Raywid, M. A., & G. Schmerler (Eds.). (2003). *Not so easy going: The policy environments of small urban schools and schools-within-schools.* Educational Resources Information Center.

Sloan, C. (director). (2005). *Bastards of the party.* HBO Films. Retrieved September 10, 2023, from https://vimeo.com/247366171

Zweig, R., & Meyer, M. (Eds.). (2007). *OES CARES: Manhattan newsletter on the Teen Talk Radio-Black Panther project.* Comprehensive Adolescent Rehabilitation and Education Service.

CHAPTER 3

Disrupting Hierarchies for New Landscapes of Learning by Action

Experiences and Reflections from a Climate Change Course

Jing Lin, Virginia Gomes, Joey Haavik, Maha Malik, Shue-kei Joanna Mok, Jordan Scanlon, Emmanuel Wanjala, and Anna Grigoryeva

INTRODUCTION

Global climate change presents many unprecedented challenges that require us all to become both teachers and learners working together to find solutions. In the collective effort to reverse the catastrophic results of climate change, we (the authors) call for a disruption of hierarchies among humans and between humans and nature, hierarchies between teachers and students, and the hierarchy of valuing rational, positivist ways of learning above inner, spiritual, and experiential learning. Jing, our professor, utilized a contemplative, holistic approach to create the course Global Climate Change and Education: Policy and Practice prioritizing the fostering of a deep love for nature at an R1 (research intensive) university (hereafter University).

The course focuses on climate change and how educational practices and policies can be transformed to meet the needs of a world that is and will be greatly impacted by climate change. Jing, who designed and taught the course, encouraged all of us to be both teachers and students, learning from each other and nature, developing a critical consciousness of the crises we are in. We critique the root causes of these crises, such as anthropocentrism, patriarchy, colonialism, and capitalism, and we explore alternative and creative ways to forge a new relationship with nature that is based on love and respect.

When theorizing human nature, Freire stated, "Human beings are not built in silence, but in word, in work, in action-reflection" (2000, p. 88). Our class, which took place during fall 2021, embraced this idea and incorporated experiential projects throughout the learning process. All students led class discussions that critically examined the intersection between our ecological environment and international cooperation, geopolitics, and transformative education. We engaged in meditation and mindfulness practices in every session of the semester, and documented our weekly and direct contacts with nature in our nature contact journals, in which we constantly reflected on our relationship with the natural world. Students and our teacher became learning partners with nature, learning from and advocating for each other, as we began seeing ourselves as proactive beings, modeling Freire's problem-posing education.

As a class, we undertook a project by joining a campaign to protect a 15-acre forest on campus called the Green Woods, which was threatened by a proposed development of private townhomes and graduate housing. The prospect of depleting the last 28% of the forest owned by the University caused an uproar among many members of the University community, who organized a campaign involving many groups to protest the project. We joined this campaign and created our own advocacy initiative, "Voices of the Woods," visualizing and vocalizing messages from the trees to the world.

We used climate change as an entry point to challenge varied hierarchies. Analyzing enablers of hierarchical thinking and action—anthropocentrism, capitalist interests, and authoritarian pedagogy—we embraced new paradigms by incorporating into the course contemplative holistic learning and interactions with nature as an intelligent, living system.

DISRUPTING HIERARCHIES: WHAT TO DISRUPT?

Freirean philosophy (1970/2000) urges us to critically challenge underlying power dynamics behind binaries by constantly engaging in attentive listening, critical reflections, and "care for the self and others with an aim toward reducing oppression, injustice, and suffering" (Hyde & LaPard, 2015, p. 3). In other words, Freire's teaching is helpful to reflect not only on the teacher–student hierarchy, but also on other forms of oppressive sociocultural and structural hierarchies.

Hierarchy Between Humans and Nature

The hierarchical human–nature relationship has set the foundation for the current climate crises; colonialist expansion treated nature as a commodity while destroying Indigenous people and their cultures (Stoltz et al., 2022). Since industrialization, capitalism has reflected human prioritization of wealth accumulation and the notion that humans are naturally self-interested. Milfont et al. (2013) explore how a human–nature hierarchy is also inextricably linked to "religious beliefs and value orientations" that reinforce the separation of humanity and nature, viewing nature's very existence as a means to provide for humanity and enhance human progress, thus justifying human domination over the natural world (p. 1128).

Challenging such a hierarchical dichotomy, Freire (1970/2000) highlights socioecological interdependencies, stressing that the "world and human beings do not exist apart from each other" but in "constant interaction" (p. 50). He further describes how ideologies and practices contribute to the exploitation of people and the planet within capitalism:

> The oppressor consciousness tends to transform everything surrounding it into an object of its domination. The earth, property, production, the creations of people, people themselves, time—everything is reduced to the status of objects at its disposal. In their unrestrained eagerness to possess, the oppressors develop their conviction that it is possible for them to transform everything into objects of their purchasing power. Money is the measure of all things, and profit the primary goal. (p. 58)

Challenging the prevailing capitalistic value system is part of transforming this hierarchical relationship in substantively responding to the climate crises (-saed, 2019).

Hierarchies in Human Society

Hierarchical forces in human society employ differential powers based on race, ability, class, gender, sexuality, age, and immigration status (among others). Legitimizing and moralizing themselves as "human beings" while dehumanizing others as undeserving "things" (the oppressed), those who control resources and powers in any given society (the oppressors) reinforce the othering of the oppressed by institutionalizing laws, media, and educational systems that reproduce oppressive sociocultural norms (Freire, 1970/2000, p. 57).

To envision transformation, Freire reminds us that "the oppressed are not 'marginals,' [they] are not living 'outside' society" (p. 74). Dismantling the concept of "otherness" requires building solidarity with the oppressed and challenging existing hierarchies and systems of power (Diggins, 2011). In the context of ecological justice and climate change, we need to empower historically disadvantaged peoples (racialized, classed, gendered, etc.) to play a central role in rebuilding an equitable world among humans and with nature.

Hierarchy Between Teacher and Students

Current education systems often reflect colonial structures and ideologies that were meant to divide and control people by cultivating obedience and passive learning (Stoltz et al., 2022). Conventional ways of teaching and learning prioritize the knowledge, perspectives, and experiences of teachers over that of students (Farkas, 2012). This type of banking education (Freire, 1970/2000) reinforces the teacher–student hierarchy and deprives students of having the chance to be critical and more fully human.

Aiming at freeing educators and students from passivity and using education for liberation, Freire promotes a dialogical and problem-posing education that empowers students to "perceive critically the way they exist in the world with which and in which they find themselves" (1970/2000, p. 83), and stimulates true reflection and action on reality. When considering the issue of climate change, a problem-posing, experiential education can help students disrupt hierarchies toward cobuilding more sustainable communities.

Hierarchy of Mind Over Body, Heart, and Spirit

Samuels (2004) traces to the Late Medieval period the emergence of dichotomies such as sense and nonsense, determinacy and indeterminacy, science and sensuousness. Figurative language such as metaphor and analogy are often ambiguous, hence heavily dependent on individual interpretations. According to him, the bourgeoisie perceived the embedded sense of agency in figurative language as a threat to the status quo, thus emphasized its fictiveness, distinguished it from facts, and moved to determine more fixed meanings and usage of words to exert and preserve power. Such a move turned words and linguistic practices used by the bourgeoisie as sensical, rational, and superior, and all others as nonsensical, irrational, and inferior.

Freire (1993) rejects this dichotomy and centers the totality of the body in the act of knowing, emphasizing that "[i]t is my entire body that socially knows. I cannot, in the name of exactness and rigor, negate my body, my emotions and my feelings" (p. 105). To Freire, the body is not just the physical constitution but its passion in knowing the world, its compassion toward its community, and its connection with its history and culture. In the context of climate change, learning needs to be body based, as we connect tangibly and lovingly, in solidarity with nature, places, and species.

DISRUPTING HIERARCHIES: WHAT WE DID AND HOW WE DID IT

In our course, a typical class session started with heartfelt greetings and catch-ups, then a meditation led by one of us. After breathing exercises and meditation that grounded us in the moment, we addressed different topics for the day through presentations and discussions. Unlike conventional assignments, which aim to assess students' ability to articulate recited concepts, the coursework guided us to use our minds, hearts, and bodies as we discussed pressing local and global climate crises, such as droughts, flooding, famine, desert locusts, and forest fires, and the role that we play in society. Our minds were enriched by reading literature and thinking and analyzing critically, and our hearts and bodies were enriched through meditation practices to open up our senses to nature, visits to the forest, direct contact (weekly) with nature, writing reflections in our journals, and developing artworks.

Step by step, we experienced holistic education in practice, from learning about different theoretical frameworks to taking actions addressing local issues. Below, we illustrate how nature contact journals, meditation, and student-centered activities disrupted hierarchies and transformed our learning experiences.

Reconnecting With Nature Through Nature Contact Journals

Keeping a nature contact journal was a novel and impactful assignment. As students, we were free to choose the format of the journal: writing entries, creating photo essays or art in any form we connected with. Such flexibility facilitated deep, organic reflection on our relationship with nature, going beyond the ways in which capitalism has characterized nature as a commodity (Marx, 1867/1990).

Modern societies are organized in a way that is largely disconnected from nature (Bai, 2001; Carrier, 2010). Even when we are physically in nature, many of us rarely take the time to focus and actively engage with the environment with all our senses. To address this disembodiment and challenge the human–nature dichotomy, the nature contact journal assignment prompted us to reestablish a connection with nature and to reflect on how nature has nurtured us, and how we have both nurtured and harmed it.

Through photo essays and journals, students shared how they reconnected with nature using all their senses. Our entries reflected experiences of awe, mystery, tranquility, liveliness, and beauty when we opened our spiritual eyes to actively see, hear, and feel nature; these are notions not often welcomed in "academic spaces." These engagements also prompted us to rethink the relationship between human and beyond human, even after the class was over. Joanna (a coauthor) wrote:

> Under the changing weather, I noticed a few species in the woods that were seemingly new to the area. I shared a photo of a heron with my partner, recalling having seen one a few weeks back, and he replied, "I'm glad he's found a home!" Indeed, as we ask people to respect our home, our personal space, at the same time, other species deserve that respect too. After all, we are part of nature. (Joanna, June 2, 2022)

Experiencing Both Inner and Outer Learning Through Meditation

Jing encouraged each of us to volunteer and lead a meditation at the beginning of each class. Some of our practices focused on breathing, while others impelled us to, for example, visualize and enjoy birdsongs and raindrops in the woods. During one of the meditations, we pictured ourselves as an eagle flying through the forest and gradually soaring into the sky. These meditation practices helped us slow down, reconnect, and experience oneness with nature. By being more present with respect and curiosity for nature, we became more aware of it as being alive with consciousness and agency.

Through meditation and fully engaging our bodies to make meaning of the experience, we also created a more accepting and inclusive space, dismantling the hierarchy among humans: We became more comfortable and open in sharing our own personal stories and views, and reflecting on our own conduct that has contributed to harming nature. One of us shared about transforming her old habit of littering, such as throwing away plastic bottles into the environment. Subsequently, she joined a local nonprofit organization to collect litter dumped in a nearby stream. Nature walks, joining pro-environmental efforts, and continuous critical reflection helped her realize the negative impact her behavior has had on the environment. (We do recognize that individual actions are not enough; rather, big corporations, and in fact, our whole society, need to experience such a wake-up and exercise their agencies.) For us, such sharing might not be easy since we are often afraid of being judged. However, in this trusting and accepting environment that we co-constructed, everyone felt safe sharing some of the most personal parts of our lives. We presented our most genuine, whole selves.

Becoming Knowledge Coproducers Through Student-Centered Activities

The course was conducted by integrating first-, second-, and third-person levels of learning (Roth, 2006). In other words, our individual and collective experiences and knowledge as a group, as well as our connections between each other and our texts, all shaped the meaning of the course and became interwoven as our "textbook." Everyone came to class prepared to discuss the assigned readings (third-person); share experiences, narratives, and insights on the concerned themes (first-person); and connect with each other's stories and perspectives through discussions and dialogues (second-person). Jing also shared her experiences and stories, from her activist work to quotidian dilemmas such as buying food in single-use containers. We live with emotional conflicts daily in such circumstances, and mindfulness gives us the awareness we need to keep track of our habits and reflect on the impact of our actions.

Student-centered presentations and discussions provided a great opportunity for us to exercise agency and explore various structural and policy-level interventions. While Jing predetermined the weekly themes, we were free to focus on a specific aspect of the theme based on our own research interests. For instance, for the theme of "Mass Migration & Displacement and Emergencies Education & Community Resilience," one group presented a case study on rebuilding education after the 2010 earthquake in Haiti, which reflected their interest in the intersection of migration and its effects on the planet. For the theme of "International Climate Change Policies & Local Responses and Technological Innovations," another group chose to act out a scenario of a town hall meeting to vividly illustrate the context, concerns, and potential solutions to sea-level rise in a coastal city. By positioning presenters as the state governor, director of tourism and business development, a local educator, and a local resident, the role-playing format made the learning more engaging and memorable, allowing us to step into different roles and understand the complexity of climate change adaptation. Students became active agents exploring critical issues and proposing solutions related to climate change, resilience, adaptation, and education.

Our final project was focused on the topic of "Tackling Climate Challenges, Re-envisioning the Future, and Actions Now." We chose the format that was best suited for our interests: research papers, action plans, website creation, TED Talk–style videos, and policy briefs, to name a few. Since we come from various backgrounds with different expertise, sharing our final projects reinforced the notion that global climate change and education is a broad and pressing issue for which no one person has all the answers; there are many powerful and important approaches in which everyone is both a teacher and learner.

By the end of the semester, our cowritten "textbook" was thick with topics such as advocacy work around refugees and girls, policy recommendations on preserving a local river, an approach to engaging youth for climate activism, an environmentally conscious framework for video game designs, and more. Although the class ended after 13 weeks, we continue to engage in (individual and collective) actions. For example, one of the main activities in the class was to design signs to wrap around trees in Green Woods voicing their protest (more details later), and Virginia went back to replace some signs that had been damaged after rainstorms. Joanna took more courses that study how language affects our perception of nature. Joey attended a summit on climate change and youth empowerment and focused his graduation thesis on climate change education. As the president of the graduate student government, he collected testimonials and was involved in writing the proposal with the University Department of Transportation to apply for a $40 million federal grant that was eventually funded to replace the University's bus fleet with electrical buses. Together, we collaboratively wrote a research article that was accepted by a journal and published in 2023 (Lin et al., 2023).

FINDING PRAXIS AND TAKING ACTIONS:
THE SAVE THE WOODS MOVEMENT

Learning theory while simultaneously engaging our bodies and hearts enabled us to view issues critically and reflect on how we could transform the world around us, which Freire (2018) says "can be done only by means of the praxis: reflection and action upon the world in order to transform it" (p. 51).

During the first class, Jing shared with the group the Green Woods development project and the local resistance effort, the "Save Green Woods" campaign. The development plan proposed to build 81 private townhomes and graduate student apartments where the forest was located. Claiming to potentially alleviate the critical graduate student housing shortage while including a commercial project, the development plan would eliminate 28% of the University's remaining campus forest. This project stood in stark contrast with the University's stated efforts to operationalize sustainability, as well as with its gold star rating awarded by the Association for the Advancement of Sustainability in Higher Education. The decimation of this forest directly undercut the University's many efforts to promote recycling, construct gardens, and enact "green" campus infrastructure such as following LEED-certified building standards. In resistance, the "Save Green Woods" action plan underlined how the development project would harm the local ecosystem by creating an urban heat island, displacing animal habitats, and destroying over 15 acres of trees.

Our class visited Green Woods several times. Juxtaposed with high-rise parking garages and stately academic buildings, the wooded paths of Green Woods beckoned contemplation. The deer grazing, the birds chirping, the creek babbling, the squirrels rustling, and the leaves shaking created a sensory experience for anyone who took the time to be still in the midst of it all. In recognizing that this ecological system is home for many, and not just for the human species, the call to protect the Green Woods became apparent. Feeling strongly that the forest should be preserved, we collectively made a commitment to contribute to the campaign.

We drew from indigenous beliefs such as the Seventh Generation Principle, which holds that anything we do could affect seven generations into the future. According to this principle, multiple human generations share an interconnected and interdependent destiny with their ecosystems, so we are therefore responsible for the impacts of our actions (Lin et al., 2021). In centering this need to respect all living creatures as our kin, we became acutely aware that one vital voice was missing from the conversation about this proposed development: "the voices of the trees." Recognizing their life energy, intelligence, and will to live, we attempted to metaphorically channel the "voices" of the trees into the protest. What might the trees feel, and how might they express themselves? How would this create a dialogue between the forest and the campus body? This was the birth of the "Voices of the Woods" project.

We hung signs on the Green Woods trees with various phrases that invited those who walked or strolled by to engage in "dialogue" with the trees, in order to educate the community about the "Save Green Woods" movement. These signs included both statements and questions, such as: "We are living beings, love us and care for us"; "Cut the greed, not the green"; "Hug me, not tug me"; "Take a moment to listen to the ecosystem around you, we all depend on its survival"; "I may be sentenced to death for no crime"; "Hello, I can feel your presence. Can you save me?"; "We all have the same roots"; and "This isn't just my home. It's yours and it's the animals; it's ours." In total, 30 trees' "voices" were amplified to prod the conscience of the larger University community.

We hung signs October 1, 2021, and each sign had a QR code that directed people to a website we created as a space for our class to connect with the community. We hoped that students and other passersby would be inspired to join in or create their own initiatives.

Jing then invited us for lunch to reflect and make meaning of our project together. A few critical reflections emerged. For instance, Joanna mentioned how the idea of "giving trees voices" still assumed certain power dynamics between the trees and us. While these pro-environmental messages were aimed at prompting passersby to reflect on their own behaviors, some of the signs emphasized the vulnerability and victimhood of the trees, risking a passive representation of nature. In response to this, Joanna proposed working with the Departments of Plant Science and Fine Art to create an art installation that displayed how trees communicate through their roots, visualizing the trees' agency in an interesting way to raise people's awareness.

On October 28, 2021, a University official announced that the University was going to pause the housing development project and reassess the situation after some time. While we saw this as a temporary win, our efforts continued. Our class decided to keep the signs in place after the semester ended, and some of us volunteered to visit the site periodically to check on the signs. On January 12, 2022, we replaced the signs with new ones, as the originals had been damaged by weather, and in March 2022, we took them down since they had deteriorated further. However, we remained in touch with the "Save Green Woods" project, and together we have continued to follow the housing development project and support the efforts to stop it.

We returned in September 2022 to put up the signs again, and included the students who were enrolled in the 2022 Global Climate Change and Education class. The new class pushed different initiatives, such as writing a research article that envisioned post-human education and creating a website on climate change education featuring young people's voices. In essence, we were creating a network of solidarity: across class sections with other students, with nature, and with the larger community.

For us, this experience demonstrated the power of community-based action. We joined the project initiated by local groups and felt empowered in this coalition. We, as a group striving to be increasingly responsible global citizens, felt the impact of connecting knowledge with self- and group-action to initiate and actualize change.

FINAL REFLECTIONS

All of us were grateful to have each other as learning partners in this transformative journey. Below, we (individually) share how the experience of disrupting various hierarchies in class has shaped our own positionalities and praxes.

Jing

I took the front seat in planning the course and coordinating learning activities. But as we built a learning collaborative, we experienced the blending of our energy and heart-mind; visible and invisible teaching and learning took place, flowing in all directions in the classroom. When we opened our heart to see the divinity of nature, a sense of awe appeared. The success of the class is that we went beyond a divided consciousness and felt a unity of heart and spirit with each other and nature. Contemplative meditation, a trusting environment, students taking agency in their learning, ownership of the process and product of their work, and social activism, all helped empower us to build a vision and take actions toward a world of peace and respect for nature and for each other.

Virginia

We moved beyond just disrupting hierarchies to building bridges of the heart between teacher and students. I see Jing and my classmates as generous individuals who not only contribute to my scholarly life but also to my personal and spiritual life. I have shared dreams and worries with them, and I feel that they care deeply for me like I care for them. And even though I have always felt energized by nature, this class experience gave me a renewed way to see and admire nature that is more present and makes me appreciate the interdependence between us and nature.

Joey

It is easy to get discouraged, frustrated, and even hopeless when imagining solutions that confront global climate crises. With the immense scale of the crisis and the potential for destruction that looms over our future, I often find myself being lulled into pessimism when thinking about how so many compounding challenges continue to accrue to our social, ecological, and political environments. However, this course foregrounded an important reminder that there is no time for pessimistic thinking. Despair fosters complacency, and complacency is the enemy of the civic and political participation that is needed to drive social change; it feeds the many destructive hierarchies that exist among human beings and between humans and nature.

This course has instilled the idea that we all have a role to play in combating global climate change. Personally, I have taken on the leadership role of president of the graduate student government at our University, and in this role, I connect with fellow student leaders to dialogue with the University and local government to identify and solve community environmental issues.

Joanna

The course is all about deep listening: listening to ourselves, our surroundings, and other points of view. No matter how technologically advanced our world gets, we will not be able to achieve a more just and equitable world for both humans and the environment unless we listen to and develop a sense of empathy for the "other." The course showed me how contemplative practices could be incorporated into higher education classrooms and its impact on both students and teachers as knowledge co-constructors, as we built a heartfelt, supportive community for sharing and growing. To put my learning into practice, I am initiating a student organization on campus to promote mindfulness practices and cultivate meaningful, cross-discipline dialogues that address and act on global challenges collectively.

Maha

It is difficult to create changes in behavior, but it starts with a mindset shift. Our coursework and time together emphasized a nonhierarchical relationship with nature where we coexist with it instead of exerting power and dominance over it. Jing challenged us to find ways to reimagine how the world could be and what attitude and behavior adjustments would be beneficial. For me, that was mentally shifting away from my one-directional perception of how the environment will negatively impact human health to a deeper understanding of how we humans impact nature, and the mutuality that connects us. I experienced this shift from the multiple exercises we did that all made room for creative engagement with the material. I picked up painting and did several artworks showing the power of nature and the beauty of trees. Such creative engagement encouraged imagination, and this was helpful because we had the space to apply multiple perspectives when exploring the various hierarchies that exist.

Emmanuel

Through this course, I was made acutely aware that climate change has dramatically affected my home country Kenya, so I wanted to find out what young people can do to fight climate change. Hence, for my final assignment, I piloted a participatory action study focusing on the role played by youth climate change activists in Kenya. Through this study, a participant, who is an environmental activist, and I created a series of Instagram posts to highlight challenges that the study participant and other youth experienced while attending COP26 (a UN Climate Change Conference held in 2021).

Alongside creating awareness about the climate change crisis in Kenya and globally, we also deliberated on ways to mainstream climate change crisis awareness in the Kenyan education curriculum and in local media. These posts attracted over 1,780 views and increased the environmental activist's following to over 2,300. The activist in this pilot study is a representative of the many disadvantaged groups that are often silenced or ignored when it comes to making global climate change policies; this despite the fact their generation is hit hardest by the impacts of climate change. This study therefore disrupted deficit narratives—that frame youth as incompetent, disinterested, and disinclined in acting as agents of change in climate crisis activism (Ritchie, 2021)—by centering the voice and agency of a young person who is passionately and proactively involved in activism around climate crisis mitigation in his own country and globally. I probably would not have conducted this kind of study had I not taken this class.

Anna

When you study and research environmental change, you cannot be indifferent (similar to Freire's statement that education is not neutral). This type of learning and disruption of neutrality is certainly "relational" because as you relate more deeply to the object of your study, to the classroom, and to nature itself, it becomes increasingly difficult to stay indifferent. Taking part in activities that connected us with nature in a direct, profound level was a new experience for me.

I was also very much surprised by how much I was impacted by the meditation practice at the beginning of our classes. This practice broke the traditional format of learning, and I became more open to learning from my inner self and my classmates. By allowing ourselves to be led by a classmate to wherever they wanted us to go in the meditation fostered a sense of trust that is integral to disrupting hierarchies.

Jordan

In realizing how much we have harmed or ignored nature, I reconnected with a place of personal significance to me: a nearby creek in my childhood neighborhood. By revisiting this place with a critical perspective, I was able to better grasp how litter and human-made infrastructure harm the environment, and how I can play a role in contributing to the well-being of the site.

CONCLUSION

As seen in our individual projects and group efforts with Save Green Woods, our class collectively attempted to disrupt hierarchies between humans and nature, hierarchies among humans themselves, hierarchies between teachers and students, and hierarchies of mind over body, heart, and spirit. In this process, we cultivated curiosity and agency in all of us as cocreators of knowledge and action in the teaching and learning process, and emphasized creating and strengthening bonds among all beings. In this way, a critical, contemplative, and holistic approach guided most of our class interactions, and engendered a substantive understanding of reciprocity and interconnectivity between people and nature, and between our inner and outer selves (Freire, 1970/2000; Freire, 1993). This class empowered us to explore solutions to counter an institutional decision that threatened the Green Woods ecosystem, and by extension, the larger natural environment in which we all exist. This solution included amplifying the "voices" of trees and partnering with other local community members and other undergraduate students to prevent the destruction of the Green Woods.

Our hope is that our actions will, like seeds in the forest, grow and blossom into larger systemic change that fully disrupts ways of thinking in the University community and beyond. Since the Global Climate Change and Education class will be offered every fall semester, we will find ways to connect with the new cohorts. In the face of catastrophic effects of human domination over the environment, our class continues to explore pedagogies that can disrupt anthropocentrism and model innovative, reciprocal relationships with nature. Ultimately, by dismantling the ways that oppressive hierarchies direct our behavior within the classroom and in our environment, we formed a connection between our class, the environment, and the larger University community.

Our class calls on communities to reimagine their engagement with their environment through revolutionary processes of dialogue, reflection, and action.

DISCUSSION QUESTIONS/ACTIVITIES

1. Why and how should caring for nature be incorporated into the education curriculum? How can we adopt critical, contemplative, and holistic pedagogies to foster deep love and respect for nature while also breaking down hierarchies of all kinds?
2. What are some of the ways that you have been hurting or nurturing nature? What can you do to start nurturing and showing gratitude to nature?
3. Is there a hierarchy between individual and systemic/collective approaches to climate change activism, and if so, how can we disrupt it?

REFERENCES

Bai, H. (2001). Beyond the educated mind: Towards a pedagogy of mindfulness. In B. Hockings, J. Haskell, & W. Linds (Eds.), *Unfolding bodymind: Exploring possibilities through education* (pp. 86–99). The Foundation for Educational Renewal.

Carrier, J. (2010). Protecting the environment the natural way: Ethical consumption and commodity fetishism. *Antipode, 42*(3), 672–689.

Diggins, C. A. (2011). Examining intersectionality: The conflation of race, gender, and class in individual and collective identities. *Inquiries Journal/Student Pulse, 3*(03). Retrieved from http://www.inquiriesjournal.com/a?id=417

Farkas, M. (2012). Participatory technologies, pedagogy 2.0 and information literacy. *Library Hi Tech, 30*(1), 82–94.

Freire, P. (1993). *Pedagogy of the city.* Continuum.

Freire, P. (2018). *Pedagogy of the oppressed.* Bloomsbury Publishing USA.

Freire, P. (1970/2000). *Pedagogy of the oppressed.* 30th anniversary edition. Continuum.

Hyde, A. M., & LaPrad, J. G. (2015). Mindfulness, democracy, and education. *Democracy and Education, 23*(2), Article 2. Retrieved from https://democracyeducationjournal.org/home/vol23/iss2/2

Lin, J., Fiore, A., Sorensen, E., Gomes, V., Haavik, J., Malik, M., Mok, S. J., Scanlon, J., Wanjala, E., & Grigoryeva, A. (2023). Contemplative, holistic eco-justice pedagogies in higher education: From anthropocentrism to fostering deep love and respect for nature. *Teaching in Higher Education, 28*(5), 953–968. Retrieved from https://doi.org/ 10.1080/13562517.2023.2197109

Lin, J., Stoltz, A., Rappeport, A., & Aruch, M. (2021). Decolonization and transformation of higher education for sustainability: Integrating indigenous knowledge into policy, teaching, research, and practice. *Journal of International & Comparative Higher Education, 13*(3), 134–156.

Marx, K. (1867/1990). *Capital: A critique of political economy* (Vol. 1, B. Fowkes, Trans.). Penguin.

Milfont, T. L., Richter, I., Sibley, C. G., Wilson, M. S., & Fischer, R. (2013). Environmental consequences of the desire to dominate and be superior. *Personality and Social Psychology Bulletin, 39*(9), 1127–1138. Retrieved from https://doi.org/10.1177/0146167213490805

Ritchie, J. (2021). Movement from the margins to global recognition: Climate change activism by young people and in particular indigenous youth. *International Studies in Sociology of Education, 30*(1–2), 53–72.

Roth, H. (2006). Contemplative studies: Prospect for a new field. *Teachers College Record, 108*(9), 1787–1815.

-saed. (2019). Nature is beyond value because we are part of nature. *Capitalism Nature Socialism, 30*(2), 143–156. Retrieved from https://doi.org/10.1080/10455752.2019.1610596

Samuels, D. (2004). Language, meaning, modernity, and doowop. *Semiotica, 149*(1–4), 297–323.

Stoltz, A., Harmon, K., Newman, R., Brooks, P., Lin, J., Ayers, S., Aruch, M., & Thomas, T. (2022). Tribal collaborations and Indigenous representation in higher education: Challenges, successes, and suggestions for attaining the SDGs. In S. Ajaps, M. F. Mbah, A. T. Johnson, & W. L. Filho (Eds.), *Indigenous methodologies, research and practices for sustainable development. World sustainability series* (pp. 117–133). Springer.

CHAPTER 4

Cala-Boca Já Morreu

Education Through Media

Grácia Lopes Lima, Mariana Casellato, and Milena Klinke

INTRODUCTION

In this chapter,[1] we chronicle how over a period of almost 3 decades our group transformed radio recorders and video cameras into educational tools for children and youth. As a Brazilian initiative that started in 1995, the Projeto Cala-Boca já Morreu (CBJM) is a nonformal educational project that uses radio and television channels to promote collective communication production with children and youth. The phrase *Cala-boca já morreu,* loosely translated, means "no more silencing." Inspired by Paulo Freire's ideas, this project aims at rupturing the traditional roles of *subjects* and *objects* of knowledge, turning children and youth participants and adult coordinators into learning partners.

Disrupting hierarchies is not a simple task. It demands time, effort, and constant praxis: reflection combined with action. Merely changing the title of positions or activities does not ensure that roles and values will be effectively transformed. Instead, focusing on critically revisiting the root and nature of interactions between group members and the values behind those interactions has proven to be more effective, though perhaps even more challenging. By presenting CBJM's story, perspectives, and methodology, we will show how reflection and engaging in a different model of human relations can be rewarding, and something to be exercised constantly, through life.

Because of CBJM's nonformal educational nature, we will not be using the terms teachers and students but rather coordinators—the facilitators of the activities—and participants—those who joined. Grácia and Donizete, the founders of the initiative, started with a group of children, and whether it was designing shows or addressing conflicts in the group, the work was guided by the ethics of non-neutrality and co-construction (Freire, 1996). As the adults coresponsible for the initiative, the founders had a full awareness of their political stance and role as educators. Committed to social change in society, they always made their opinions clear, but they would *coordinate*, or organize *with* the group (and not *for* the group). They helped amplify the participants' ideas, opinions, and feelings, and mediated conversations and conflicts, while cobuilding individual and collective self-awareness. By creating and nourishing the space for participants to express themselves, Donizete and Grácia were putting into practice their political beliefs in partnership with the young people. These terms—coordinators and participants—represent the initial roles, which did admittedly change over time in this learning partnership, as the children from the original group grew over the years.

CBJM is rooted in the work of revolutionary Latin American scholars Paulo Freire and Mario Kaplún (an Argentinian Uruguayan communicator who left mainstream media to work with peasant communities producing communication for political engagement during the dictatorship). We have come to understand that, though part of Freire's work was translated into English, some key terms around this practice do not have direct synonyms in English; therefore, part of our effort in this chapter will be to introduce some concepts from Portuguese.

The authors of this text are three women, each representing different generations and phases of this initiative. Grácia Lopes Lima, one of the professors who founded the initiative in 1995, represents the early years of CBJM's creation and writes about its historical/theoretical framework. Mariana Casellato first started at CBJM in 1996 at the age of 10 and remains part of the organization. She represents the initial development of the project during the 1990s through the early 2000s. Milena Klinke joined CBJM in 2012 at the age of 20 and represents the development of our work in recent years. The following sections showcase each of these generational perspectives.

THE UNPREDICTABILITY OF THE TREE

Grácia Lopes Lima

I am a teacher and psychotherapist by training. In 1995, I was 45 and director of the Gens Institute for Education and Culture (GENS), an education consulting agency, with Donizete Soares (a philosopher and teacher by training), in São Paulo. Together, along with *Rádio Cidadã* (Citizen Radio), a community radio station, we founded CBJM. It was a radio show produced and run entirely by a group of students from nearby schools and broadcast on community-owned channels. This educational initiative was created to provide 7- to 12-year-old children with a platform to share their thoughts and feelings where they would not be silenced. The name of the project is an adaptation of a saying in Portuguese that stands in opposition to undemocratic movements, such as past dictatorships of Latin America.

The origins of this initiative are closely connected to Freire's ideals of fostering an informed and critical citizenry as a responsibility of all of society, where every person should contribute to emancipatory teaching and learning processes, in contrast to the banking education model he criticizes. This conceptual platform was central to our work because we believe that to silence a human is to dehumanize them (Freire, 2014).

Our overall process and approach illustrated what Freire wrote in *Pedagogy of Autonomy* (1998):

> [O]nly in this way—when learners are effective subjects of the construction and reconstruction of knowledge—can we speak authentically of knowledge that is taught, in which the taught is grasped in its very essence and therefore, learned by those who are learning. (p. 33)

Therefore, with our coordination and guidance, participants learned to create scripts, produce interviews, and comment on issues related to the environment, culture, health, education, and human rights. Excited by the learning, they soon grew interested in also exploring other roles, such as aspects of production (e.g., operating the sound equipment and framing of a camera shot), hosting programs, answering listeners' calls, and writing the topics of discussion and questions for interviews.

This learning, exploration, and creation was the work of the participants, and as coordinators, Donizete and I supported these processes. We were not specialists in communication, but we shared the little knowledge that we had from domestic use of recorders; from there, we all learned together. Inspired by the idea of generative themes Freire used for literacy, the participants brought their rich ideas from their own repertoire and experiences for radio show topics and, together, we cocreated knowledge to "read the world," subverting the teacher and student roles defined by the banking education model.

In a short span, GENS and *Rádio Cidadã* teams remarked on the "growth of the seeds" we had planted together: The radio station had been transformed into a stimulating educational environment. By producing radio shows, the participants' learning was driven by their curiosity. Working collaboratively, they explored topics covered by school curricula and beyond. We would pick topics as a group, and each person would conduct their research and later share it with the group and the listeners during the live show.

For example, one of the show's sections was dedicated to space: A boy passionate about this topic would check NASA's website on a weekly basis to bring news about outer space. Another section was focused on complaints: Participants would discuss a range of problems, some that they had with their parents, or with a nearby store that was charging exorbitant prices for stationary materials, or with a denim company located in a poor part of the neighborhood that was dumping toxic waste in the river.

Within less than a year, two other communication formats were added to our project: print and audiovisual media. Both were a result of new partnerships established between GENS and community communication broadcast channels of São Paulo. This expansion was possible because the project was highly relevant to the participants since they were the ones in control, selecting topics of discussion, interviewees, and formats. The children invited, interviewed, and learned from adults from varied fields. The interviewees were not school professionals but instead, politicians, authors, scientists, and sound technicians. These interviewees took on the joint responsibility of raising conscious citizens while also incorporating new perspectives into their own work, based on the participants' questions and knowledge. This process demonstrated Freire's conception of the "teacher" also being a "student," and the "student" being a "teacher" too. For example, when interviewing a biologist about snakes, the children asked him "if snakes get the flu, like people?" I, as the "educator," was initially embarrassed by that question. However, our guest laughed, mesmerized by the participants' untamed curiosity, and answered that "yes, snakes do indeed get the flu." I, too, was always learning, and the CBJM show was becoming an initiative that was disrupting hierarchies on different levels.

Our practice, rooted in Freirean praxis, challenged the traditional roles of teachers and students, and from there we derived our methodology combining two areas, education and communication, to ensure that the participants were respected and free to engage fully in the communicative exercise (as Mariana and Milena will describe later).

We based our methodology on Freire's liberatory education theories, and in libertarian education theories represented by Emma Goldman and Mikhail Bakunin. Some of the fundamental elements of our approach were individuality, affirmation of freedom, equal rights, and shared management. With Mário Kaplún as our main reference in the sphere of communication, we believed that community communication channels could facilitate experimental projects and the participation of nonprofessionals, and nonhierarchical management could create space for diverse voices and promote community economic development and solidarity.

These methodologies and theories underpinned our commitment to promoting autonomy, but we also took our responsibility as adults seriously in nurturing that space. We acknowledged that aiming for a total disruption of hierarchy in this context was risky when working with children and youth in their early development phases, because that could lead to a failure in appropriately caring for those individuals and in respecting their age-specific needs.

We provided the structure necessary for the well-being of the children while coordinating the process, instilling relational awareness among group members, teaching them what we knew, and posing questions that generated critical reflection. With time, participants became more knowledgeable and comfortable with taking on many of the coordination and production roles, even becoming coordinators when they felt confident in doing so. They became savvier around technologies, taking the lead and teaching one another. Within a few years, the children became young adults who started giving communication production workshops to other children and youth. Throughout the following decade, we grew nationally and internationally.

Personally, I learned to extract theory from practice with the participants, which years later informed my doctoral thesis, *Education Through Media* (Lima, 2009). This thesis expounded on educommunication, the intersection between communication and education, a growing field of study in Latin America (rooted in Freire's theories of autonomy and agency, and a repudiation of the banking education model). Different from media education studies, educommunication has a strong political lens, with liberatory interventions being a fundamental part of the work (Lima, 2009). Starting off as an experimental radio show with kids, we found ourselves to be one of the founders of the educommunication field. And it has been through that intersection of education and communication that we have been promoting an emancipatory education that has been able to disrupt hierarchies.

FIRST SPROUTS

Mariana Casellato

> The new generations are readers of audiovisual communication still in their intra-uterine state. (. . .) [They] are formed within this context from the moment they open their eyes to the world. They already understand what the television and the cinema is showing. They bring this knowledge, this reading, into the classroom. They are all post-graduates in audiovisual language when they enter school illiterate.
>
> —Franco, 1996, p. 109

In 1996, I was 10 years old and had just started writing classes with Grácia—my mother had taken me there because I loved to write. One day, Grácia showed me one of CBJM's radio programs. I listened to the children discussing their experiences as kids: a radio soap opera, curiosities about a Brazilian wolf, a chocolate cake recipe. I started writing them letters that they then read and answered live on their shows. Not long after that, I was facing a microphone for the first time at the small house that hosted the radio studio on a Sunday afternoon. Other kids taught me how to operate the equipment and how to position the microphone to speak.

We were 10 to 12 kids meeting weekly to plan and present the live 2-hour radio show. With time, we were also producing newspapers, videos, and photography. At a certain point, every day after school I would go to GENS to meet with the group and plan our activities. We enjoyed ourselves there; we would often play games and eat together before participating in discussions. We felt like we co-owned the meetings and were coresponsible for organizing them, something that not even my most participatory class in school provided. In CBJM, I had the space to do everything Grácia and other coordinators did; I led conversations and shared my opinion freely.

At first, Grácia modeled this process: She taught us the name of each step, how to create an agenda, and how to organize meetings. This process reflected Freire's distinction between the educator being authoritarian—owner of absolute truths—versus an educator as an authoritative figure—who knows themselves to be a reference, responsible for sharing their knowledge rather than imposing it (Freire, 1998). She abided by her ethical commitment to respecting the autonomy and dignity of each learner (Freire, 1998). In modeling trust and these Freirean principles, she invited us to cocreate and take turns leading each step.

Later, we, as participants, discussed making changes to the structure of meetings. We suggested implementing icebreakers and different ways of time management. The lead person for a meeting would ask the group for agenda items, who would document the ideas in our shared notebook, and who would be responsible for specific tasks. For example, if we were going to be interviewed by a media channel, we discussed who wanted to participate and who would conduct research on the media channel; determined our audience; and brainstormed potential questions that we might be asked and discussion points we wanted to raise.

Even as kids, we already carried a lot of knowledge regarding communication. Although at first we did not know the formal terms relating to radio production, we knew what radio shows sounded like. For example, we understood different types of transitions, intros, and outros, and our familiarity with some of the equipment facilitated quick learning of their functionality. As soon as I shared my interest in the technical aspects, the radio station's operator taught me how to use the sound operating table. Within a few months, I was ready to teach others these technical skills I had accrued. The process of learning from each other was how we all gained many new skills and knowledges.

The world grew "bigger" than the radio station and GENS headquarters, because children speaking their opinion drew wide attention. As a teenager, I found myself participating at panels and having critical discussions with adults on citizenship, health, and the environment while also teaching other kids how to produce communication. We were invited to join important events. In 1996, we were panelists on a training for environmental education teachers, and in 1997, our group made an opening statement at the launch of a project aimed at involving students in environmental action in their school areas. In 2000, we joined a training by the biggest Brazilian public university's school of medicine on health for community radio station broadcasters. These engagements were indeed a form of citizenship education for us.

I remember the first time I traveled by myself to Acre, a state in the north of Brazil, to give a radio workshop to a group of 100 students from the municipal education network. I was 18 at that time and had been part of CBJM for 8 years. We were all young people then, with only a few new children among us. We were producing radio, giving workshops, and joining events as lecturers quite frequently. The invitation came to the group, but we had to choose one person to go. I was active among the participants, but others who were more extroverted often spearheaded those initiatives, and as much as I thought I could do it, I felt insecure, because it was a large responsibility. I remember a silence within the group when we talked about who should go. Someone suggested that I should go, and different people supported and encouraged the idea. I was scared, but I knew I could do it because I had been working with that group and they believed I was capable. I accepted the challenge and together we prepared for the workshop. We thought about the workshop's context, gathered information, brainstormed, wrote a script, created an agenda, and finally conducted a mock session so I could practice. A friend my age had more experience traveling than me, so she gave me tips on how to prepare for the 6-hour flight.

In the end, leading this workshop was an incredible experience. I was able to visit a place completely different from where I lived. I tasted new food and got to see what public schools looked like in another part of my country. I faced my insecurity and conducted that workshop, creating the space for other kids to talk about their own life experiences. Together with my CBJM peers, I was encouraged to take on a more active role, which enabled me to see the world in a different way, and to collaborate on expanding our sphere of influence beyond just our radio station. I felt important and empowered.

Grácia and Donizete always discussed the importance of building a space of encouragement, freedom, and autonomy. When we were kids, they would mention Freire occasionally, telling us that he was a teacher who talked about freedom. When we were teenagers, as we discussed group dynamics, they would cite Freire more specifically, talking about his work and theories. In my 20s, we started giving weeklong trainings on CBJM's methodology. On those occasions, as we led the more technical and practical activities, we would hear Grácia and Donizete's lectures on Paulo Freire. It was around that time that I decided to read Freire myself. I started with *Extensão ou Comunicação?* (2001) (*Extension or Communication?*), and his ideas impacted me deeply while they also felt quite familiar, since I could identify that I had experienced those ideas in practice since childhood. His work helped me understand even further the importance of empowering people to think critically about their roles in society. Little by little, the empowering task of producing communication equipped us with skills to disrupt hierarchy, share power, and deepen our relationship as learning partners.

More relevant to the disrupting of hierarchies—was the development of people skills, or what we call in Portuguese *convivência*. Sometimes translated as *conviviality* in English, *convivência* is a word that defines the experience of sharing a routine encounter and engagement with someone or with a group of people, the set of routine interactions that slowly craft relationships among people. As Baró (1997) attests, "there is no knowledge capable of transforming reality that does not involve a change in relations among human beings" (p. 17). *Convivência* encapsulates how relationships, bonds, and conflicts are shaped. The spaces of *convivência* we experience throughout life shape our personality and existence. The collective communication production exercise as praxis is not focused on producing a product but rather is a means to exercise *convivência*, or transform how we relate to one another.

The focus of our work is the process and how relationships are formed. We addressed tensions, including disagreements over who appeared more frequently on the show, insecurity, envy, competition, jealousy, and resentment. By naming our feelings, we were able to reshape our relations to make them less centered in individualism and competitiveness and more in solidarity. Addressing these tensions honestly and openly was essential to building/maintaining our relationships as learning partners.

Early on we used a box of emotions: When we were angry with someone for any reason, we anonymously wrote how we felt on a piece of paper and added it to the box, and every week we opened the box and discussed everything inside. Due to the practice and development of our conflict resolution skills, addressing conflict became more organic. Even though addressing and transforming conflicts is a difficult task, we became increasingly better at it. All these tools helped us name and transform our world (Freire, 2014).

Praxis was enshrined in this naming of the world: We reflected just as deeply as we engaged in the creation of critical communication. For example, in a weeklong radio workshop we led, we would debrief each day and discuss improvements for the following day. These reflections were not bureaucratic conversations about tasks to be completed. Instead, these were moments when we focused on our own *formation*. I opt here for the word *formation* instead of *training* because that is the word—*formação*—we use in Portuguese to describe this kind of process. *Formação*, according to the Brazilian Michaelis dictionary, is a "way of raising a person, forging their character, personality and education." *Formação* is much more connected with the idea of the long-term education process focused on *convivência* (rather than just skills development), reflecting a commitment to fostering human beings who care about liberation for all.

Grácia regularly discussed the connection between education and life. That connection is what constitutes CBJM. We are engaging in a lifelong praxis of *convivência* and building a new way of living together that requires constant thinking and doing. My own praxis has been a deeply meaningful journey, eventually leading up to my becoming a coordinator for the radio production process at the age of 26. It is at that juncture that we welcomed Milena to CBJM, from whom you will hear next.

LATE BLOSSOMS

Milena Klinke

I arrived at CBJM in 2012. By then, the coordination role was not exclusive to Grácia and Donizete. The children you read about were young adults at this point, highly knowledgeable in CBJM's methodology, working mainly with other young people interested in learning how to use radio to communicate. I was 21, and a 2nd-year psychology student at a traditional private university in São Paulo. I was a hardworking, low-income student on a scholarship living in a faraway neighborhood.

I had never done radio before and had some time to spare before taking my bus home after class, so I decided to join. Grácia was sometimes present as an invited lecturer, and Mariana was one of the coordinators, working directly with me and other young people.

I was impressed with how participants and coordinators at the CBJM had been producing communication for so long using a collective and participatory approach. I participated in Rádio Ambiente 21 (Radio Environment 21), an 8-month long workshop that was organized in weekly sessions and focused on environmental topics. It culminated in youth media coverage of Rio+20, an environmental conference held by the United Nations in Brazil that year. After 6 months, my role as a participant in Radio Environment 21 began to shift to a place of creation, belonging, and greater autonomy within CBJM. So, I produced a radio show for the first time.

The first thing that stood out to me was how the members of CBJM related to each other. This, I learned, was the result of their intentional praxis—*convivência*. Brazilian philosopher Pedrinho Guareschi (2007) affirms:

> what constitutes a group are its relations. If you want to know if you are looking at a group or not, observe if relations among its participants are present or not. If you want to know what type of group that is, observe what is the nature of the relations among the people involved. . . . if you want to transform a group, begin by transforming the existing relations in this group. (p. 86)

From my initial observations, I was quickly able to see that CBJM's structure was different from other organizations; I was witnessing and participating in their disrupting of hierarchy in real time.

Participation in CBJM was based in *auto convocação* (loosely translated to English as *self-convocation*, or the intentional will to join an activity). This involved participants intentionally opting into activities, which reflected the exercise of freedom, something that we had to unlearn from the banking education model. Despite broad interest, participation varied based on our comfort level and interests. Those who were not confident to speak on the air joined as timekeepers or script writers.

For me, at first, talking live felt difficult and made me nervous. I remember listening to our shows and finding the sound of my voice weird, but I was also deeply empowered in recognizing myself, my words, and the final audio product that tangibly represented our group's work. Radio production created a sense of belonging and confidence that was the basis for later embracing the coordination role. Participating in this process together as learning partners was the source of our liberation, the path to learning about ourselves individually and in a group, finding support to build our confidence, while learning how to critically read the world so that even outside of that space we would feel empowered to challenge injustices and organize alternatives.

Another element that stood out to me was the transparency around sharing information about the project. This made me feel safe and comfortable with asking questions and, eventually, offering suggestions and criticism. I felt free and had the space to be creative. Freedom and creation, however, did not come easily to me. My experience of learning had been mostly in school, and freedom was not present there—we had to sit straight, obediently accepting times, rules, and curriculum. Knowledge was centered on the teacher (Freire, 2014). I had not experienced freedom like those who had been in CBJM since childhood—roughly half of the group at this point. It was through routinely meeting and relating to participants and coordinators that I started learning to exercise my freedom and overcome the distance that initially existed between us. We became jointly responsible for the learning process (Freire, 2014). As Donizete used to put it, responsibilities were individual (e.g., I would be responsible for hosting the show or researching a specific topic), but power was always shared (e.g., decision-making).

I remember moments at the start of my participation when I recognized Freire's (2001) dialogic approach. All steps of the collective production process required collaborative and generative dialogue. To produce an interview, for example, we had to think about and discuss our lived reality together, determine what to bring to a radio program, and create partnerships with the people we wanted to interview. In this process, coordinators did not do the work *for* us but *with* us.

During the work, I became closer to one of the other coordinators, Mariana Manfredi. We discussed my reflections about the process, as well as the connections I made between this work and the theories I learned in my undergraduate psychology course. I was a sophomore and had recently been selected for a paid internship in a mental health program for socially vulnerable children and youth. As part of my job, I assisted other professionals in facilitating activities with the children. After 6 months participating in Radio Environment 21, I decided to bring that experience to my workplace.

Mariana shared details on the methodology and preparation steps used by the coordinators, composed of four nonlinear steps for organizing a collective communication production session:

- **Pitching:** Ideas flow freely to define the topic and format of the production. It is the time to exercise freedom, negotiation, and critical thinking.
- **Production:** This is when the idea takes form, is turned into a script, and gets recorded; it is usually the most chaotic and creative phase.
- **Sharing:** This is the moment to close the communication circle, reaching the listener, viewer, or reader. In this phase, listening to one's own voice can be a powerful exercise of self-confidence.
- **Considerations:** Participants share impressions on the final product and, most importantly, the production process, such as challenges and joyful moments, to raise self-awareness about one's emotions and behavioral patterns.

Understanding the underlying methodology helped me shift from the role of participant to that of coordinator. I learned that there was a methodology, an agenda, predefined times for each part of a session, and a clear set of goals for each step. In speaking to Mariana about these details, I felt like her equal. She sent me an agenda model as a reference and gave me feedback with tips on how to prepare within a limited time frame and how to make participants comfortable during the production. We went back and forth in a very safe environment until I felt confident to lead activities.

CBJM's values—centered on dialogue, transparency, and generosity—fostered a space for the cocreation of knowledge. My experience with group work in psychology was informed by CBJM as I learned about their critical perspectives. This was an individual and collective exercise in which dialogue materialized as "the loving encounter of [people] who 'pronounce' knowledge, that is, transform it, and by transforming it, humanize it for the humanization of all" (Freire, 2001, p. 43).

The more I got involved with the group and became responsible for planning and other tasks, the more I learned how to bring this exercise in *convivência* to life. This opened a world of possibilities beyond CBJM for me. I started to exercise autonomy in other spaces, including the university and my practice as a psychologist.

CONCLUSION

Knowledge emerges only through invention and re-invention, through the restless, impatient, continuing, hopeful inquiry human beings pursue in the world, with the world, and with each other.

—Freire, 2014, p. 72

Through our voices, we hope to have made clear that CBJM is a collective project focused on developing the vocation of becoming more fully human (Freire, 2014) by dismantling hierarchical differences. Since 1995, we have been transforming radio into a tool that creates a path to liberation, to the constitution of autonomous individuals, people committed to themselves and to the world around them. Our nonformal practice enables us to step away from the banking educational model more easily.

Grácia and Donizete, dreaming of the possibility of a different society, sparked an educational process based on Freire's ideas. As following an authoritarian model was not an option, it was through praxis and radio that we invented and reinvented what *convivência* could look like. We connected action and reflection toward a collective freedom built *with* all, opening space to become coinvestigators in dialogue (Freire, 2014).

We use radio as a means to promote conversations about the world and to build community, from participants' individual life experiences to a range of global topics. For this to exist, structures have to be broken, as institutionalized roles too often maintain hierarchy. Breaking through these roles is needed for coliberation.

In memoriam
Donizete Soares, 1958–2022

DISCUSSION QUESTIONS/ACTIVITIES

1. How can you imagine the disrupting of hierarchy beyond school spaces? What are the challenges to do so? What possible partnerships are needed?
2. During the Radio Environment 21 workshop, one of the topics discussed was consumerism and how it is related to what Donizete called *garbage ideas*, which are values and opinions that shape our lives and consumer habits without us even realizing—such as

competitiveness, selfishness, or comparison. In order to identify and interrogate those thoughts, Donizete proposed these questions:

a. Do you think about *what* you think?

b. Have you ever stopped to think about your opinions and where they come from?

c. Are ideas we consider natural or obvious really that natural or obvious?

NOTE

1. This chapter was written initially in Portuguese and later translated into English. Among the authors, only Mariana is fluent in English, and she was therefore responsible for the translation. Language was a challenge due to the complex cultural differences between English and Portuguese—which you might sense while reading the chapter. Due to that, we decided to keep a few terms in Portuguese, with accompanying explanations, in order to give the reader a more precise sense of our perspectives.

REFERENCES

Baró, I. M. (1997). O papel do psicólogo [The role of the psychologist]. *Estudos de Psicologia, 2*(1), 7–27. Natal.

Franco, M. (1996). *As linguagens audiovisuais no processo educativo* [The audiovisual languages on the communication process]. In Comunicação e Plano decenal de Educação: Rumo ao ano 2003. Publicação dos Anais Faculdades Claretianas.

Freire, P. (1996). *Pedagogia da autonomia: saberes necessários à prática educativa* [Pedagogy of autonomy: Necessary knowledge for the educational practice]. Paz e Terra.

Freire, P. (1998). *Pedagogy of freedom: Ethics, democracy, and civic courage.* Rowman & Littlefield.

Freire. P. (2001). *Extensão ou Comunicação?* [Extension or communication?]. Paz e Terra.

Freire, P. (2014). *Pedagogy of the oppressed.* 30th anniversary edition. Bloomsbury.

Guareschi, P. (2007). Relações comunitárias—Relações de dominação. [Community relations—Relationships of domination]. In R. Campos (Ed.), *Psicologia social comunitária, da solidariedade à autonomia* [Community social psychology, from solidarity to autonomy]. Editora Vozes.

Lima, G. (2009). *Educação pelos meios de comunicação, na perspectiva da educomunicação ou produção coletiva de comunicação na perspectiva da educomunicação.* [Education through Media, in the perspective of educommunication or collective production of communication in the perspective of educommunication]. Instituto GENS de Educação e Cultura.

Part II

INSTITUTIONALIZING SOCIAL CHANGE

SKILLS AND PROGRAM DEVELOPMENT

CHAPTER 5

Education for Revolutionary Nonviolence
Enacting Decolonial Praxis

*Hakim Mohandas Amani Williams,
Christina M. Noto, and Daniel Jones*

Adolescents and young adults often report being told that they lack the credentials, wisdom, and expertise to contribute to the serious challenges that confront our global society (Leistyna, 2009). Excluding youth from engaging in certain conversations and from co-crafting solutions reinforces hierarchy, reduces opportunities for youth to develop leadership and collaborative skills, and robs societies of valuable youth insights. The work we document in this chapter reflects our efforts to institutionalize spaces within higher education where youth (namely undergraduates) can assemble, organize, innovate, and build skills so that they are self-empowered as radical change-makers.

Christina, Daniel, and Hakim are friends, mentors, and collaborators, but our relationship started in a classroom at Gettysburg College in Pennsylvania (USA) as traditional "student" and "professor," and evolved into something much stronger as we applied the "Freirean classroom" to the world beyond it.

Gettysburg College is a small and rural campus set amidst the site of the brutal and consequential Battle of Gettysburg that occurred in 1863 during the U.S. Civil War; even some of the college's buildings were used as field hospitals for both Union and Confederate soldiers (Mahr, 2021). Today, those in the Peace and Justice Studies Program at Gettysburg College are reappropriating this higher education space (Joseph-Salisbury & Connelly, 2021) to create decolonial (i.e., critiquing and delinking from Eurocentric hierarchies of knowledge, and implementing alternatives) discourses and practices around revolutionary nonviolence.

Higher education is a complex space. In our opinion, some of the best ideas, discourses, and solutions have been and are generated there, and yet it remains a violent space where power is often abused and supposedly critical values and goals (such as scholar-activism; diversity, equity, and inclusion;

and decoloniality) often ring hollow when folx try to employ them as platforms for actual structural transformation. Against the historical backdrop of Gettysburg, and higher education as hierarchical, violent, and colonizing, we frame our work as education for revolutionary nonviolence.

Admittedly, violence is not exclusive to higher education. U.S. society itself was built on genocide, dispossession of land, and slavery, and more contemporaneously, we contend with gun culture, police brutality, and deep inequities. Much of this has been (and continues to be) shaped by a globalized coloniality (Mignolo, 2011). We, therefore, concur that decoloniality, which includes processes of dismantling and reenvisioning, is a globalized imperative (Abdulla et al., 2019; Patel, 2016). In playing our small part, we offer our vision of positive, nonviolent, and decolonial praxis (Schockman et al., 2019).

Dellinger (1971), Deming (1985), Finley & Minch (2020), Jackson et al. (2020), and Lawson (2022) write on revolutionary nonviolence. Although there are conceptualizations of similar (and important) types of critical education, such as education for peace and human rights, and education/pedagogies for revolution (see Brown, 2021; Hantzopoulos & Bajaj, 2021; McLaren, 2000; Romo, 2020), there is not much on *education* for revolutionary nonviolence (ERN) (Williams, 2022a, 2022b). This is the first extensive writing on ERN that uses this phrasing. Revolutionary nonviolence—which is different from the Gandhian nonviolence of spiritual and direct action, and the strategic nonviolence of the methods and tactics of Gene Sharp (a political scientist whose writings on nonviolence influenced many resistance movements)—is defined as:

> forms of individual and collective political action directed at fundamentally changing social structures, political subjectivities, modes of power and ways of being for individuals and communities—as opposed to reformist nonviolence which is aimed at changing leaders or particular policies. (Hallward & Norman, as cited in Jackson et al., 2020, p. 6)

Simply put, instead of using nonviolence to make tweaks or changes in the margins of societies, revolutionary nonviolence is centered on fundamentally transforming societies at their roots and the violent, authoritarian, and colonizing ways in which we (individuals and communities) relate to each other and the planet.

ERN is therefore about cofostering the knowledges, skills, dispositions, and visions to create and sustain a revolutionary, justice-oriented, nonviolent world with learners. To this end, we have disrupted hierarchies to create projects that reflect ERN and constitute prefigurative, decolonial praxis. In other words, our projects are a combination of critical reflection and action (praxis; Freire, 2000) that models the radically just and sustainable world we envision; "prefigurative" here means that as we dream of and sketch a more just world, we simultaneously enact foundational elements of such a world (Boggs, 1977).

Before detailing our cocreated projects, we offer reflections on our relationships, because those provided the sturdy foundation for the work that we did/do together.

HOW WE MET: IN A CLASS ON CRITICAL PEDAGOGY

We found inspiration to collaborate from our class entitled Education for Social Change. The cornerstone of this class is *Pedagogy of the Oppressed* (*PotO*), alongside other readings on critical pedagogy, and in it, students conduct semester-long social change projects to develop skills in creating, implementing, and assessing their work.

In one project, a group collected data about centralized support for students with disabilities at peer institutions and then presented findings to Gettysburg College administrators with hopes of replicating a similarly cohesive support structure. Through this, and similar projects, students learn to resolve conflicts and how and why systems and bureaucracies are too often resistant to change. The aims of the projects are not necessarily in the achievement of the project objective, but rather the learning students gain from having to engage with real-life obstacles, interpersonal and intragroup dynamics, and applying theory from class/recognizing the dissonance that sometimes exists between theory and practice.

The goals are the same for other low-stakes assignments like creating a critical questions journal about the readings in that no one assignment is weighed too heavily. These assignments are about reflection versus regurgitation of materials, and they combine theory and practice so that students find them useful and engaging. Another example is a politico-educational autobiography in which students critically analyze an aspect of their educational history through the lens of what they have been reading in the course; this is meant to partially highlight educational violences at the individual and systemic level.

The course thus centers on critical reflection and critical action to create what Freire calls praxis (2000). Students learn theory and must engage in action to discern for themselves the challenges in fostering change. The course was intentionally a space that prepared us for the out-of-traditional classroom work that we document.

In January 2018, Christina met Hakim during a college trip to Rwanda, after which she became involved in the Peace and Justice Student Council, and they have been working together since. She took this course during her senior year. In 2019, Daniel took Hakim's other class on human rights in his first year, then took this course in his second. Daniel became president of the Peace and Justice Student Council and Hakim's teacher's assistant, and their work together took off. Although we come from different backgrounds, our commitment to challenging the status quo in education has strengthened our relationships and spawned amazing collaborations.

A LABORATORY FOR DISRUPTING HIERARCHY AND RELATIONSHIP BUILDING

Our individual positionalities (i.e., sociocultural identities and privileges) shape the ways we view(ed) education and thus how we collaborate and engage in our work.

Positionality

Christina

I am a White, middle-class woman who was born to two teachers with master's degrees. I grew up in politically conservative upstate New York where I completed school. I was a three-sport athlete who cared about gender equality, partly because I experienced sexism while playing sports and in the classroom. Additionally, I was involved in Democratic politics because of my dad's involvement in local government. Going to college was an expectation. After my first year at Gettysburg, I realized that although I cared about social justice and effecting change, a career in the government was not something I wanted; instead, I wanted to create change from the grassroots level. I graduated in 2019 with a history major and minors in peace and justice studies and women, gender, and sexuality studies. After graduation, I completed an alternative teacher certification program and taught for 3 years.

Daniel

I am a White, middle-class man who was raised by my mom (an elementary school teacher) and my father (an engineer) in central Virginia (USA). Growing up, I commuted about 2 hours round-trip daily to the better-funded school system where my mother teaches. Through this, and by volunteering in my mom's school, I became aware of inclusive teaching (i.e., valuing students' ideas and different learning styles) and curriculum building. Reading *PotO* in the course gave me the inspiration and framework to then turn educational social change theory into praxis. I did this through research, leadership positions, and in my day-to-day life trying to center the ideas of undergraduate and high school students in projects for social change. These experiences helped me identify and define aspects of education-based traumas and hierarchies for myself and those around me. I graduated in 2022 with bachelor's degrees in religious studies and public policy, and completed my master's in international relations with the University of Chicago's Committee on International Relations in June 2023.

Hakim

I'm a Black, queer, immigrant man, from a poor/working class community (Laventille, Trinidad). Growing up, I was sensitized to bigotry, bullying, and inequality. Reading *PotO* in graduate school helped me analyze my reality and better understand the structural violence in which I grew up. This text informs my visions of radical social change today as I teach at a predominantly White institution located in a politically conservative part of the United States.

Living and working in this part of the country, with my particular identities, exacts an emotional toll. I insist on all undergraduate students calling me Dr. or Prof. Williams until they graduate. Frankly, I do not like this practice, but the times when a student has called me by my first name, the engagement has not felt respectful. Amidst the landscape of race and class in the USA, I too am still navigating the balance between being a teacher–student and setting boundaries regarding my professional personhood.

In the classroom, I readily share my encounters with racism and homophobia. Students from marginalized backgrounds tell me that the intersectional representation of my identities is powerful because they see reflections of their present and future selves. I think my identities are also important to the students for whom I am their first Black, queer, and/or immigrant teacher because the totality of who I am often unsettles their assumptions and exposes their biases for self-reflection.

Additionally, because education was my "way out of poverty," I am passionate about my work, and sometimes my emphasis on taking education seriously is jarring to students for whom higher education is not among their highest priorities. I thus try to proceed with compassionate accountability: I challenge students and invite them to challenge me, with deep respect and kindness, as we co-construct a liberatory education. This kind of critical co-construction has animated my pedagogy, research, and activism since I first read *PotO*.

Encounters With *PotO*

We describe our encounters with the text, how the course reflected its elements, and how we disrupted hierarchy by modeling vulnerability, co-construction, and so on.

Christina

During our in-class discussions, I realized the power of Freire's work, specifically praxis. Our classroom was an attempt at putting praxis into practice through:

- The physical space: Almost every class was discussion based; we sat in a circle to ensure everyone could see each other. Our physical space embodied the intellectual space we were trying to cocreate.
- Shared vulnerability: Hakim shared his struggles with mental health, which is so rarely done by professors. This helped me recognize the power of vulnerability and the reality that even people older than me, in positions of power, also struggle.
- Community of learning: Hakim regularly told us not to put people on pedestals, and to stop looking to him for all the answers but to also look to our classmates. This reinforced that students could contribute to knowledge production.

Daniel

In some academic settings, we avoid embracing the heart, spirit, and physical body; students sit still at a desk for hours (body), learn primarily through textbooks rather than personal relationships (heart), and are socialized to resist spaces that encourage building on their cultural and religious beliefs/traditions (spirit). In such classrooms, the resulting lack of both holistic teaching and vulnerability is harmful. I saw this all around me, but after reading *PotO*, I understood that instead of being nurtured in cocreated and empowering educational spaces, I was restricted and silenced by status quo pedagogies, structures, hierarchies, and student/teacher binaries.

During my undergraduate education, many of my professors were so afraid of being labeled as oppressive and authoritarian (read racist) that they often shied away from being key facilitators in classroom spaces. They shirked their responsibility to scaffold a rigorous and stimulating environment and to guide difficult discussions, which resulted in spaces that lacked empowering structure and critical thought. Yet still, I could not articulate what specifically was wrong with these kinds of environments until engaging with *PotO*. This text helped me define and reflect on what educational environments *should* and *could* be.

Hakim

Diverse violences in schools (e.g., banking education, deficient funding/resources, increasing surveillance, militarization, and hyper-securitization of some school spaces, to name a few; Harber, 2004) cause woundedness and trauma. I see problem-posing education as education for revolutionary non-violence that can facilitate healing, and a fairly nonhierarchical classroom as a powerful site for modeling nurturance and healing. As part of my peda-gogy in analyzing said violences and enacting alternatives, vulnerability is a key part, because we cannot heal the world and craft just societies if we do not work on healing ourselves and our communities.

To disrupt hierarchies, and to humanize myself and normalize dis-courses that are taboo for some academic spaces, I model vulnerability and healing practices by speaking about my personal struggles. We specifically do this in restorative circles (a conflict-resolution/community-building tool), which is a safe space for disrupting hierarchies between emotional and theo-retical analyses. After a restorative circle, the class atmosphere always shifts to a deeper resonance, in which more openness and active listening are in-tentionally embraced within our discussions.

Navigating Challenges and Boundaries

Christina

My relationship with Hakim is fluid. I am active in its cocreation, and it has evolved over time. We recognize the complexity of relationships, the care that is required to sustain them, and that our methods may not work in all contexts. The following are steps we took to break down hierarchy:

- Discussing my imposter syndrome and generalized anxiety during office hours and more deeply after graduating with Hakim; he listened without judgment and shared his experiences.
- We text via WhatsApp, making it easier to communicate; our conversations flow freely and support us in developing rapport.
- After graduation, he told me to call him "Hakim" to reinforce our relationship as colleagues, vs. "Dr./Professor Williams"; this is still difficult for me because I was taught that using formal names shows respect.
- I was nervous to cowrite this chapter. Although I believe in disrupting hierarchy, acting on it is difficult. There were several questions of doubt: Are my ideas valuable? Will they contribute to this book? What if I am not "academic" enough? Initially, it was hard for me to tell Hakim and Daniel, but after I did, they were encouraging and provided suggestions to support my writing process. For example, on WhatsApp, Hakim told me to just write down my ideas and editing would come later.

Although we disrupted hierarchy, there is still much work to be done. For example, hierarchy existed in our classrooms: We earned a grade (centering the teacher's opinions on classroom knowledge production), and many readings were incredibly dense, making them less accessible to students.

Additionally, even when hierarchy is disrupted, there are still boundaries that should not be crossed between teachers and students (i.e., harassment, oversharing, projecting emotions or feelings, hostility, etc.). For me as a woman I must note: I am comfortable having a close relationship with Hakim (as a queer man in his position of power), so I do not worry about our relationship being misunderstood or overstepped. These boundaries and care, which are specific to our relationship, will of course be different for other people based on their own positionalities. Teachers are in positions of power, and thus they need to be mindful of how power can be experienced differently in different spaces.

Daniel

Schools serve as a unique arena where the potential for critical disruption coexists with barriers to profound social change; this explains why schools are often sites of contentious power struggles. By shifting the classroom into a space of multidirectional mentorship, however (e.g., a web of mentorship ties in which Hakim mentors Christina and me, we mentor him, and each other), we can create humanizing spaces for both students and teachers.

In reflecting on my schooling, I appreciate the learning environments in which teachers and I were able to humanize each other; where academic and socio-emotional lesson content were blended; and where I was empowered to challenge and think innovatively and critically. I found those classrooms to be truly liberatory. I have long forgotten the more "fundamental," often traditional expectations of quiet obedience.

As Hakim and I continued our joint work planning an international peace conference, and this chapter, I still struggle with seemingly inconsequential changes such as calling him Hakim, a remnant of the preceding hierarchy. However, having simple changes such as addressing one another as "brother" helps tremendously. I now more deeply recognize his humanity and better understand the dynamics between his personal and professional lives, more than was possible in a classroom space where students are often more focused on managing peer relationships, instead of also developing one with their professors. We now both maintain our relationship by sharing our burdens and triumphs, ensuring we stay updated with one another's personal and professional lives; if one of us is carrying a heavy emotional load one day, the other will offer to listen or provide guidance.

Instead of being "typecast" as only "teacher," or "student," our identities are progressively fluid—to each other, we are now student, friend, mentor, brother, imperfect, human.

Hakim

Balancing student engagement and teacher authority is difficult (Tierney, 2020). I do challenge students in the classroom to think more deeply about the readings, our discussions, and their connection to life in the "real world"; this causes (mostly positive) tension. At the start of the semester in this course, when students engage with *PotO* and other readings on critical pedagogy, they are sometimes disheartened when they realize how violent and stifling their education has been. Others resist critical pedagogy perhaps because of their familiarity with the banking model; they expect exams, detailed notes, and teacher-centered classrooms. A co-constructed classroom is therefore perceived as a threat because while sharing power is a stated goal (and entirely a possibility), some of my students view a teacher-decentered classroom as a chaotic abandonment of strong teacher control.

Another challenge in my current context concerns grades. Because professors are compelled to submit final grades, this may sometimes contribute to students performing "wokeness" or vulnerability, or focusing more on the grades than the actual learning and my feedback for improvement. To diminish some anxiety around grades, I strive to make the assignments relevant to meaningful student learning, critical reflection, and skills development. Therefore, to build musculature around disrupting hierarchies in the classroom, I have students present on the readings before I share my thoughts so they foster trust in their own sense-making and to reduce the primacy of my "teacher" voice. I also do not give exams; instead, for each class, students use their critical questions journals to challenge the texts, troubling taken-for-granted assumptions, revealing underdeveloped or missed areas, extending the arguments presented, and connecting to past and/or out-of-class materials (e.g., newspaper articles, movies, etc.). Overall, I am interested in expansive and creative student analysis without the narrowing impact of the students hearing my thoughts first.

Navigating these challenges while intentionally power sharing often feels fraught; for example, sometimes (but not often) students have weaponized my sharing and vulnerability. However, when I do err, I try to take ownership because modeling how to address these challenges is an important part of my philosophical and pedagogical scaffolding of an education for revolutionary nonviolence.

ELEMENTS OF AN EDUCATION FOR
REVOLUTIONARY NONVIOLENCE (ERN)

We believe that revolutionary nonviolence (as praxis) can be taught via active and experiential learning that is embedded in communities that prize ongoing reflection (Romano, 2022). ERN as prefigurative praxis does not mean we are naïve about our current realities, but we do believe that we can simultaneously hold ideal visions of the future alongside flawed realities (Romano, 2022). Freire (2000) characterized problem-posing education as revolutionary futurity, and to us, this encapsulates ERN *as* a prefigurative decolonial praxis.

As an introductory theorization, we list below some elements of ERN. The list is not exhaustive, so we invite others to customize it to accommodate their contexts, needs, resources, and visions:

1. **Abolitionist teaching** (Love, 2019): Teaching how to analyze systems of oppression and their causes, and how to co-craft solutions for delinking from (and eventually abolishing) them (Mignolo, 2011). Part of this is learning about past successful, nonviolent revolutions.
2. **Freedom dreaming** (Kelley, 2003) **and futures envisioning**: We often describe what is wrong in societies but struggle in sketching clear visions of what does not yet exist. We also have to think of what freedom means for everyone and envision futures outside the confines of the status quo.
3. **Iterative praxis**: In our social change projects, a feedback loop of constant critical reflection and action must be fostered (Freire, 2000) to elude comprehensive co-option and dilution by larger systems and structures that resist major transformation.
4. **Holistic**: One product of the "Age of Reason" was a split between mind, body, and spirit; this atomization leads to disjointed intra- and interpersonal and communal relationalities. ERN needs to be holistic, where we reconnect all parts of our "selves."
5. **Community-oriented**: Colonialism denigrated and disintegrated community-based relationalities; we must move beyond the individualism of Western and capitalist thinking and practices that divide us.
6. **Planetary in scope and pluriversal in implementation**: We must foster systems thinking and action that sees us as co-stewards of and in solidarity with the planet. Local actions must be considered with the planet in mind, and global actions should be in conversation with culturally varied ways of being. At the core is a recognition of the sentience of the natural world (Williams & Bermeo, 2020).
7. **Design thinking**: We need pedagogies and praxes of sustainable innovation to foster an entrepreneurial spirit that considers past wisdoms without generating clutter and perpetuating exploitation.
8. **Skills for nonviolent conflict transformation**: We need skills to transform what hinders us from our higher selves (individually and communally), including skills in nonviolent communication, mediation, restorative justice, and so on.

9. **Intrapersonal work:** This is ongoing and cannot be overstated. We must engage in reparative work—for example, therapy, finding ways to meditate, healing from our traumas, and radical self-care (Williams, 2016).

The two cocreated projects described below, and the Education for Social Change course itself, are informed by and/or reflect these elements of ERN, and we believe that institutionalizing these elements is important so that there is a foundation on which to build *within* existing institutions that possess the resources to support this kind of work. In other words, our projects tried to cement (with institutional resources) the disruption of hierarchy as a student-centered organizing practice.

INSTITUTIONALIZING SOCIAL CHANGE PROJECTS

The two related projects that we cocreated are the Consortium of North American Peace Programs (hereafter referred to as the Consortium) and the Peace and Justice Transformative Leaders Fellowship (hereafter referred to as the Fellowship).

Hakim envisioned these projects several years ago (based on reading *PotO*), but to actualize them, he invited student leaders to partner with him since the aim is to cocreate spaces that are student centered and codirected.

Consortium of North American Peace Programs

Hakim, Christina, and other students formed the Consortium, an undergraduate student-directed organizing and leadership development hub of peace and justice (and similar) academic programs across North America (Canada, Mexico, and USA). Its main goals are to plan a biennial conference where students learn more about (and enact) the elements of ERN; organize; build community; share research and cutting-edge ideas around peace, justice, and conflict; and offer peace and justice leadership development opportunities (such as the Fellowship).

The inaugural conference was slated for June 2020, but was postponed due to COVID-19. Student leaders are currently determining when it would be best to have the conference in the next few years (we did, however, host a virtual convening of about 40 students in 2020 to discuss varied peace and justice issues). The conference intends to flip the usual script of academic convenings. Students would submit work online in advance, and then folx would attend sessions having already read the main presentation points, with questions for the presenters. Sessions would reflect iterative praxis: The first half would be critical dialogue between presenters and attendees, and the second half would be discussion about implementing the ideas emerging from the dialogue. We intended to provide seed funds for the implementation of a few feasible ideas. We raised $30,000 to offset the conference attendance costs for about 100 students.

The Consortium is meant to facilitate the institutionalization of skills development, design thinking, community orientation, and freedom dreaming/futures envisioning within student organizing.

Some ways we disrupted hierarchy during planning:

- We met on a Sunday morning, a time convenient for most students in our group. The Peace and Justice Studies program paid for food because meeting over mealtime could be a barrier for attendance.
- Everyone's ideas were welcomed and seriously considered. Hakim insisted that student opinions were integral to this project (especially around major decision-making).
- We created a shared online drive to which everyone had equal access.
- After creating a shared vision, students took the lead on thematic (interest-driven) subcommittees (for accountability's sake), which made it easier to divide the tasks. Students volunteered based on skill sets and personal expertise.
- Christina created a website and social media for the project, making it more accessible to students outside Gettysburg College. Note: The website is written in English, which is a barrier for other language speakers.

Many elements of ERN with which we imbued the Consortium project, we had received/experienced (in different ways) from our time together in the Education for Social Change course. For example, in that class

- We explored and analyzed abolitionist teaching (reading *PotO* helped with analyzing systems of oppression), and freedom dreaming/futures envisioning (the end-of-semester educational blueprint for social change allowed students to dream boldly while thinking through details such as funding, how to create a nonprofit, etc.).
- We created semester-long projects for social change that organically leaned on elements of design and systems thinking, and community orientation since the projects were meant to benefit the immediate social ecosystem.
- We received restorative circle training as part of skills development for conflict resolution, and together as a classroom community, our pedagogy was steeped in intrapersonal, holistic, self-reflective work that invited the whole person into that space (Hakim modeled this by openly discussing his mental health struggles and encounters with racism in the wider community).

The class thus equipped/deepened the Consortium's founders with the requisite skill and mindset, which were then reinforced by this out-of-class student–faculty collaboration. This iterative, community-oriented approach provided the space for our expansive dreams for the Consortium.

Peace and Justice Transformative Leaders Fellowship

Hakim and Daniel, assisted by fellow Gettysburg College students and staff, cocreated the Fellowship (in 2021), a partnership between the Consortium, the Gettysburg College Garthwait Leadership Center, and the Peace and Justice Studies Program. For this Fellowship project, we reappropriated Gettysburg from a site of war memorialization to a radical space of peace and justice leadership development. We received over 80 applications from students across North America.

The weeklong series of workshops (offered by current students and alumni, staff and faculty, and a few external associates) included

- effective facilitation and transformative leadership,
- public speaking and communicating one's vision,
- grant writing for social impact,
- conflict resolution (restorative circles and mediation),
- lessons from the U.S. Civil War for today's polarized times,
- fostering community partnerships,
- policymaking for social change,
- developing and mobilizing an entrepreneurial mindset,
- political organizing, and
- sustaining social movements.

These workshops (and the construction of the entire program) reflected ERN elements of abolitionist teaching, skills in nonviolent conflict transformation, systems thinking, iterative praxis, and intergenerational and intrapersonal work. A beautiful example of intergenerational work and systems thinking: One evening after the workshop on building and sustaining social movements, most of the fellows gathered for an hours-long informal discussion with an elder who has been part of several global movements; it was such a joyous and intimate exchange.

Additionally, these are some of the ways in which we disrupted hierarchy through the Fellowship:

- Applications from undergraduates of any age and background were welcomed and considered equally following a rubric drafted by students and professors. All applications were reviewed by two Gettysburg College students and two professors, and the students' ratings weighed equally as the professors'.

- We met over winter break, a time that was convenient for the fellows (nine in person, following COVID-19 guidelines, and two virtual). With funding from the Garthwait Leadership Center and the provost's office, we paid for food, travel, and accommodation for the fellows to avoid any cost-related barriers to their participation.
- Fellows engaged in workshops and informal settings (e.g., over meals) with workshop and program leaders, allowing them to disrupt the hierarchy of the traditional classroom model by discussing/challenging each other on an equal playing field.
- Workshop leaders and fellows exchanged phone numbers and emails for continued collaboration *as colleagues*, rather than resorting to a student–teacher relationship after the program.
- To further honor the fellows' leadership potential, they were tasked with reinvigorating the Consortium's Leadership Council and recruiting other colleges and undergraduates.

In the spirit of freedom dreaming and futures envisioning, the fellows also planned and presented their social change projects that they would pursue on returning to their communities. In preparation for this, Daniel led three mini-workshops focused on blending critical thought with innovative, community-based research design and project implementation, evaluation, and sustainability. Afterwards, each fellow was assigned a mentor (Daniel, Hakim, or Logan Grubb, a Gettysburg College alumnus), who served as a sounding board throughout the fellows' project implementation during academic year 2022–2023.

In the next iteration of this fellowship, we hope to have 10 college students and 10 high school students who will be paired as mentors for their social change projects. Some inaugural fellows will return to conduct workshops (to build an alumni base and cement the student-centeredness of this enterprise). We will include high school students so they are primed with more skills for this kind of work by the time they start college.

CONCLUSION

These projects and our work rest on a continuously intentional disruption of hierarchy to nurture prefigurative and decolonial relationalities, and the conduit for this work has been education for revolutionary nonviolence.

This work fuels us to apply the lessons learned here to other contexts/ communities of which we are a part.

We therefore conclude by remarking on what the elements of ERN and Freirean principles mean to each of us beyond the Education for Social Change course and our cocreated projects.

Christina

As a former teacher, I used aspects of interpersonal care, iterative praxis, and community building to improve my teaching. Some hierarchies I tried to dismantle, and others I unfortunately let be (because of finite energy and resources). Although I had little institutional power, I would reflect daily and try to change something "small" the following day. For example:

- not separating elementary students by gender to diminish the reinforcement of gender norms,
- implementing restorative justice by having conversations with students about the impact of their actions and then giving students strategies to self-regulate when they were frustrated instead of using punitive justice (e.g., taking away recess), and
- adding my pronouns to my Zoom name. When students asked, I explained. Students then started adding their pronouns to their names.

These changes often helped me to operationalize ERN within a space that I did have the power to shape, and thus my relationships with the students. Similar to how my relationship with Hakim demonstrates how the teacher–student hierarchy can be dismantled and can be beautifully co-constructed, I continuously try to see such re-creation in my professional life as well.

Daniel

Before leaving Gettysburg, it became crucial to me to operationalize ERN through relationship-building and by helping the next year's Peace and Justice Student Council leaders (my peers), in this style of multidirectional mentorship. Although I was in a position of power as the president, I often met one-on-one with each member, because I wanted them to feel comfortable challenging me, specifically in a nontypical leadership role, with the hope that this confidence would transfer into them critically challenging older students, professors, and administrators as well.

ERN is about providing learners with the knowledges and visions to create and sustain a revolutionary world, so as an active researcher, author, and recent teaching assistant in graduate school, I now constantly utilize ERN to involve my peers. I work to foster intergenerational, multidirectional relationships and co-construct youth-led mechanisms meant to disrupt and replace traditional hierarchies. For example, I am now coauthoring with one of the participants of the Fellowship a toolkit for youth peace-building praxis that will showcase the incredible work of other youth. As a teaching assistant I help students to think critically through international relations-based diplomatic simulations and co-led peer review processes as well as by leading youth-community organizing simulations and workshops. My goal is to share elements of ERN in academic as well as non-academic ways.

Hakim

Every opportunity I get to work with Daniel and Christina, I take (such as coplanning an international peace conference in 2023). My intention has long been to cocreate spaces *with* youth for them to develop into the revolutionary leaders that our world needs, not tomorrow, but now! I am truly overjoyed to see Daniel and Christina using Freirean principles and elements of ERN in life beyond Gettysburg College. To me, this is a kind of revolution that is understated because it is not flashy; it is methodical, slow, granular, and interpersonally strategic.

All

We acknowledge that there is not any perfect formula for disrupting hierarchy; this work is contextual, and ongoing. Coloniality runs deep; therefore, the work of dismantling, healing, and reenvisioning requires patience. Through our projects, hopefully you were able to see how intentional, decolonial relationality formed the bedrock for the work that we do. This kind of work takes time and emotional labor, but it is supremely rewarding. We are hopeful that a commitment to revolutionary nonviolence will birth a more justice-oriented, sustainable planet, and we will continue to use radical education as one of the conduits.

DISCUSSION QUESTIONS/ACTIVITIES

1. How can you gather critically minded students/youth on your campus/in your community to work intersectionally to co-construct a pipeline that fosters a diverse cadre of leaders, and to operationalize the skills needed to effectuate radical and sustainable change in your context?
2. What are specific ways you can balance your visions of more just and sustainable tomorrows with the flawed realities of today?
3. What is one aspect of your life in which you do (or would like to) practice nonviolence? Reflect and journal the challenges, progress, and opportunities for growth. You can do this activity with friends or colleagues, and as an exercise, you can together visually map out the ripple effects.

REFERENCES

Abdulla, D., Ansari, A., Canlı, E., Keshavarz, M., Kiem, M., Oliveira, P., Prado, L., & Schultz, T. (2019). A manifesto for decolonising design. *Journal of Futures Studies, 23*(3), 129–132.

Boggs, C. (1977). Marxism, prefigurative communism and the problem of workers' control. *Radical America, 11*(6), 99–122. Retrieved from https://library.brown .edu/pdfs/1125404123276662.pdf

Brown, N. (Ed.). (2021). *Revolutionary education: Theory and practice for socialist organizers.* Liberation Media.

Dellinger, D. (1971). *Revolutionary nonviolence.* Bobbs-Merrill Co.

Deming, B. (1985). *On revolutionary and equilibrium.* A. J. Muste Memorial Institute.

Finley, L., & Minch, M. (Eds.). (2020). *Revolutionary nonviolence in violent times.* Cambridge Scholars Publishers.

Freire, P. (2000). *Pedagogy of the oppressed.* Continuum.

Hantzopoulos, M., & Bajaj, M. (2021). *Educating for peace and human rights: An introduction.* Bloomsbury Press.

Harber, C. (2004). *Schooling as violence: How schools harm pupils and societies.* Routledge.

Jackson, R., Llewellyn, J., Leonard, G., Gnoth, A., & Karena, T. (Eds.). (2020). *Revolutionary nonviolence: Concepts, cases and controversies.* Zed Books.

Joseph-Salisbury, R., & Connelly, L. (2021). *Anti-racist scholar-activism.* Manchester University Press.

Kelley, R. (2003). *Freedom dreams: The Black radical imagination.* Beacon Press.

Lawson, J. (2022). *Revolutionary nonviolence: Organizing for freedom.* University of California Press.

Leistyna, P. (2009). Preparing for public life: Education, critical theory, and social justice. In W. C. Ayers, T. Quinn, & D. Stovall (Eds.), *Handbook of social justice in education* (pp. 51–58). Routledge.

Love, B. (2019). *We want to do more than survive: Abolitionist teaching and the pursuit of educational freedom.* Beacon Press.

Mahr, M. (2021). *Medical care on the Gettysburg College Campus.* Retrieved from https://www.civilwarmed.org/gettysburg-college

McLaren, P. (2000). *Che Guevara, Paulo Freire, and the pedagogy of revolution.* Rowan & Littlefield.

Mignolo, W. (2011). *The darker side of Western modernity: Global futures, decolonial options.* Duke University Press.

Patel, L. (2016). *Decolonizing educational research: From ownership to answerability.* Routledge.

Romano, A. (2022). *Racial justice and nonviolence education.* Routledge.

Romo, A. (2020). *Education in revolutionary struggles: Iván Ilich, Paulo Freire, Ernesto Guevara and Latin American thought.* Routledge.

Schockman, H., Hernández, V., & Boitano, A. (2019). Introduction: On peace, reconciliation and social justice. In E. Schockman, V. Hernández, & A. Boitano (Eds.), *Peace, reconciliation, and social justice leadership in the 21st century: The role of leaders and followers* (pp. 1–10). Emerald Publishing Limited.

Tierney, A. (2020). Who's in charge? Teacher authority and navigating the dialogical-based classroom. In J. Kirylo (Ed.), *Reinventing pedagogy of the oppressed: Contemporary critical perspectives* (pp. 105–114). Bloomsbury Press.

Williams, H. (2016). A neocolonial warp of outmoded hierarchies, curricula and disciplinary technologies in Trinidad's educational system. *Critical Studies in Education, 60*(1), 93–112. Retrieved from https://doi.org/10.1080/17508487.2016.1237982

Williams, H. (2022a). Afterword. In W. Marshall & M. Meyer (Eds.), *Insurrectionary uprisings: A reader in revolutionary nonviolence and decolonization* (pp. 383–386). Daraja Press.

Williams, H. (2022b). *Education for revolutionary nonviolence.* Lecture at University of Illinois: Urbana-Champaign.

Williams, H., & Bermeo, M. (2020). A decolonial imperative: Pluriversal rights education. *International Journal of Human Rights Education, 4*(1). Retrieved from https://repository.usfca.edu/ijhre/vol4/iss1/1

CHAPTER 6

From Transformative Pedagogy to Transforming Collegiate Spaces

Creating a Network for Multicultural Scholars

Roberto Garcia, Paulina S. Lim,
Jacqueline Nguyen, and Natalie M. Schneider

In the summer of 2020, there was a collective call to action against racism spurred by the murders of George Floyd, Breonna Taylor, and other Black Americans whose deaths became a flashpoint in the ongoing reckoning with racial relations in the United States. At a large public university in the midwestern United States, administrators offered grant funds for projects to address institutionalized social change toward equity and anti-racism.

The authorship team was awarded a 1-year grant to create a network of multicultural scholars and an anti-racism resource database.[1] This project was rooted in principles of praxis and transformative pedagogy (i.e., Freire, 1970; Giroux, 2010), requiring the disruption of established hierarchies and institutional norms in higher education: imbalanced institutional power relationships, uncompensated labor expectations, and colonized expertise. Disrupting these hierarchies resulted in the creation of a network of BIPOC (Black, Indigenous, and People of Color) scholars, a fellowship for graduate BIPOC scholars, and a resource database.

The network and resource database enhances the research productivity of individuals whose voices have been historically and institutionally erased from U.S. culture, namely BIPOC faculty and graduate students (Garcia, 2020). By doing so, the network promotes retention of BIPOC faculty and improves student continuation along the academic pipeline. Over time, this initiative and the efforts of the learning team led to more widespread outcomes, including payment for (typically uncompensated) labor done by BIPOC scholars, establishment of a BIPOC graduate student advisory group to the graduate school, and creation of a BIPOC graduate student campus gathering space. This learning team advocated for these efforts to increase the sustainability of equity, diversity, inclusion, and anti-racism (EDIA) efforts while maintaining the network members' independence, and resistance to oversight, from institutional structures.

This chapter details the transformative practices and activities in which our learning team questioned critical assumptions, particularly about the status quo of unpaid labor, and grappled with social issues, including the institutional barriers faced by BIPOC scholars at historically White institutions. These practices led our graduate student team members toward social action. We discussed the process of disrupting the following hierarchies: imbalanced institutional power relationships, uncompensated labor expectations, and colonized expertise. Indeed, we encountered these hierarchies while writing this chapter and challenged the institutional power through authorship contribution; by listing authors in alphabetical order, each author became equally responsible, counteracting the expectation that faculty are the leaders in student–faculty learning relationships. Authors from four disciplines developed consistent vocabulary throughout the project and writing of this chapter to disrupt hierarchies of colonized expertise. For example, conversations persisted regarding use of the terms "minoritized vs. non-dominant group," with co-learning around the history of these terms informing decisions. Still, the writing process violated uncompensated labor expectations. All authors contributed time in service of a scholarly publication, which is a more acceptable practice since scholarly publications yield greater merit rewards than service activities.

While transformative pedagogy shaped the course in which our initial praxis occurred, the change mechanisms to disrupt campus norms occurred outside the confines of the classroom through three hierarchy-disrupting practices that resulted in permanent institutional changes. This chapter focuses on graduate students as critical members of the academic pipeline who are most vulnerable to the harms of uncompensated labor but are also best positioned to question and disrupt the hierarchical norms that have shaped academia.

NAMING INSTITUTIONAL NORMS

Norm of Invisible and Uncompensated Labor

In the United States, there is a long history of underrepresentation of BIPOC individuals in the professoriate due to challenges at all levels of school; as a result, historically minoritized group members leave or are pushed out of academia, leaving a small number of individuals who must meet the needs of an increasingly diverse student body. In 2020, about one-quarter of faculty in tenure-track positions identified as BIPOC across all U.S. degree-granting postsecondary institutions. Yet 48.4% of the students identify as BIPOC (National Center for Education Statistics, 2022). U.S. college students are more than twice as likely to be Black than faculty and more than four times as likely to be Hispanic (Davis & Fry, 2019). At our institution, the disparity matches the national average: 19.1% of the faculty body is non-White and 33% of the student body is non-White. These numbers include international faculty; therefore, the number of U.S. ethnic minority group members is even lower.

Despite these low numbers, historically White institutions in the United States have relied on BIPOC scholars to provide equity and diversity-related services, mentor students from minoritized backgrounds, and "represent" the voices of diversity in the institution (El-Sabawi & Fields, 2021; Zambrana et al., 2016). This additional form of labor is termed "cultural taxation" (Hirshfield & Joseph, 2012), or "inclusion taxation," and involves expending additional resources (specifically by Black women but applicable to other marginalized groups), "including time, money, mental, and emotional energy in order to be allowed in white institutional spaces and to adhere to or resist white norms" (Melaku, 2019, p. 1517).

Although these diversity-related responsibilities benefit the broader institution, they are seldom acknowledged, rewarded, or compensated. At times, they are discounted or devalued, particularly during the promotion and tenure process (El-Sabawi & Fields, 2021; Evans & Moore, 2015). Rather than invest in resources to bring EDIA initiatives to fruition, historically White institutions rely on the "invisible labor clause" of BIPOC scholars, implying their expertise and emotional investment in anti-racism as a term of employment (Melaku, 2019). The increase in this invisible labor burden in recent years hinders BIPOC scholars' academic and research activities, furthering disparities in the academic pipeline.

Graduate students are particularly vulnerable to these labor burdens and have historically been the labor force in academic institutions (Goonen & Medina-Shore, 2021). Higher education has created a reward system that promotes extracurricular activities, leadership opportunities, and service provision as necessary experience to build one's CV, or as mandatory hours to graduate from postsecondary education. These practices devalue the labor and expertise of graduate students because, despite increased service provision to academic institutions, graduate students are paid below the poverty line (Quarterman, 2008). Lack of financial compensation disadvantages students from poor or working-class backgrounds, some of whom might have to take out loans and/or work throughout their education to support themselves (Kornbluh et al., 2021; Mendoza, 2007), which perpetuates disparities based on socioeconomic status.

Three out of four members of our learning team are BIPOC scholars, and three are also graduate students. We have all experienced these forms of taxation. Our collective frustration as undervalued experts led us to identify ways faculty and administrators normalize these injustices by tacitly demanding students complete uncompensated labor for professional development. It was vital that our team explicitly name these institutional issues to disrupt those barriers to BIPOC scholar success and disrupt their perpetuation. One way we did so was in the labor acknowledgment on our website, the first to exist at our institution to our knowledge:

> We must acknowledge that much of what we know of this country today, including its culture, economic growth, and development throughout history and across time, has been made possible by the labor of enslaved Africans and their ascendants who suffered the horror of the transatlantic trafficking of their people, chattel slavery, and Jim Crow. We are indebted to their labor and their sacrifice, and we must acknowledge the tremors of that violence throughout the generations and the resulting impact that can still be felt and witnessed today. (Stewart, 2021)

This acknowledgment was prioritized by the media and web consultant whose professional and personal insights are informed by her experience as a Black woman; as such, she desired to call attention to the history of uncredited labor on which institutions of higher education were built.

Norm of Disciplinary Silos

Academia rewards narrow, discipline-specific expertise, and therefore, segregated silos of knowledge are upheld by the institutional hierarchy. As a result, bias toward that perspective and ignorance of other disciplines occur, also known as "narration sickness" (Freire, 1970). The solution may be interdisciplinary instruction and discourse (Warner, 2012). For example, one learning team member from the business field noted that narration sickness likely led to a lack of knowledge about EDIA within their field. Finding her knowledge base lacking as an instructor, she enrolled in the course discussed in the next section and learned that the language, norms, and ideologies around anti-racism, prejudice, and discrimination are vastly different outside of business.

However, not all scholars are fortunate to enroll in a course to learn outside their discipline. Several flawed practices often result from the institutional norms of separated disciplines. For example, White faculty may rely on students' uncompensated labor to teach them "how to be anti-racist," as experienced by several of our team members. Alternatively, individuals may reproduce existing knowledge, potentially colonizing the work of others and claiming it as their own and potentially denigrating information from outside the field. To truly create institutional change for anti-racism, institutions of higher education must disrupt hierarchies maintained by disciplinary silos and instead, effectively collaborate on EDIA practices.

DISRUPTING POWER IMBALANCE

Classroom Genesis

All team members first met in an upper-level graduate course in social psychology facilitated by the faculty team member during spring 2020. The course focuses on exploring prejudice, discrimination, and stereotyping, and its structure was informed by *transformative pedagogy*—classroom practices resulting in "radically democratic social relations" due to student changes (Mayo, 1993, p. 3)—and *liberation psychology*, in which participants seek to understand the ways power structures manifest in psychological and behavioral ways for oppressed and marginalized individuals and groups, who then act to change those systems (Comas-Díaz & Rivera, 2020).

Course participants validated different ways of knowing and different experiences through self-awareness, responsivity by attending to how they respond to and engage with classmates, and reflective dialogues. In doing so, class participants engaged in continuous questioning of epistemologies and assumptions of their own worldviews. The course endorsed students as change agents for whom praxis ought to be a core element of their varied pathways as scholars and practitioners through a "transformative" final project, a labor-based grading model in which final grades are determined primarily by students' assessment of their efforts toward understanding the material, and explicit discussion about ways in which problematic norms and practices must be disrupted in all disciplines.

We practiced critical consciousness to break free from existing practices and paradigms in psychology and higher education (Giroux, 2010) that were historically so harmful for minoritized individuals to the extent that the American Psychological Association issued a public apology for past wrongdoings (2021). The student members of the learning team were particularly adherent to principles of liberation by questioning the privilege and perspective of key theorists in social psychology and consistently asking, "For whom?," "By whom?," "Who benefits?"

In applying this critical consciousness, we questioned the norms of our disciplines, from the labels used to describe groups (Latinx vs. Latine) to instruments used in assessment (e.g., intelligence tests) to how multicultural efforts on campuses center the emotions and needs of White individuals. These interrogations exemplify the ways critical consciousness influenced our class discussions.

Student–Faculty Interactions

Despite the increasing number of BIPOC scholars in higher education, many still feel powerless and lack a sense of belonging in academia, leading to diminished professional relationships, support, and access to information and knowledge (O'Meara et al., 2017). One solution is to create spaces outside of the institution where BIPOC scholars can build personal and professional relationships (McKee & Delgado, 2020). Doing so disrupts institutional norms and, importantly, allows for open discussion of structural racism and inequities.

Given their positions of authority, faculty can utilize hierarchy-disrupting practices in their relationships with students (Guzzardo et al., 2021). Formal student–faculty interactions occurring in classrooms or mentoring promote student success (Cuseo, 2018; Miller et al., 2019), but informal mentoring can increase opportunities for transformative faculty–student relationships and anti-racist praxis.

Freire's (1970) critical pedagogy deconstructs the power imbalance and sustained oppressive circumstances students may experience, such as those commonly found in a traditional student–faculty relationship. This relationship is inherently hierarchical because by definition "teacher" has a different status than "student" and is traditionally considered more knowledgeable (Freire & Macedo, 1995). However, reciprocal knowledge through critical dialogue can disrupt this hierarchy and redefine who is a learner vs. teacher in the academy. There is a notable positive effect of informal interaction with faculty on academic self-concept for first-generation BIPOC students (Cole & Griffin, 2013). Graduate students may have more access to these interactions than undergraduates because they are often treated as junior colleagues.

Our team disrupted the teacher–student hierarchy first through classroom interactions, then in informal interactions outside the classroom, such as meals, conversations about non-academic subjects, and mutual informal emotional support such as sharing our experiences with microaggressions. Importantly, sharing personal adverse experiences within higher education catalyzed our collaborative thinking about dis-belonging in historically White institutions and the value of community in engaging and retaining BIPOC scholars.

Horizontal student–faculty relationships can buffer negative campus climates, experiences of oppression, feelings of marginalization, and/or dis-belonging (Cole & Griffin, 2013). In higher education, these practices are impeded by faculty–student boundaries enforced both informally, such as through the internalization of beliefs around antiquated hierarchies of knowledge (Freire & Macedo, 1995), and formally, through institutional policies that restrict faculty–student fraternization. The latter exists to offer protection for both parties due to cases of misguided faculty–student interactions when faculty overreached their authority or when social interactions affected the student's academic experience. However, they may increase wariness to disrupt the hierarchies of vertical faculty–student relationships.

To increase horizontal faculty–student relationships while maintaining protection for all parties, the following steps may be helpful: (1) outline the nature of the relationship, (2) continually affirm consent from both parties, (3) ensure that any evaluative role by either students or the faculty member is not influenced by the potential horizontal relationship through explicit agreement, and (4) make a third party aware of the agreement to allow for independent expression of any concerns as the relationship progresses. These recommendations refer to platonic social relationships, not the romantic or sexual relationships for which all universities have existing guidelines.

Student–Administrator Disruption

While faculty and students can develop horizontal relationships, they are both subject to institutional hierarchies and the power of administrators. These administrators, such as deans, provosts, and presidents, have significant control over decision-making regarding new initiatives. Our learning team collaborated with an administrator ally to disrupt the administrative hierarchy for this project.

Administrators are gatekeepers to change and are most prone to upholding hierarchical norms (McKee & Delgado, 2020). In this project, we overcame the power imbalance among administrators, faculty, and students within our group through explicit role identification, individual and group engagement in reflexivity about our positionalities, dialogue, work toward more horizontal relationships, and cocreation of knowledge, drawing from Freire's (1970) ideas on reciprocal faculty–student relationships.

In a hierarchy-disrupting move, the student authors became collaborators with equal status to the administrators (outgoing and incoming deans) who sought institutional strategies to better support the success of BIPOC graduate students. This collaboration fostered Freirean horizontal relationships of democratic co-learning and mutual respect, which were solidified through three primary actions: (1) students were invited to call administrators by their first names; (2) students were involved in decision-making; and (3) administrators used their power to amplify student voices by requesting a physical BIPOC graduate student space on campus, paying student representatives on a governance committee, and funding community events for BIPOC scholars.

These disruptions of everyday practices and discourses are simple but led to cumulative change. The opportunity for student team members to address a dean by their first name was monumental, as it disrupted social status hierarchies and fostered trust. An opportunity to challenge hierarchical power structures arose when a (White, male) administrator joined the project, acknowledged his privileged place, and used that position to support the liberation of other team members while working as an equal team member specifically when the team was reviewing applications to select the network's fellowship recipients.

In traditional institutional hierarchical structures, administrators are assumed to have more valuable time than faculty or students and as a result, tend to delegate laborious tasks such as application reviews, preferring to instead participate only in ceremonial aspects of awarding fellowships. In contrast, our administrator team member reviewed fellowship applications willingly, signaling that his time was equal in value to the rest of the team. Moreover, he deferred fully to the student team members to lead the application and review processes.

This associate dean respected the learning team and never attempted to subvert, monopolize, or pass judgment on their efforts. Instead, he learned from the student members and uplifted their expertise and identities as BIPOC scholars. Our team never felt "out of the room" when decisions pertaining to this project or our advocacy efforts were made. Unfortunately, this is atypical, as students often have their ideas used without consent or are excluded from decision-making about policies that benefit or harm them.

Disrupting the hierarchy of administrator–student–faculty relationships was instrumental to achieving this project's anti-racist goals. Still, we recognize that a single administrator's individual actions, rather than an institutional cultural shift, helped strengthen the project's outcome.

DISRUPTING GRADUATE STUDENT MENTORING
AND LABOR EXPECTATIONS

The horizontal relationships among graduate students, faculty, and administrators were essential in disrupting the systems that led to the internalization of expectations for uncompensated labor among graduate students. This disruption helped reduce the likelihood of expectations that future faculty will comply with those labor expectations.

As a group, Freire might consider graduate students a class of "oppressed" individuals for, with, or by whom radical pedagogy and systematic change must be undertaken. Unpaid labor perpetuates class disparities for all students but is compounded for several groups in particular: (1) first-generation students and those who are working poor and therefore lack generational wealth that might allow those from social groups with a traditionally higher socioeconomic status or with greater access to historical and familial wealth to better absorb the harm of uncompensated labor, and (2) graduate students from racially minoritized backgrounds who contend simultaneously with low wages and the additional stressors of cultural taxation and inclusion tax (El-Sabawi & Fields, 2021); these students are themselves most likely to be first-generation students from families with lower socioeconomic status. These intersectional identities create challenges that are compounded by the expectation of unpaid labor within higher education institutions.

ALTERING PERCEPTIONS OF UNCOMPENSATED LABOR

To disrupt norms around uncompensated labor for BIPOC scholars, we formed a network of multicultural scholars that enables the small numbers of BIPOC scholars on campus to support each other and their scholarly pursuits through writing retreats, mentorship, and networking. The network exists solely to support BIPOC academics' research and development with the explicit intention of "asking nothing" of the scholars—namely, no institutional demands on their time and service such as committee work, labor in service of the institution, nor external demands for time or other resources. The network further supported a fellowship to reward two BIPOC graduate students for past uncompensated social justice engagement and mentoring of BIPOC undergraduate students in the academic pipeline. In this nascent initiative, other activities are collectively and democratically determined by members and facilitated by a lead convener.

The network contributes to eliminating racism on campus by dismantling institutional assumptions that BIPOC scholars will engage in EDIA work without support or remuneration (Evans & Moore, 2015). Its presence continues to disrupt discourse around uncompensated labor and brings attention to the problematic nature of these practices. Investing resources to pay for and protect the labor of BIPOC scholar-advocates engaged in social justice efforts demonstrates institutional commitment to EDIA and prevents exploiting these students who use their free time to enact institutional change. In a democratic partnership, compensation should be defined and collectively outlined by the institutions and the BIPOC members of the academy.

INTERDISCIPLINARY COLLABORATION AS DECOLONIZATION

To disrupt the norm of disciplinary segregation as well as reliance on uncompensated labor, the resource database (see http://uwm.edu /multiculturalscholarscollaborative) was created to serve as a comprehensive, accessible collection of anti-racism resources for faculty, staff, and graduate students to decolonize disciplinary silos of knowledge in academia. The learning team acknowledged that individuals interested in anti-racism often expect BIPOC scholars to provide education. By consolidating and sharing collective resources, the resource database serves as an accessible collection for all campus members interested in anti-racist work, thereby relieving individual BIPOC scholars of emotional and resource labor and shifting anti-racism education toward a more collective and democratic space.

The resources database project team comprised individuals from different disciplines (media studies, strategic management, development science, and clinical psychology), including the learning team plus a paid graduate student consultant from media studies to develop the database. A public web-form allows anyone from any background or discipline to submit resources. During development, the project team identified four resource categories—anti-racist teaching practices, anti-racist research practices, resources for BIPOC graduate students, and general anti-racism education—to address institutional expectations that anti-racism practices be implemented across levels of the institutional hierarchy. This database provides EDIA resources for academics across disciplines and levels of training to voluntarily educate themselves. The resource database disseminates anti-racism resources to the campus community, thereby alleviating the burden on BIPOC faculty to head these efforts.

At the time of this book's publication, the project team has listed all resources submitted to the database publicly, but may need to censor future submissions or address pushback from departments that do not see the value in interdisciplinary resources. Processes for addressing censorship and critique remain to be determined.

PHYSICAL AND INSTITUTIONAL HOME FOR ADVOCACY

As this network of BIPOC scholars has become increasingly visible, several outcomes have cemented its place in the fabric of the institution and campus community. The timely restructuring of the university's division of diversity, equity, and inclusion and hiring of a permanent administrator for the division allowed the network to be considered as a key collaborator with this division and the graduate school, two of the largest divisions on campus with budgetary and staff capacity to support the network. Resulting directly from our advocacy, these two entities partnered in 2022 to successfully push the campus to make the large monetary investment of a multiyear institutional membership in a national faculty development program supporting the productivity and retention of BIPOC scholars. The graduate school continues to ally with the network's goal to provide faculty mentoring with the understanding that such support will ultimately improve the graduate student experience, particularly that of BIPOC students, and alleviate labor demands on BIPOC faculty.

Through engagement with this project's team of students, the graduate school and its faculty governing body created a student advisory board for BIPOC students. This advisory board is compensated financially and has a codified voice in affecting the policies, procedures, and decisions of the graduate faculty and graduate school.

Finally, the graduate school is funding the creation of a physical space for BIPOC graduate students to promote belonging and academic camaraderie across disciplines and address dis-belonging in historically White institutions. Whereas undergraduate BIPOC students are supported by various campus cultural centers, graduate students often face isolation within their programs. The creation of this space was requested by student members of this authorship team, and funding was shifted to institutional offices/divisions with annual budgets and capacity to maintain the offices, in consultation with our project team and network members.

CONCLUSION: TOWARD LIBERATION FOR BIPOC SCHOLARS

Transformative pedagogy can inspire students to effect sociocultural change. The activities undertaken to disrupt the institutional structures emanated from the pedagogical experience shared by the authors in a classroom but embraced key pillars of Freire's notion of praxis wherein knowledge is accepted as inherently collective, contextual, and created (not discovered) (Freire, 1970; White, 2007).

Higher education is slow to systemic change, relying on uncompensated service from individuals including emotional and cognitive labor graduate students are trained into this paradigm, supported by faculty and administrators, perpetuating the system. While the efforts of the authorship team in creating this network of multicultural scholars have helped to disrupt these higher education practices, there remain several challenges due to the lack of a budget line for the network: sustainability, ongoing maintenance of the resource database, and funding for the graduate student fellowships. The partnering division of diversity, equity, and inclusion and the graduate school provided shared support for the lead network convener (the faculty author) in the initiative's 2nd year in the form of one month's summer salary; fellowship funding, however, continues to be solicited.

To sustain the network's efforts, it must be integrated into the university's structure and given an annual budget line. However, it must also retain its autonomy to prevent becoming a tool of the institution it aims to disrupt. The institution benefits from the network's existence in recruiting and retaining BIPOC scholars, but it is essential that the network remain a space for liberation rather than be co-opted by the institution.

Now in its 2nd full year of existence, the network is increasingly viewed as a resource on campus and a collaborating partner with the division of diversity, equity, and inclusion and the graduate school. The lead convener continues to present the network as an independent group primarily focused on supporting scholarly productivity. It will require ongoing praxis, collaboration, and commitment to disrupting the hierarchy of students, faculty, and administrative norms to retain the network's original aims of enhancing the research productivity of scholars of color, promoting retention of BIPOC faculty, and improving student retention within this pipeline.

DISCUSSION QUESTIONS/ACTIVITIES

1. What are your field or institution's expectations (i.e., unwritten rules) about labor and service, particularly related to equity, diversity, inclusion, and anti-racism? Who is disproportionately affected by those expectations (and why)? What actions could you take to disrupt expectations and eliminate disproportionate burdens of labor?
2. Who are the learning partners in naming and disrupting hierarchies found in your educational institutions (or other institutions of learning)? What will help create and maintain horizontal relationships among learning partners? What interdisciplinary discourse and partnership will be created to overcome "narration sickness"?
3. Name specific hierarchical structure(s) that you/your group are attempting to disrupt.

NOTE

1. The authorship team consisted of three doctoral students who identify as Asian American (she/her), Latino (he/him), and White (she/her) from multiple disciplines at the same institution, and one (Asian American) faculty member. Two of the students received the grant to form the network, and the third contributed to activities resulting in several changes outlined in this chapter.

REFERENCES

American Psychological Association. (2021, December). *Apology to people of color for APA's role in promoting, perpetuating, and failing to challenge racism, racial discrimination, and human hierarchy in U.S.* Retrieved from https://www.apa .org/about/policy/racism-apology

Cole, D., & Griffin, K. A. (2013). Advancing the study of student-faculty interaction: A focus on diverse students and faculty. In *Higher education: Handbook of theory and research* (pp. 561–611). Springer, Dordrecht.

Comas-Díaz, L., & Torres Rivera, E. (Eds.). (2020). *Liberation psychology: Theory, method, practice, and social justice.* American Psychological Association.

Cuseo, J. (2018). Student-faculty engagement. *New Directions for Teaching and Learning, 2018*(154), 87–97.

Davis, L., & Fry, R. (2019, July 31). *College faculty have become more racially and ethnically diverse, but remain far less so than students.* Pew Research Center. Retrieved from https://www.pewresearch.org/fact-tank/2019/07/31 /uscollege-faculty-student-diversity/

El-Sabawi, T., & Fields, M. (2021). The discounted labor of BIPOC students & faculty. *California Law Review Online, 12,* 17–29.

Evans, L., & Moore, W. L. (2015). Impossible burdens: White institutions, emotional labor, and micro-resistance. *Social Problems, 62*(3), 439–454.

Freire, P. (1970). *Pedagogy of the oppressed* (M. B. Ramos, Trans.). Continuum, 2007.

Freire, P., & Macedo, D. (1995). A dialogue: Culture, language, and race. *Harvard Educational Review, 65*(3), 377–403.

Garcia, S. E. (2020). Where did BIPOC come from? *New York Times*. Retrieved from nytimes.com/article/what-is-bipoc.html

Giroux, H. A. (2010). Rethinking education as the practice of freedom: Paulo Freire and the promise of critical pedagogy. *Policy Futures in Education*, 8(6), 715–721.

Goonen, N. M., & Medina-Shore, S. (2021). "Hot" issues in workers' compensation in colleges and universities: Graduate assistants and teaching assistants. *Compensation & Benefits Review*, 53(3), 144–154.

Guzzardo, M. T., Khosla, N., Adams, A. L., Bussmann, J. D., Engelman, A., Ingraham, N., Gamba, R., Jones-Bey, A., Moore, M. D., Toosi, N. R., & Taylor, S. (2021). "The ones that care make all the difference": Perspectives on student-faculty relationships. *Innovative Higher Education*, 46(1), 41–58.

Hirshfield, L. E., & Joseph, T. D. (2012). "We need a woman, we need a black woman": Gender, race, and identity taxation in the academy. *Gender & Education*, 24(2), 213–227.

Kornbluh, M., Johnson, L., & Hart, M. (2021). Shards from the glass ceiling: Deconstructing marginalizing systems in relation to critical consciousness development. *American Journal of Community Psychology*, 68(1–2), 187–201.

Mayo, P. (1993). When does it work? Freire's pedagogy in context. *Studies in the Education of Adults*, 25(1), 11–30.

McKee, K., & Delgado, D. A. (Eds.). (2020). *Degrees of difference: Reflections of women of color on graduate school*. University of Illinois Press.

Melaku, T. M. (2019). *You don't look like a lawyer: Black women and systemic gendered racism*. Rowman & Littlefield.

Mendoza, P. (2007). Academic capitalism and doctoral student socialization: A case study. *Journal of Higher Education*, 78(1), 71–96.

Miller, A. L., Williams, L. M., & Silberstein, S. M. (2018). Found my place: The importance of faculty relationships for seniors' sense of belonging. *Higher Education Research & Development*, 38(3), 594–608. Retrieved from https://doi.org/10.1080/07294360.2018.1551333

National Center for Education Statistics. (2022, May 31). *Characteristics of postsecondary faculty*. U.S. Department of Education, Institute of Education Sciences. Retrieved from https://nces.ed.gov/programs/coe/indicator/csc

O'Meara, K., Griffin, K. A., Kuvaeva, A., Nyunt, G., & Robinson, T. N. (2017). Sense of belonging and its contributing factors in graduate education. *International Journal of Doctoral Studies*, 12, 251–279.

Quarterman, J. (2008). An assessment of barriers and strategies for recruitment and retention of a diverse graduate student population. *College Student Journal*, 42(4), 947–967.

Stewart, T. (2021). *On labor acknowledgements and honoring the sacrifice of black Americans*. Retrieved from https://diverseeducation.com/article/206161/

Warner, C. K. (2012). A cure for narration sickness: Paulo Freire and interdisciplinary instruction. *Journal of Thought*, 47(4), 39–49.

White, J. (2007). Knowing, doing and being in context: A praxis oriented approach to child and youth care. *Child & Youth Care Forum*, 36(5), 225–244.

Zambrana, R. E., Wingfield, A. H., Hoagland, T. L., & Burciaga Valdez, R. (2016). Blatant, subtle, and insidious: URM faculty perceptions of discriminatory practices in predominantly white institutions. *Sociological Inquiry*, 87(2), 207–232.

CHAPTER 7

A Trio of Co-Conspirators

Teacher Educators, (Preservice) Teachers, and Elementary Students Working Together as Activist Researchers for Social Change

Katie Allison, Jessica Barnett, Vickie Godfrey, Jasmine Hashemi, James Hoffman, Beatrice Kyle, Catherine Lammert, Julie Mazur, and Theresa Nguyen

INTRODUCTION

This chapter documents how, in 2017, a university professor, two doctoral students, 16 preservice teachers (PSTs), and hundreds of elementary students disrupted teacher–student binaries by collectively conducting a practice-based research study (Sailors & Hoffman, 2019). This disruption occurred on three levels: (1) Teacher educators practiced activist research in the enactment of our preparation program, (2) PSTs developed activist research knowledge and practices that shaped their inservice teaching, and (3) Elementary students became activist researchers by identifying topics of concern and taking action for change.

We are three university professors and six 3rd-year inservice teachers reporting on how this research experience has continued to create change in our classrooms near Austin, TX. In this chapter, first, the former doctoral students—now professors—recall the preservice phase of the project. Next, six former PSTs—now several years into their careers—share their perspectives (via individual narratives) on developing instructional practices that disrupt teacher–student hierarchy through activism and research. Finally, we all close with a collaboratively written discussion of the challenges and possibilities afforded by our research on preservice teacher education.

PST EDUCATION: REFLECTIVE VS. TRANSMISSION MODELS OF LEARNING

In PST education, transmission models—those based on banking education (Freire, 1970)—are common (Hoffman et al., 2018). Traditionally, faculty, as experts, pass down their knowledge to novice teachers, who pass down knowledge to their students. This model appears logical since future educators must learn basic pedagogical routines (e.g., using "turn-and-talks") and classroom management (e.g., creating classroom norms). However, we argue that knowledge transmission, like banking education, is insufficient to develop critically engaged teachers and students. In this program, we relied on a reflective model rooted in collective growth and aligned with a knowledge-mining approach (Freire, 1970).

The reflective model, in contrast, centers the idea that learning to teach entails deepening commitments to humanizing practices (Freire, 1970) rather than simply learning subject-matter content. This view centers learning through communities of practice (Lave & Wenger, 1991). Lave and Wenger describe these communities as spaces where less experienced members, that is, new teachers, engage in "Legitimate Peripheral Participation" (1991, p. 27) as they engage with seasoned community members. LPP is "an empowering position" (Lave & Wenger, 1991, p. 36) where newcomers can observe, experience, and reflect on the practices of experts. Consistent with Freirean (1970) views of education, this reflective model makes learning to teach an intellectually freeing experience that prepares teachers to create liberatory spaces with their students.

STRUCTURE OF THE PROGRAM

Turning a reflective, Freirean stance into a tangible teacher education program is no small task. In 2017, the PSTs in this research enrolled in a program to earn an elementary teaching certification. The program explicitly emphasized literacy and research. To create a community of practice (Lave & Wenger, 1991), we maintained a cohort model where PSTs stayed together across 3 semesters of their junior and senior years. Instead of discrete classes, a university mainstay, these students' courses connected across domains of reading, writing, equity, and activism. The program relied on a core group of doctoral students and faculty to co-teach courses and supervise practicums. The physical location of this coursework was not the university campus but a spare classroom in a local elementary school. As part of the university teacher education program, methods courses were held on an elementary campus where PSTs, supported by instructors, mentored elementary students in reading, writing, and literacy experiences. This school was chosen because of its high number of second-language learners and location in a low-socioeconomic-status neighborhood. At this school, teacher educators mentored PSTs as PSTs honed their instructional practices through Legitimate Peripheral Participation.

Within this program, the literacy focus involved PSTs learning to teach through critical and humanizing pedagogical lenses (Freire, 1970), invoking imagination to make change in the world (Hoffman, 2020). We centered transformative practices by moving from the traditional emphasis on mastery of skills with the teacher positioned as deliverer to an emphasis on literacy learning as building tools for activism. For instance, one PST developed student interest on pets into an activist stance by moving from readings about cats and dogs to readings about pet shelters and volunteerism. Additionally, PSTs learned to teach reading and writing by positioning themselves alongside their students and engaging in exploration together (Leland & Harste, 2000). The PSTs' research focus was disrupting the idea that only university-based scholars can conduct meaningful research. Together, we emphasized the role of practice-based research in designing curriculum that engaged with social justice topics (e.g., racism, sexism; Janks & Vasquez, 2011) and socio-scientific issues (e.g., climate justice/injustice).

THREE DIMENSIONS OF PRACTICE-BASED RESEARCH

The practice-based research emphasized questions of who can consider themselves a researcher and what activism is enabled when the concept of research is broadened to include individuals who are often marginalized and/or excluded from being researchers (in this case, undergraduate college students and elementary students from underserved communities). We now describe each of the three research levels.

Teacher Educator Research

Research conducted by faculty and doctoral students was driven by the question: How can PSTs' engagement in research support their learning as literacy teachers? This question developed out of previous semesters, experiences, and conversations with cohort students; thus, knowledge from PSTs formed the basis for this project. Our multiple case study analysis showed that engagement in research supported their learning as reflective practitioners who thought deeply about each comment or action their students made and relatedly grew their pedagogical practices to differentiate for a wider range of literacy strengths and needs (Lammert, 2020).

PST Research

The research conducted by PSTs was driven by their self-selected research questions. PSTs began forming these questions during the first weeks of the program. Rather than waiting until the teacher educators had imparted enough of our "expert" knowledge, we trusted that research would be the way PSTs would grow their knowledge of teaching through Legitimate Peripheral Participation. Instructors encouraged them to choose a problem of practice that was important to them, ideally connecting literacy and/or activism. PSTs' research questions included: "How does intentional relationship building between student and teacher influence the student's literary practices and creativity?" and "What spaces best encourage my students to take risks in their writing?" PSTs learned to collect field notes and classroom artifacts as data sources in coursework. Then teacher educators supported the analysis process by asking questions and helping PSTs look for patterns in their data. The first and last semesters culminated with a research symposium (see Lammert & Steinitz Holyoke, 2020).

Elementary Student Research

The elementary students taught by these PSTs also self-selected research topics. The students initially considered a variety of engaging topics (Hoffman et al., 2020), such as mythology, chiropterology (i.e., the study of bats), performing arts, feminism, pirates, and ancient Egypt. Through book floods (a large quantity of various texts), students explored books and materials across multiple topics. Afterward, they discussed their interests with PSTs and chose a topic with the intention that the elementary students, through problem-posing pedagogies, would find and/or grow their own interests.

Then students formed small groups and began an extended inquiry into their subject. This inquiry involved reading informational and narrative texts while also recording evidence in support of views they gained from readings and dialogue with PSTs. Work sessions occurred twice per week for 45 minutes. Our belief was that the more a student learned about any topic that mattered to them, the closer they would come to finding some element of that topic that demanded an activist stance. As Freire (1970) has demonstrated, all human systems include elements of injustice and oppression, so we believed that regardless of whether a young person was interested in bats, Egypt, or performing arts, a social issue would eventually reveal itself through their study. This Freirean premise was supported in our case. The prime example was a group of students who selected gemology as their topic. As Dr. Hoffman recounts:

> Last fall, as I was picking up a group of 3rd-graders at the cafeteria to come to mentoring, one of the girls looked up at me with this very furrowed brow and said, "I still don't know how to change the world with rocks." I could tell how much she had been thinking and worrying about the challenge we had expressed from that first day. I had observed and interacted with her group many

times in their study of rocks and gems. The PST standing next to me said, "It's going to be alright; we still have time. You will find a way."

Eventually, her group moved from the study of rocks to gems to diamonds and the world of diamond and gem trading, ultimately discussing the abuses of people and the environment. She found her voice and a new term, "boycott," that she and her co-researchers took not only into their classroom but into their homes and community (2020, p. 12).

This shift occurred as students, in conversation with PSTs, read and thought about how social issues were present in their interests. Importantly, elementary students and PSTs compared options for what products could be created to support their activism (e.g., emails to a museum curator, signs to encourage peers to keep the school clean). Each group created different products. These experiences indicate that the elementary students' interests guided their choices. Instead of asking them what they already wanted to be activists for, our beginning point was for PSTs and teacher educators to provide tools and ask how they could help—an uncommon move for teachers (authority figures) to make. From there, activism emerged.

Graduation

Before these PSTs graduated in May 2019, one of the doctoral students found a passage that described Paulo Freire as "medium height, slender body, *eyes the color of honey*" (Freire & Macedo, 1998, p. 42). As teacher educators, we agreed that it was fitting for the graduates to have an honor cord representing their work. Naturally, we chose one that was honey-colored. Our sentiment was clear: May we all read the world through Freire's eyes as we bring humanizing pedagogies into our daily lives.

The following section provides individual narratives from six PSTs that describe their experiences disrupting hierarchies in the early years of teaching. Each individual shares how this process occurred in their classroom, and in the final narrative, challenges in attaining humanizing pedagogies are described.

DISRUPTING HIERARCHIES: TEACHER PERSPECTIVES ON INQUIRY, ACTIVISM, AND RESEARCH

These educators, now inservice teachers and professors, continue to reflect together on their commitment to humanizing teaching practices. To extend these reflections into the present, these inservice teachers describe how their undergraduate experience influenced their first years of teaching. They share how they continue to disrupt teacher–student hierarchies in the literacy classroom using activism and research.

Katie Allison, 3rd-Grade Teacher

My philosophy of teaching is influenced by Paulo Freire's statement, "to exist, humanly, is to *name* the world, to change it. . . . Human beings are not built in silence, but in word, in work, in action-reflection" (1970, p. 69). As a teacher, it is my commitment to leverage power in the classroom and not only guide students in developing skills to understand the world but to elevate their voices as they name and challenge their experiences. My development as an educator has been a spiral of action and reflection that would not continue without the opportunity to work in communion with my students, their families, and our community.

I credit my understanding of young children's language practices to the first group of children I worked with as an undergraduate student in a bilingual kindergarten class. I explored practice-based research with a student who had been identified as a "struggling reader." As we wrote together, I encouraged her to take ownership of the writing by choosing a topic and dictating a story, honoring her language choices, and noticing and naming what she had accomplished (Lammert & Steinitz Holyoke, 2020). She expressed agency by making choices in tools (sticky notes, thick markers, etc.), directing me as a coauthor, deciding to revise and redesign certain parts, and intentionally using translanguaging (i.e., multiple language resources) in her stories to convey the importance of words she held dear, such as *spiky tacones green* (green high-heeled shoes) and *going to el parque* (going to the park).

As I continued student teaching, my understanding of student agency expanded to account not just for how students interact with words but how they interact with the world (Freire & Macedo, 1998). In my senior year, I became interested in Youth Participatory Action Research (yPAR). I wanted to explore how I could apply this type of problem-posing education to a 5th-grade ELA classroom. My three classes, my mentor teacher, and I entered this project as co-conspirators. Together, we investigated tensions and wonderings we had about our worlds, built an argument for what we thought could/should change, and then chose how to take action. Students took up this work in a wide variety of ways. Some chose to educate their community about topics like deforestation and police violence, utilizing multimodal literacy projects, including videos, zines, graphic novels, and posters. Others opted for more direct actions, including writing a letter to a senator and organizing a canned food drive. I was moved by my students' passion for their topics, and we spent a lot of necessary time working together to reflect on the many feelings that world-changers experience: anger, success, failure, joy, and more. Their authentic motivation to create change fueled their research process.

As an inservice teacher, I continue to be impressed with how my students connect activism to their lives. For example, when my 2nd-grade class and I discussed a video about children learning to speak Wampanoag with the Wôpanâak Language Reclamation Project, one of my students shared a powerful reflection, "Losing your language? That's like losing your free will . . . if I lost my Spanish, I wouldn't be able to talk with anyone in my family anymore." This deepened everyone's perspective about why we nurture our traditions and stories. Throughout the pandemic and other challenges, I have found so much hope in my students' literacy practices. Sharing stories and celebrating each other's words have grounded our classroom community. Teaching is so much more than prescribing a set of skills; it is about growing ways of thinking and being that students will carry with them far beyond our classroom.

Jasmine Hashemi, Pre-Kindergarten Teacher

Based on my experience, the idea of the traditional classroom dynamic between teacher and student is one that is slowly becoming extinct. Some educators realize that our students play more than just the learner role in the classroom; therefore, the student–teacher hierarchy shifts in ways that benefit both the adult and child. During my student teaching and the past 3 years as a pre-K educator, my understanding of building relationships with students has grown. The connections we built come to life by getting to know each other on a personal level; this includes understanding the things students love. Students' curiosity should drive teaching, not just the curriculum guide provided by the school district. Thus, I've found multiple ways to foster curiosity in my current practice, which is my purpose for teaching.

In early childhood classrooms, much of learning happens through play. By providing open-ended activities called *centers*, I invite students to bring in their literacies and experience content using their own methods. During October, for example, one unit is about pumpkins. Before we begin, I transform the dramatic play center into a pumpkin patch, fill the sensory bin with fall-related items, and sprinkle pumpkin-themed puzzles, games, and toys throughout the rest of the centers. My role as an educator is to guide their play through inquiry, so I provide materials for students to manipulate in their own ways and take control of their education. Children connect experiences from their lives as they build a fall carnival in the blocks center or pretend to make pumpkin pie in the kitchen center. Within the first few minutes of exploration, dialogues that may not have happened in a more restricted and traditional learning environment occur.

As a student teacher, I found that I was inspired by my students' curiosity and realized engagement happened the moment a child's eyes lit up. I realized that students thrive when they take ownership of their experiences and engage in the inquiry process. Through play and writing, students carry their knowledge outside of the classroom and advocate for themselves and others, such as sharing their experiences with the community. As a practicing teacher, I create space for students to be curious, ask questions, and make suggestions. This practice allows me to view myself as a teacher–researcher, always on the lookout for things to try to provide the best environment for children. By using my students' curiosities, I am able to plan instruction that is tailored to their interests. It is not only the child who learns but I the teacher as well. For example, the students teach me how they make use of the materials I put out for them to manipulate, and many times, they show me ways that I could not have come up with myself. The learner and teacher roles are interchangeable between adult and child; this is the foundational idea to disrupt the teacher–student hierarchy.

Jessica Fisher, 1st-Grade Teacher

During student teaching and undergraduate work, our program focused on research that allowed us to unpack stereotypes seen in classrooms through reflection on our teaching practice, instructional choices, and our students. For instance, students often view the teacher as having all the answers and knowledge. However, through reflection, I was able to disrupt this process. For example, initially, when a student was unable to solve a problem, I would simply suggest a new strategy for them to use; however, after reflecting, I thought, "What ways could I have students problem solve rather than giving them a solution?" I realized that when you are continuously questioning and reflecting on your practices, you become a teacher who co-constructs learning rather than being the one knowledge source, and when you bring the research perspective into the classroom, these practices of questioning and reflecting are enriched.

Students can provide a wealth of new thoughts and ideas, but it is important for the teacher to create an environment that values these student assets so that knowledge is intentionally co-constructed. In order to create this environment, you need to have strong relationships with your students, be willing to make mistakes and acknowledge them, and be vulnerable enough to step back and let learning be co-constructed. For example, during the year, our class read a book about a klutzy teacher who was constantly being taught simple tasks like spelling and arithmetic by her students. My students found the book hilarious, and they realized that they, too, could teach the teacher. Originally, the purpose of the reading exercise was to teach setting, plot, and character development. However, it revealed to students that they have a voice and knowledge that could, and should, be shared with others. In another instance, the class was working on program coding as an enrichment activity. I knew one student who loved robots and coding, so I asked if he knew of any applications we could use. I had him take on the teacher role, and I sat with other students while we all learned from him how to use the coding applications.

Creating an environment where students use their voices and explore their ideas gives them opportunities to teach others and the teacher. This space creates a team dynamic rather than a strict teacher–student hierarchy. The teacher is not obsolete, but rather, now plays the harder role of guiding and facilitating.

Julie Mazur, 4th-Grade Teacher

For my research, I chose collaborative student–student partnerships because I was interested in the ways students worked together. Anecdotally, I found that the best collaborations came when students had the opportunity to choose their partners or groups. Simply giving students the power to choose their groups and to look to each other for answers disrupts the traditional teacher–student hierarchy in the classroom. Because of my research, I now try to encourage teamwork and collaborative learning as much as possible. For example, my school put a strong emphasis on preparing for the state test. Almost every day, I was required to use a passage from a previously released state test. I disrupted this process by creating collaborative groupings. Students would work in teams to read the passage and create their own strategies to answer the questions. After the teams were finished working, the students would then create new teams to go over their answers. When students did not get the same answer, they needed to use the strategies they created to determine the correct answer collaboratively. This opportunity gave them the space to learn and to creatively develop skills in conflict resolution and decision-making.

In my experience, students often look to their teacher to give them the answers, creating a have/have not hierarchy. One way I disrupt this hierarchy in my 4th-grade classroom is by not giving my students answers to all the questions they ask. It usually starts in writing. A student will ask me how to spell a word. I will tell them to "try your best." This moment can sometimes feel frustrating, especially at the beginning of the school year. Later in the year, a student may ask me a question about a topic we have covered in class before, such as, "What is a metaphor?" Instead of just telling them the definition, I will ask them, "How can you find that answer?" or "Who in the class can help you with that answer?" By not giving my students on-demand answers, they develop stronger problem-solving skills.

Beatrice Kyle, 1st-Grade Teacher

Relationships are a vital component to disrupting the teacher–student hierarchy in the literacy classroom. Building relationships starts from day one by greeting students by their name, asking questions about them—activities they enjoy, members of their family, holidays they celebrate—and making connections with them. Throughout the year, relationships are built by getting to know students even better by understanding their preferred style of learning, what subjects excite them (and which ones do not!), and their academic and behavioral strengths.

When I reflect on my student teaching, I realize there was much more to my PST experience than sitting in a classroom, watching the teacher to whom I was assigned. Instead, I became an active participant and learner in the classroom community while interacting with both my teacher and the students. Because I was a learner alongside the students, I was given a unique perspective into the inquiry, activism, and research projects we worked on during my student teaching semesters. I worked alongside the students as a guide or facilitator of their understanding, not as a teacher directing their process. I got to know them by talking with them about their families, their friends, and their lives outside of school, which all worked together to help build a strong, trusting relationship with the students.

Observing students interacting with each other, noticing what makes them happy, sad, angry, or scared, and responding in a way that validates their feelings and equips them to respond appropriately are all part of building a relationship. But relationships are two-sided, which means, as an educator, I have to be willing to let my students get to know me beneath the surface too. My responsibility, then, in the relationship is to be honest with them about where my feelings are coming from and how I responded— including when I need to apologize for responding inappropriately. As a teacher, I have an opportunity to teach and model vulnerability to my students. Sharing information and admitting when I am wrong or unsure of an answer shows them I am human. It shows I am still learning and growing, just like them, and that connection with them helps grow our relationship even more.

Theresa Nguyen, 5th- and 2nd-Grade Teacher

Disrupting the teacher–student hierarchy in the literacy classroom sounded easy to me at first because I was so motivated and eager to change the system, but I have realized this disruption is difficult to achieve. Based on my preservice experience, disrupting the teacher–student hierarchy meant moving away from a teacher-centered classroom and moving more toward a student-centered classroom. In my eyes, a student-centered classroom looked like students taking charge of their learning while the teacher takes more of a back seat in the room. I attempted to implement this approach. For example, in both my classrooms, I hoped to develop shared classroom rules with my students. I thought it would be best for them to come up with the classroom rules themselves, but when I asked what they thought, only one or two students shared their thoughts about classroom rules. The classroom rules they suggested were common, such as "treat others the way you want to be treated." I thought students would be naturally excited to create their own rules since it would be different from the typical structure of the teacher giving the rules, but the rest of the class nonchalantly agreed or were not paying attention. Students signed the classroom agreements but did not really follow through with them. I thought rules like "treat others the way you want to be treated" were commonly known, but I failed to establish a mechanism in my classroom for my students to follow that rule. I wanted to take a step back and let my students have more control of the classroom, but my lack of authority in my own classroom led to many student conflicts and frustrations.

I did not know what to do and sought support from the school coach, my former field supervisor, and my teaching partner. My attempts to disrupt the teacher–student hierarchy led to many students feeling upset and less trusting toward me. Eventually, two of my students' parents requested that their children move out of my classroom and into the teacher's classroom next door, where the "teacher is the authority" approach was being used. I felt defeated. What I was doing by disrupting the teacher–student hierarchy was supposed to be the "right" way, but it turns out that it was not always the "easy" way. This lack of support for my use of humanizing pedagogies ultimately led me to take a break from teaching. I was not prepared for the challenges that came with trying to disrupt the hierarchy and did not realize that there would be so much pushback for this approach.

Looking back, I understand the significance of disrupting the teacher–student hierarchy, but it is a difficult task to achieve. When my students had the opportunity to have more power in the classroom, they often had hesitation toward those opportunities (reminding me of Freire's [1970] insight that people are often afraid of freedom/liberation). For example, when I give out assignments that have questions that are free response, my students would rather have me tell them what to write than come up with their own answers. I think there is so much hesitation toward disrupting teacher–student hierarchy because it feels safer for students to stay within the system they are familiar with and into which they have been socialized. Disrupting the hierarchy could be a success if most people in that environment were on board with it, but it feels impossible to implement in a system that seems hostile to it. I felt like I had to give up on this approach to disrupt the hierarchy as a beginning teacher because there was little support for me to implement it successfully. This approach did not help me as a beginning teacher, and I needed to switch to the "authoritative teacher" approach to "survive" for the rest of the school year. There was much more support from my coworkers, students, and parents when I was using the standard "authoritative teacher" approach. Someday I want to return to the classroom and teaching, but I feel overwhelmed by a system that "seems to be against" humanizing pedagogies, and overworks and does not support teachers.

MOVING FORWARD: POSSIBILITIES FOR PST EDUCATION

In this chapter, we unite by exploring how teacher educators, PSTs, and elementary students can work together to disrupt hierarchies through combining research and humanizing pedagogies. We found that by disrupting the notion that conducting research is inaccessible to practitioners and is solely the domain of academics, elementary students and PSTs were able to find their own power as activists. The lasting impact of engagement in a reflective teacher education model is that these individuals can conduct research inquiries into their communities as they work toward liberatory schooling, which equally values teacher and student voices. This path is not without challenges; dismantling hierarchies in education systems is a continuous act of navigation and change, as evidenced by Theresa's experience.

In contrasting mining and banking stances (Freire, 1970) toward teacher preparation, we do not deny that it is helpful for teachers to learn content and practices. In particular, Theresa's story provides a window into what can happen when reflective approaches lose their grounding in practice. We believe that Theresa is not alone in her sentiment that disrupting hierarchies can sound better in theory than reality. In fact, this view is held by many scholars and policymakers who believe newly certified teachers are incapable of early expertise and therefore promote transmission models of teacher education (Hoffman, 2020). No method is without limitations, but for many teachers, reflective teacher education prepares them for powerful practice. We continue to view Theresa, and teachers like her, as helpful guides in pointing out the places where our practices as teacher leaders and educators can grow. The lack of support for humanizing pedagogies that she experienced from her students and their parents/caregivers has pushed us to wonder: How might we better support teachers as they experience tensions? How might we disrupt binaries that exist between university and K–12 schools to support teachers? These questions linger in our work as educators committed to liberatory education.

Importantly, most of these teachers' narratives focus on student autonomy, respect for students' language(s) and ideas, and faith in students' ability to grow. Further, it is noteworthy that many practices infused in the PSTs' research continue today. For example, Jasmine's teaching centers play and values curiosity, not just as something fun but as a teaching tool. Julie is intentional about withholding easy answers to help students become confident in their ability to solve problems themselves. These teachers center humanizing pedagogies that honor student identity, choice, and decision-making. These are pedagogies that began in the preservice program and, with the support of their students' parents and school leaders, extended into their inservice years.

We also note that despite their preparation to conduct research, by the 3rd year, only a few of these teachers reported continued engagement in research. Just one, Katie, named specific research methods, such as practice-based research and yPAR, and contrasted the two. Has the research education that these teachers received gone to waste? We think not. Jessica points out the beauty of being able to laugh at one's mistakes, even as an authority figure and teacher. Beatrice describes the need for a similar vulnerability by explaining that relationships are "two-sided," and teachers need to share about themselves if they expect the same from students. In our work together, we disrupted hierarchy by altering the narrative of who is an authority and who conducts research. We argue that the experience of trilevel research may have contributed to these teachers' continued humility and willingness to work toward more humanizing pedagogies.

We conclude with a reflection on the design of the chapter itself. This chapter foregrounds the experiences of classroom teachers, once PSTs, as they developed instructional practices using research and activism. We, teacher educators, facilitated this writing due to our familiarity with academic publishing. In doing so, we acknowledge the seemingly hierarchical relationship present in the publication process. To disrupt this hierarchy, teachers wrote freely to address how they disrupted student–teacher binaries. Looking across these narratives, it is evident that we view teaching as an impetus for change and advocacy for students' rights. Together, we write this chapter to challenge traditional hierarchical structures and to blend our voices to advocate for humanizing pedagogies in classroom teaching. Furthermore, we invite other teacher educators to consider research as a tool for building humanizing teaching practices.

DISCUSSION QUESTIONS/ACTIVITIES

1. How might you use research to identify hierarchical structures in your teaching practice or in another profession?
2. Once you have identified hierarchical structures, how might you disrupt those structures?
3. How might you develop professional networks that disrupt hierarchical systems in education? How might these networks build more humanizing educational experiences?

REFERENCES

Freire, P. (1970). *Pedagogy of the oppressed*. Continuum.

Freire, P., & Macedo, D. (1998). Literacy: Reading the word and the world. *Thinking: The Journal of Philosophy for Children, 14*(1), 8–10.

Hoffman, J. V. (2020). Practicing imagination and activism in literacy research, teaching, and teacher education: "I still don't know how to change the world with rocks." *Literacy Research: Theory, Method, and Practice, 69*(1), 1–19.

Hoffman, J. V., DeJulio, S., & Lammert, C. (2018). *Transforming literacy teacher preparation: Practice makes possible.* International Literacy Association. Retrieved from https://www.literacyworldwide.org/docs/default-source/where-we -stand/ila-transforming-literacy-teacherpreparation.pdf

Hoffman, J. V., Lammert, C., DeJulio, S., Tily, S., & Svrcek, N. (2020). Preservice teachers engaging elementary students in an activist curriculum. *Research in the Teaching of English, 55*(1), 9–31.

Janks, H., & Vasquez. (2011). Critical literacy revisited: Writing as critique. *English Teaching: Practice and Critique, 10*(1), 1–6.

Lammert, C. (2020). Preservice literacy teachers "bringing hope back" through practice-based research. *Literacy Research: Theory, Method, and Practice, 69*(1), 1–18.

Lammert, C., & Steinitz Holyoke, E. (2020). Supporting English learners through practice-based research. *Reading Horizons: A Journal of Literacy and Language Arts, 59*(1), 24–40.

Lave, J., & Wenger, E. (1991). *Situated learning: Legitimate peripheral participation.* Cambridge University Press.

Leland, C., & Harste, J. (2000). Critical literacy: Enlarging the space of the possible. *Primary Voices K-6, 9*(2), 3–7.

Sailors, M., & Hoffman, J. V. (2019). *The power of practice-based literacy research: A tool for teachers.* Taylor & Francis.

CHAPTER 8

Brooklyn Arts Council's Wellness Studio

Educational Praxis in Slow Curating for Social Change

Chief Baba Neil Clarke, Daniela Fifi, Desiree Gordon, David Gumbs, Miguelina Rodriguez, Griselda Rodriguez-Solomon, and Zane Rodulfo

INTRODUCTION

As the global community confronted the COVID-19 pandemic and the rise of other global health emergencies, wellness continues to be a major concern. Artists and cultural practitioners were uniquely affected and are still recovering from the vulnerability experienced during the pandemic and the lasting effects on their livelihoods and stability (National Endowment for the Arts, 2022; Villarreal, n.d.). In response to these growing concerns, the Brooklyn Arts Council Wellness Studio (BACWS) was a program designed in 2020–2021 to investigate the intersection of arts and culture with wellness. Funding was received from various sources including the National Endowment for the Arts, New York State Council of the Arts (with the support of the Office of the Governor and the New York State Legislature), New York City Council members and former members through the Cultural Immigrant Initiative, the New York City Department of Cultural Affairs Cultural Development Fund, and the TD Charitable Foundation.

This chapter reflects on how curators and artists developed BACWS through an inclusive, iterative approach. The two public program curators and four cultural practitioners and artists who created BACWS (and are the coauthors) explore the possibilities and vulnerabilities of ceding power by applying educational philosophies to curatorial work, focusing on Paulo Freire's (2018) philosophies of praxis and Megan Johnston's (2021) slow curating. Through this hybrid theorization, we show how Freire's work can be applied to settings beyond the traditional classroom.

In this chapter, the two public program curators refer to Ms. Desiree Gordon and Dr. Daniela Fifi (who also served as Brooklyn Arts Council's director of programs and strategy, and cultural research consultant and community liaison, respectively); artists (such as musicians, dancers, visual artists, etc.) are represented by David Gumbs and Zane Rodulfo; cultural practitioners (i.e., those who engage in traditional cultural and folk practices/art) are represented by Chief Baba Neil Clarke and the Bruja Sisters (Drs. Miguelina Rodriguez and Griselda Rodriguez-Solomon); the Brooklyn Arts Council senior management team is represented by the executive director and the development & external affairs director; and the Brooklyn Arts Council Cultural Heritage Advisory Group is constituted by the senior management team, cultural practitioners, artists, and community stakeholders (e.g., cultural and business leaders).

THEORETICAL FRAMING: PRAXIS AND SLOW CURATING

The Brooklyn Arts Council Wellness Studio's public program curators looked to Freire's concept of praxis and the gradual work of slow curating to guide the program's development. The conceptual and theoretical frameworks of praxis and slow curating are founded on inclusiveness, reciprocity, mutual regard, and humanizing methods of meaning-making. Slow curating is a term developed by Megan Johnston (2014) that emerged in response to the educational turn in curation. It is used to describe a method of socially engaged curation that undoes the top-down hierarchy of curatorial practice, instead prioritizing artists and cultural practitioners as cultural experts/knowers in a way that promotes and enhances audience engagement. The process is "slow" because it involves a cyclical and iterative system of engagement and evaluation with cultural practitioners and artists throughout the curatorial process, as opposed to the curator conceptualizing the process individually. During the 1960s and 1970s, Freire's work was used to reconsider the status quo in curatorial work, causing an ideological change in cultural institutions known as the educational turn (which is essentially the integration of education concepts in curation). Curation began to be considered an educational process as it determines the ways in which audiences experience or interact with art and culture.

Freirean praxis focuses on critical reflection and action toward freedom and positive transformation in the world. Central to this approach is valuing students' abilities to contribute to knowledge production and learning through their own expertise in their local cultural domains, instead of viewing them as passive recipients of knowledge (Freire, 1970).

In her 2021 article "Slow Curating: Re-Thinking and Extending Socially Engaged Art in the Context of Northern Ireland," Johnston posits that engaging in slow curating results in "a dialectical approach that is an open model for knowledge production; a site for many people and not just the few" (p. 24). Thus, slow curation aligns with Freire's liberatory theorization of agency, dialogue, co-construction and revolutionary possibilities, integrated into critical cultural programming for social change.

To meet BACWS's goals, an artist-centered approach to designing this program emerged. The cultural community's input was central to the establishment of a program that emphasized the health care and wellness needs of the arts population of Brooklyn. To bring this program to fruition, artists and cultural practitioners assumed a position that is traditionally held by a public program curator. Traditionalist curatorial frameworks call on the specialized academic and professional skill sets of the curator as an authoritative voice that shapes cultural programs and provides narrative around cultural production (Fowle, 2007). Curators are esteemed as the bearers of culture; "with the charge of researching, acquiring, documenting, and publicly displaying art [and culture], the curator becomes the propagator of taste and knowledge for the public good" (Fowle, 2007, p. 28). Thus, often artists and cultural practitioners are passive participants in the display and representation of their own work and culture. Given the weight of social responsibility associated with this program, it called for the dismantling of these hierarchies for a more democratic process that placed the curator and artist/cultural practitioner together as co-constructors of knowledge and programmatic elements, hence the choice to employ the paradigms advocated by Freire and Johnston.

HEALING AND THE ARTS

BACWS offers wellness content and resources, such as podcasts, blogs, curricula, training opportunities, wellness on-site installations, and live community performances to artists and the wider Brooklyn community. The program is rooted in research that suggests the act of creating art and participating in art programming has powerful healing properties (Lane, 2005). The discipline of the creative arts and traditional cultural practices (such as Qigong, yoga, and Salpuri) are beneficial to mental health, stress reduction, and improving diagnostic outcomes of severe illnesses (Seaward & Lissard, 2020). Music engagement, for example, reduces anxiety, improves auditory stimulation, and calms neural activity in the brain; it is also used to control pain in cancer patients (Stuckey & Nobel, 2010). Aligned with these research findings, BACWS invests in the prosperity and spirit of Brooklyn by supporting the well-being and health of Brooklyn's artists through empowering cultural programming.

BACWS is primarily a digital initiative with site-specific physical activations, discussions, performances, installations, and demonstrations. The virtual delivery facilitates both local and global accessibility for Brooklyn Arts Council's (BAC) programming, an important characteristic since Brooklyn's creatives represent a large immigrant population (U.S. Census Bureau, 2022). The site-specific installations allow BAC's audiences to intimately engage with artistic and cultural practices that enhance wellness.

BACWS launched two programs in 2021 that continued into 2022: the Neighborhood Clinic Healing Installations and BAC's Sonic Clinic. Both programs focus on the healing properties of the arts and culture. They offer BAC's public and the Brooklyn artist community the opportunity to connect with culture through restorative and meditative avenues. The Neighborhood Clinic Healing Installations were interdisciplinary, with broad entry points for healing to allow cultural practitioners and the community opportunities to create and engage in forms of healing from varied aspects of practice. In BAC's Sonic Clinic, the program focused on healing and culture through music and sound. Both programs center on cultural practices and traditions that are indigenous to the local and immigrant populations of Brooklyn. These immigrant communities include those from South Korea, Trinidad and Tobago, Colombia, Morocco, West Africa, Dominican Republic, and India. BAC's director of programs and strategy as well as the cultural research consultant (Desiree and Daniela, the two public program curators) facilitated conversations virtually with the artistic community and cultural practitioners.

During these conversations in the early stages of developing the program, themes of community, spirituality, grounding, celebration, nature, and connectivity surfaced as important elements of healing through cultural traditions and art. These anecdotal insights are backed by research highlighting that cultural traditions assist not only in defining a community but also in the actual formation of communities (Stuckey & Nobel, 2010).

Indeed, the process of investigating and critically reflecting on one's own cultural traditions and practices can make a significant contribution to one's road to recovery and overall well-being (Stuckey & Nobel, 2010). Yet, despite the benefits of cultural programming, ongoing budget cuts, closure of cultural centers, increased unemployment, and heightened restrictive measures due to the COVID-19 public health crisis have threatened the livelihood of artists, particularly freelance, self-employed, and small-scale creatives (Villarreal, n.d.). The pandemic has highlighted the vulnerability of artists' access to resources and health care that are generally available through standard employment, while simultaneously emphasizing the crucial relevance of wellness for these groups. The inaccessibility of health and wellness resources for these populations raises the question: Who has comprehensive access to public health care, mental health care, and wellness programs? It is clear from the pandemic that serious racial, cultural, health care, and economic inequities exist in New York City communities (New York City Council, n.d.).

BACWS: A SPACE FOR CHANGE

BACWS responded to these inequities by being a dedicated space for social change through providing paid opportunities to Brooklyn's cultural community. BACWS's offerings included presentations, open forums, and research about the healing components of cultural heritage traditions and contemporary art; wellness resources for artists and freelancers, including affordable health insurance, affordable counseling/therapy, and accessible support groups; international exchange and partnerships; and affirmation and validation for artists from mentor artists. For example, through paid Neighborhood Healing Clinic Installations, artists were provided with commissioned opportunities that were scarce during COVID due to budget cuts in cultural institutions and closure of cultural and artistic spaces. Through these initiatives, BACWS redressed inequity through increased investments in artists and communities; increased content for greater accessibility and reach; and increased connectivity for building capacity, networks, sustainability, and solutions for a more just and joyful Brooklyn.

BACWS is a hybrid program that lives online as well as in site-specific locations. On-site programs were developed in areas that historically faced socioeconomic and health challenges. In designing this program, we also came together (curators and artists) to imagine what new spaces of wellness could look like in areas that faced health care inequities in Brooklyn.

We (the two public program curators) asked artists and cultural practitioners a series of questions developed by the senior management team and the public program curators. Questions included: Where would you imagine these programs can live in Brooklyn? What form should these cultural wellness programs take? How can they contribute to your communities? Artists agreed that programs should be created to support areas of Brooklyn where artists were faced with harsh unemployment realities due to the pandemic. Together, we envisioned programming that took the shape of small-scale wellness music festivals throughout Brooklyn, healing workshops, and a space to distribute wellness resources (such as COVID-19 home testing kits).

BAC's public program curators collaborated with community stakeholders in regular monthly virtual meetings through BAC's Cultural Heritage Advisory Group to determine how the BACWS project would be presented both online and offline. In these meetings, we asked participants what they required from BAC in terms of programs, overall direction, and even the goals of the meetings. The team ensured that the privacy of all members was respected by not recording sessions, and this in turn created intimate environments to share and express views openly. If participants could not make it to meetings or preferred to chat one-on-one about topics, we followed up with individual meetings, building trust and safety, which made it easier for them to express difficult or uncomfortable views. We welcomed all opinions and maintained a level of flexibility regarding the direction of the program to reflect the concerns and preferences of participants.

During a monthly meeting, one artist remarked that wellness and healing are associated with an intimate experience in his community and that spaces should be created for private engagement and reflection. He addressed personal ritual practices of the Yemenite Jewish tradition where communities wail and mourn together after a death as a form of wellness, healing, and community support (Gamliel, 2014), noting that these traditions called for privacy and not public display. Other artists and cultural practitioners supported these notions through their own practices, which led to the creation of community blogs on the BACWS website where members of the public could contribute from their own homes, in their own time, allowing them the space and privacy to engage (see the Wellness Studio Community Voices page on the website https://www.brooklynartscouncil.org/what-we-do/wellness-studio/neighborhood-healing-clinic).

The methodology for producing this chapter also dismantled notions of hierarchy by including an iterative process of approvals by each contributing author. The progression and development of this chapter was as a result of conducting interviews with the artists and cultural practitioners involved as coauthors (as seen from personal communication, later on in the chapter). The approval of the chapter's segments, writing, word choices, ideologies, and conceptual framing was also granted by all contributing authors; the creation of this work, therefore, was essentially a collaborative endeavor, with one individual serving in the role of scribe based on their availability.

In the following sections, we will explore how the theories of praxis and slow curating apply to curatorial work in the field of arts and culture. We will reflect on their incorporation into BACWS through co-constructing knowledge and designing equitable wellness community spaces.

REFLECTIONS OF BAC WELLNESS STUDIO AS PRAXIS: CO-CONSTRUCTING KNOWLEDGE AND ACTION TOWARD CREATING EQUITABLE SPACES FOR WELLNESS

For the BACWS program, artists and cultural practitioners took on the role of the public program curator. The following section is a reflection by the six authors about the co-construction of BACWS (i.e., two curators, Daniela and Desiree, and four artists/cultural practitioners: Chief Baba Neil Clarke, Zane Rodulfo, David Gumbs, and the Brujas of Brooklyn). We reflect on the program's development as effectively and successfully integrating praxis as a curatorial method through slow curating. We will also review the meaning of praxis and its role in dismantling hierarchy. The tenets of praxis explored in this section specifically apply to those utilized by us to develop the BACWS. We will look at the following ideas in relation to critical reflection as a foundation for praxis that deconstructs hierarchy:

- Open communication enables reflection and meaning-making through equal exchange, thus removing hierarchy.
- Critical reflection encourages imagination and innovative thinking to create equitable spaces in wellness that break the status quo.
- Using language in critical reflection and action draws on the expertise of the marginalized (i.e., artists and cultural practitioners) rather than those who traditionally assume power (curators).

- Critical reflection dismantles hierarchy by renegotiating established concepts of truth in wellness and critical action.
- Programmatic spaces align with the concepts devised through critical reflection.

We do note that these ideas are relevant not only to our setting but also to other educational spaces. BACWS drew on Freire's notion of praxis to challenge the "teacher–student contradiction" by promoting vulnerability and reciprocity between curator and artist. A curator in a traditional context is often a doctoral-educated professional with specific expertise in subject matter pertaining to the arts. The evolution of artwork and the narratives around cultural output are typically driven by curators. For exhibitions in particular, commissioned artists are often driven and imposed on by curators to create a certain kind of work. This dynamic can result in commissioned artists becoming accustomed to leaning on the curator's vision and direction instead of their own (Kelly, 2014). The curator is seen as a specialist instructor or professor, while the artists are seen as pupils in need of guidance. This relationship is reminiscent of Freire's banking model, which erases students from the process of knowledge production.

In this section, we detail how we disrupted the curator-artist hierarchy using Freirean concepts. Central to dismantling this hierarchy in BACWS was ensuring that the program collectively prioritized artists' voices and expertise over that of the public program curators. By engaging in slow curating, we cocreated dialogic structures that facilitated mutual exchange of knowledge and expertise among the multiple participants in curatorial practice, including artists/cultural practitioners, audiences, and curators.

Thus, program development processes began with public program curators turning to artists and cultural practitioners as the main source of knowledge-making and compensating them for their input. This collaboration was facilitated through monthly dialogue-based sessions, where we employed a Socratic method and inquiry-based approach. In the critical classroom setting, many educators use the Socratic approach to "draw out" student understandings of a topic. Instead of just telling students what they need to know, a critical educator will ask them questions that get them thinking critically and talking with each other, which will ultimately help them to formulate their thoughts on a topic and justify their thinking. Through our monthly meetings, we employed this approach on themes of wellness with artistic and cultural practitioners by asking probing questions on wellness and art to stakeholders and asking for justification in their practice or cultural settings that supported their thoughts.

In each monthly dialogue-based session, artists, cultural practitioners, community stakeholders, and the public program curators engaged in discussions about what healing, culture, and wellness meant to them in their respective communities. This development came about in response to outcry from artistic communities during the pandemic to meet a communally expressed need. This need was that of proper health care for artists who were out of work due to places closing. During these sessions, cultural practitioners articulated what they understood by "culture" and "healing," and these varied meanings were documented by the public program curators present at the meeting.

We all also engaged these specific questions: What does healing mean in your cultural community? What does it look like? How does healing sound? What areas of healing are needed in your communities? How does your artform converge with healing in your community? At the first monthly meeting with the community stakeholders for BACWS Sonic Clinic program, for example, cultural practitioners and artists expressed 13 specific entry points to healing as sound from their respective cultural communities. Their responses were:

- "Healing is a state of mind";
- "Healing is holistic and integrated into the body, mind, and soul";
- "Healing in music is a cathartic experience birthed in legacies of resistance";
- "The body is an instrument of healing that is used to create music and sound";
- "Healing is a form of solace";
- "Healing is a personal relationship with music, sound, and art";
- "Healing is multiplicitous with various entry points. It isn't linear";
- "Healing through sound, art, and culture is a state of transformation, being transcendent";
- "Healing is a deeply personal and intimate experience";
- "Healing is therapeutic";
- "Music is a healing prayer";
- "Healing is spiritual"; and
- "Music is healing in praise."

(Brooklyn Arts Council Cultural Heritage Advisory Group, personal communication, September 2021).

The curators then met with artists individually to discuss their notions and insights of healing, art, culture, and its relationship with their communities. Musician Zane Rodulfo expressed:

> Finding forms of healing, especially when rooted in one's own cultural memory and community, is tantamount to the progress of my community and myself. Healing allows us to not only reclaim, but also transform and regenerate ourselves into newer forms, discovering and negotiating both old and new patterns and finding a healthy medium through which we can progress. . . . Trinidad and Tobago's musical heritage is rooted not only in healing, but serves as an epicenter and benchmark of change and evolution. (Z. Rodulfo, personal communication, May 20, 2022)

The oral and written responses collected from participating community stakeholders, artists, and cultural practitioners were coded and reviewed by the curators and senior management team to devise thematic categorizations as the starting point for program creation. These were reviewed during monthly meetings to ensure that the categorization, coding, and development into themes were reflective of the data received and captured by the community of artists and practitioners. After reviewing all responses, the curators then narrowed down categorizations for the project into five thematic buckets:

- Healing as resistance
- Healing as spirituality
- Healing in tradition
- Healing through the body
- Healing as celebration

These categories were then taken back to community stakeholders, artists, and the cultural community for review, feedback, and approvals. Then, based on the approvals and feedback provided, these five themes set the foundation for the entire program (see BAC Sonic Clinic website for more detail: https://www.brooklynartscouncil.org/what-we-do/wellness -studio/sonic-clinic). Thus, these monthly dialogue-based sessions were an integral part of program development as the views expressed by cultural practitioners and artists centered, oriented, and shaped the direction for the program, and therefore disrupted the traditional curator/artist relationship.

Artists involved in the process were encouraged to define program terminology as it resonated with them and brought their own interpretations of these themes to their work. BAC wanted to make sure that the program's language and meanings came from a community of artists, which is a key component of Freirean praxis. Freire believed that for reflection and dialogue to be liberating, it must respect the common language of the knowers (in this case, artists and cultural practitioners rather than public program curators), seek to understand their way of life, and create settings in which knowers may express their goals and intentions fully (Freire, 1970/2007).

Philosopher Maxine Greene (2000) argued that imagination also plays an important part in Freire's theory of praxis. Through dialogue, knowers must feel free to envisage the possibilities of altering their current lived realities. This, according to Greene, is the work of the imagination, a jolt of possibilities that rouses us from the slumber of the status quo (Allsup, 2003). Through the community voices page, artists and curators created an online space to reflect and visualize what we propose as a healing community, thus connecting praxis to their vision for a better world.

BACWS also made room for artists to collaborate with each other across disciplines. Consistent with Freire's praxis model, during meetings, the public program curators acted as facilitators rather than gatekeepers of knowledge. David Gumbs, the digital artist creating the artwork for BAC Sonic Clinic programs, discussed the means by which collaboration was supported and the effects of this:

> From the start, BAC introduced me to each musician and encouraged me to reach out to gather further information individually [learning about each community's sense of culture and wellness]. . . . The liberty [and trust] to experiment with a variety of mediums and techniques allowed me to draw inspiration from my own visual vocabulary. This freedom was the key to create and experiment with the art. (D. Gumbs, personal communication, May 20, 2022)

The freedom to move through the creative process was central to establishing the artist's voice at the core of the artwork developed. Furthermore, BAC provided David with the space to imagine healing and wellness as it emerged for him as he interfaced with his collaborators. He explains, "throughout the whole creative process [and through conversations with my collaborators], I was inspired to associate healing with a sort of cosmic, and surreal feeling in the videos [digital art created for the program]" (D. Gumbs, personal communication, May 20, 2022). David drew on his own cultural memory, and this, along with notions of healing derived from group conversations with participating artists, led him to create visual manifestations of healing soundscapes (see landscapes at https://www .brooklynartscouncil.org/what-we-do/wellness-studio/sonic-clinic).

The curators, in the spirit of slow curating, prioritized the desires of participating artists in the creation of their art. At the end of each monthly dialogue session, BAC collaborated with artists to develop online programs, site-specific installations, and activities that invited audiences to engage with the artists' ideas in embodied ways. Dialogue sessions became spaces of constructive reflection in each stage of the programs' development, calling to action elements of the program that did not address social inequities. Iteratively, BAC collectively revisited, redefined, and reshaped programs with participating artists to ensure that they mirrored the needs of their communities. Participating artist Chief Baba Neil Clark commented during one of these cyclical sessions, "praxis requires practice" (N. Clark, personal communication, April 29, 2022). He further reflected on the public program curators' involvement as mainly supportive, describing his conversations with the organization's representatives as an exchange of ideas rather than the engagement feeling authoritative and unidirectional.

Other cultural practitioners, such as the Brujas of Brooklyn, had a similar report. The Brujas of Brooklyn (Griselda and Miguelina) are doulas and certified yogis merging "ancestral medicine with sharp intellect" to address internalized oppression and intergenerational imbalances. The programs team (led by Desiree as director of programs and strategy) collaborated with the Brujas of Brooklyn on the Neighborhood Healing Clinic Installation to present wellness tools that promote personal power and progress using breath, song, and movement. The Brujas explained that BAC's main involvement was to offer logistical support for the artists' participation. Griselda explains: "Desiree and [the team] were very thorough in explaining [the parameters of the program] and then Miguelina and I kind of just go with the flow of how we want to fill the container" (the Brujas of Brooklyn, personal communication, April 26, 2022). Both artists interviewed felt a sense of agency in determining the nature of their participation.

MANAGING PRAXIS

The cyclical and inclusive nature of developing programs in line with notions of praxis did not come without its challenges. Because of this nontraditional approach, some tensions arose around authority and hierarchy. One member of BAC's Cultural Heritage Advisory Group expressed strong desires for a clearer institutional presence and voice in the framing of the projects. This was met with resistance from the invited artists, who insisted on their autonomy. This member of the group strongly encouraged the program to focus on education more directly and asked for scholarly educational references in programming, whereas community stakeholders present in the Cultural Heritage Advisory Group sought to elevate the significance of intergenerational wisdom. To navigate these tensions, the senior management team facilitated conversations, centering vulnerability and honesty, to allow both groups to express themselves and be heard. This meant asking the artistic community questions such as: How would you prefer the work to be represented, and how should it be framed? These conversations led to heated tensions and conflicts between those who leaned toward academic scholarship as knowledge versus those who embraced Indigenous ways of knowing.

To facilitate this process, the curators worked out a satisfactory compromise. Together with the artists and cultural practitioners, we devised and included scholarly blurbs and interactive activity aides. These were included on the website, along with artist statements that spoke to community-informed beliefs, highlighting the educational, Indigenous, and theoretical groundings of the work. Thus, these iterative and inclusive processes of knowledge-making and action contributed directly and tangibly to program development. These components struck a compromise between the competing desires of the artists for their voices to be at the center of discourse while still making space for scholarly input (see website for examples of artists' statements and activity aides). Navigating these challenges by using liberatory praxes truly forged us as learning partners.

CONCLUSION

Freire (1994) contends that praxis and freedom are essential to both the individual effort of self-actualization and the communal effort to produce culture. He explains that the fight to be human includes both processes of humanization and dehumanization. Dehumanization reduces humans to objects of their culture, denying them the potential to be self-defining subjects who create and define culture. Processes of humanization allow persons to situate themselves within their culture, within their art, and within their cultural-political circumstances. For Freire (1994), the ultimate expression of one's humanity is to generate one's own sense of self through deliberate and conscious reflection, followed by purposeful action. Artists were called on to be the voice of their cultural creation rather than being objects of it. The success of BACWS as an equitable space for health is more crucial than ever to hold onto optimism in these trying times, when so many people throughout the world feel burdened and separated, and cooperation feels increasingly rare (Finkelpearl, 2013).

Freire's voice is still essential as we try to find solutions to our challenges in constructing a better future for Brooklynites. Our hope is that cultural institutions will continue to turn to our creative and cultural communities to participate in and co-construct/codevelop knowledge and programs, and that curators and the creative community will continue to interrogate who selects content and how it is represented. We believe that in order to do this, disrupting the curator/"teacher" and artist/"student" hierarchies is important, and although some may not automatically think of education vis-à-vis art and culture, our work demonstrates how Freire's theories can be applied to settings beyond the traditional classroom.

DISCUSSION QUESTIONS/ACTIVITIES

1. Outside of the traditional classroom, to what other settings can Freire's theories be applied?
2. How can your lived cultural experience better inform the programmatic life in our institutions?
3. In what ways can you incorporate the concept of slow curating in your practice?
4. How can we mobilize art and culture to both disrupt hierarchies *and* promote wellness? How do we critically teach others how to balance this?

REFERENCES

Allsup, R. E. (2003). Praxis and the possible: Thoughts on the writings of Maxine Greene and Paulo Freire. *Philosophy of Music Education Review*, 11(2), 157–169. Retrieved from http://www.jstor.org/stable/40327208

Finkelpearl, T. (2013). *What we made: Conversations on art and social cooperation.* Duke University Press.

Fowle, K. (2007). Who cares? Understanding the role of the curator today. In S. Rand & H. Kouris (Eds.), *Cautionary tales: Critical curating* (pp. 26–35). Apexart.

Freire, P. (1994). *Pedagogy of hope: Reliving pedagogy of the oppressed* (R. R. Barr, Trans.). Continuum.

Freire, P. (2007). *Pedagogy of the oppressed* (M. B. Ramos, Trans.). Continuum.

Freire, P. (2018). *Pedagogy of the oppressed.* Bloomsbury Publishing USA.

Gamliel, T. (2014). *Aesthetics of sorrow: The wailing culture of Yemenite Jewish women.* Wayne State University Press.

Greene, M. (2000). *Releasing the imagination: Essays on education, the arts, and social change.* John Wiley & Sons.

Johnston, M. (2014). Slow curating: Re-thinking and extending socially engaged art in the context of Northern Ireland. *Oncurating.org, 24,* 23–33.

Johnston, M. (2021). *Curating in context: Slow curating as a reflexive practice* [Doctoral thesis, Ulster University]. Ulster University.

Kelly, N. (2014). *Artists and curators.* Visual Artists Ireland. Retrieved June 22, 2023, from https://visualartists.ie/artists-and-curators/

Lane, M. R. (2005). Creativity and spirituality in nursing: Implementing art in healing. *Holistic Nursing Practice, 19*(3), 122–125. Retrieved from https://doi.org/10.1097/00004650-200505000-00008

National Endowment for the Arts. (2022, March 15). *New data show economic impact of COVID-19 on arts & culture sector* [Press release]. Retrieved from https://www.arts.gov/news/press-releases/2022/new-data-show-economic-impact-covid-19-arts-culture-sector

New York City Council. (n.d.). *The impact of COVID-19 on NYC artists.* Retrieved June 22, 2023, from https://council.nyc.gov/data/artists-covid/

Seaward, B. L., & Lissard, C. (2020). A spiritual well-being model for the healing arts. *Journal of Holistic Nursing, 38*(1), 102–106. Retrieved from https://doi.org/10.1177/0898010120907528

Stuckey, H. L., & Nobel, J. (2010). The connection between art, healing, and public health: A review of current literature. *American Journal of Public Health, 100*(2), 254–263. https://doi.org/10.2105/AJPH.2008.156497

U.S. Census Bureau. (2022). *Quick facts: New York City, New York.* Retrieved from https://www.census.gov/quickfacts/newyorkcitynewyork

Villarreal, J. (n.d.). *How COVID-19 has affected the arts industry.* Artdaily. Retrieved July 10, 2022, from https://artdaily.com/news/130517/How-COVID-19-Has-Affected-The-Arts-Industry—#.Yt9CLsHMIyg

Everybody Teach! Upending Traditional Disciplinary Curriculum to Create Co-Taught, Praxis-Based, Higher Education Courses

Alexander Fink, Bemnet Habtamu, Angela Kunkel-Linares, Morgan Pence, Kaiya Woller, and Ilene Dawn Alexander

In this chapter, we outline the transformation of an undergraduate course across 2 years of collaboration. Working together, we upended typical hierarchies and challenged embedded myths of the classroom as a container of learning and the teacher as a dispenser of knowledge. Influenced by Highlander Folk School activist educators Myles Horton, Septima Clark, and Bernice Robinson, and their contemporary Paulo Freire, we grew Adolescent and Youth Development (AYD) from a traditional youth studies major course to a co-created learning community with three of four semesters between fall 2020 and spring 2021 conducted online due to COVID-19.

Additionally, several course participants collectively designed and facilitated AMPLIFY2020, a conference designed to support youth and social work professionals' understanding of issues young people face. Having learned from these experiences through reflective writing and conversation, we highlight our co-creating practices and share several insights (that we call Glimpses) into disrupting educational hierarchies in order to upend destructive aspects of conventional education.

GATHERING

We worked within the University of Minnesota Youth Studies program, which purposefully engages students in collaborating with professors and in reflecting on the principles of critical pedagogies. Our writing collaboration, which includes one teacher, four junior- and senior-level students, and one teaching consultant, emerged from Alex's invitation to AYD and AMPLIFY participants to continue reflecting and co-creating.

In our own voices, we are:

Alex: I came to teaching this course having spent a decade trying to sort out how to be a cis White guy supporting students from backgrounds different than mine to do critical, participatory, activist work with young people. Myles Horton, Septima Clark, and Bernice Robinson served as disrupting hierarchy models whose work we could adapt to our context.

Bemnet: Coming into our course I found myself initially hoping to have an easier class in which I could thrive academically, but also mid-pandemic I was looking forward to engaging in something I knew I was passionate about. I simply felt like I was "getting by" each day of the pandemic, and I wanted more than that!

Angela: As a Latinx student in higher education, I entered this course pessimistic, burnt out, and looking for a university space in which students who are critical of the way our world treats young people would be listened to and engaged.

Morgan: I always wanted to work with young people and thought that a career in education was my only option. I came to this course seeking a different way to engage with young people: to learn from them, understand their experiences, and amplify their voices. I did that, and learned more about myself and my interests in the process.

Kaiya: As a student during the pandemic, I felt disconnected from chances to be involved in the community. I saw the struggle, deterrents, and feelings of burnout folks experienced when working with young people, and I felt discouraged in traditional methods of youth work. This new approach to a college course intrigued me, and I felt invested and engaged in the learning and work.

Ilene: I am a White, queer, first-generation, 60-something, activist academic who participated in the course as a teaching consultant. I first worked with Alex when he was a graduate student taking Teaching in Higher Education, a class that I still regularly teach. Across a dozen years, we have co-designed and co-taught multicultural learning and teaching courses, and now we make space for intergenerational discussions of social justice teaching and learning.

HIGHLANDER FOLK SCHOOL

In our work together, we centered practices linked to Highlander Folk School, a popular education center founded in rural Appalachia in 1932 that played a critical role in the U.S. Civil Rights Movement. For example, Highlander supported student-led activism in organizing Mississippi Freedom Schools in 1964, and later worked in communities to launch Citizenship Schools focused on developing adult reading, writing, and social justice literacy so that participants might register to vote and work as activists and organizers in their communities (Clark, 1986; Fink, 2015).

Highlander's processes and outcomes resonated deeply with Paulo Freire, as reflected in Horton's and Freire's published conversations (Horton et al., 1990). The conversations highlight beliefs central to our work: Everybody is a teacher and learner; collectives are better at solving problems than individuals or traditional experts; people should be put in charge of directing their own education as much as possible; and education's goal ought to be creating a better society (Horton et al., 1990). Teaching and learning in the spirit of Highlander requires applying Horton's "two-eyed" view: first to see people as they *are* to understand where they are coming from, and then to see where they *could be*. In designing courses, teacher-facilitators enact this practice by noting who and where participants are, how they show up, and the orientations they bring to learning, and by actively creating and holding space for the kinds of learning spaces we want to co-create (Horton et al., 1997).

FOUR STAGES OF CO-CREATING

Introduction: Planning for Disrupting and Bridging

Frank Coffield offers "acquisition" as a metaphor to describe standard hierarchies structuring university classrooms; he also theorizes "participation," which we use to describe our approach to teaching–learning work. It is an approach that prioritizes building community and active engagement as learning goals, connects all participants as dialogue partners, and centers interaction with peers as essential for learning (Coffield and Learning Skills Network, 2008, p. 10). Participation informs Coffield's definition of learning as requiring "significant changes in capability, understanding, knowledge, practices, attitudes or values by individuals, groups, organisations or society" (2008, p. 7). Coffield's participatory learning framework aligns with Horton et al.'s approaches to praxis and informs our work in educational spaces and in the broader world.

Throughout our YOST3032 experience re-design, Alex and Ilene asked "How can this university course . . ."

- embody a model of expertise that invites participant expertise and active roles in decision-making, rather than a top-down, hierarchical, authoritarian "banking model"?

- offer significant projects inviting students to develop and share their ways of knowing and expertise with each other and the broader world?
- develop (whether in-person or online) a community that supports organizing and change-making work beyond the classroom in both space and time?

We designed a course curriculum to (1) practice Highlander's "everybody is a teacher and a learner" approach, (2) enact Coffield's participation mode, and (3) disrupt hierarchies to share roles associated with expertise. In making bridges from the disruptions, course participants reinvigorated a knowledge acquisition–focused higher education course into practice-oriented, transformative learning experiences with opportunities for learners to engage in co-creation of knowledge and provide leadership in professional development. Throughout the course, learners developed a range of communication, research, collaboration, and presentation skills as they participated in real social change work as learners and (future) professionals.

Stage 1: Participatory Learning

Adolescent and youth development courses should address theories of youth development such as participatory facilitation and youth-led program models, and ideally, embody those approaches (Fusco, 2012). Further, to be relevant to students' lives and experiences, youth development courses should also infuse social justice pedagogies and practices that upend dysfunctional divisions between "teacher" and "student." YOST3032 provided an opportunity to model participatory learning and youth-led development work by inviting students to, for example:

- join in shaping early-semester class sessions;
- draw on their experiences and research to design and teach, later in the semester, their own workshop sessions on youth development topics (Fink, 2020b); and
- set up individual learning contracts focused on seeking feedback rather than on traditional grading mechanisms.

During the initial 5 weeks of class, Alex drew on the standard practice of Highlander facilitators, selecting key resources and springboard questions that created an invitation for students and the instructor to draw from scholarly knowledge, practical experience, and community and cultural wisdom. He also noted points of agreement, disagreement, and dissent. From such invitations, students and instructors began interacting differently—as collaborators with shared goals rather than as actors fulfilling traditional "student" and "teacher" roles (Smith & MacGregor, 1992). Students began by facilitating team-building and eventually, with support from Alex, taught each other through facilitating class sessions they designed.

Primary challenges to adapting critical pedagogies to college classrooms include creating course assignments that are significant for learners during a course and meaningful beyond the classroom, and moving away from A–F grading systems that reassert teacher authority. To meet these challenges, Alex developed transparent assignments, introduced learning contracts to support student feedback and evaluation choices, and worked as a learning partner with students in sharing goals for developing and revising curriculum, and for facilitating interactive workshops for different audiences (Alexander, 2021; Fink, 2020a).

Stage 2: Everybody Teach

We also drew on practices Highlander developed in running primarily race-, gender-, and class-integrated learning circle workshops aimed at acknowledging the agency of individuals (predominantly Black, poor, rural, young/old, Southern) who were told, and taught, to rely on the knowledge of others (predominantly White, culturally and economically elite men in community and national leadership roles). Highlander focused on the knowledge brought together by participants: A key part of the model involves asking relevant questions to invite participants to uncover problems communities face by sharing stories and experiences to better understand peers' perspectives, and ultimately to build next strategies, share resources, and create new networks beyond the workshop (Alexander & Fink, 2018).

For the primary project of this course, students selected youth development topics (such as youth experiencing houselessness, mental health and trans youth, or supporting youth with substance-abusing caregivers), explored these topics through research and conversation, and then developed them as workshops with learning aims, preparatory activities, and informative informal assessments based on the project outline Alex adapted from course design resources (see also Fink, 2020c; Learning4All, 2015).

Each workshop would build on the learning atmosphere created through session plans and invitations that Alex and guest facilitators modeled in the first few weeks of the semester. For the remainder of the semester, students facilitated their workshops and learned about their chosen topics, many of which are significantly underrepresented within youthwork and social work continuing professional development.

By positioning the teacher as a learning partner, students as knowledge builders, and all parties as involved in feedback, the workshop project transformed the roles of students, teachers, and mentors, and the very purposes and practices of university learning spaces.

Stage 3: Broader Change

In practicing co-teaching and co-learning, the perspectives of course participants on knowledge, expertise, and problem-solving led to profound shifts in their understandings about shaping and interacting within community-based projects and youthwork roles. Highlander had similarly served as a springboard for the formation of the Citizenship School, wherein a Black community member, rarely a professional teacher, would take it on themselves to teach other Black people in their community how to register to vote. The model and curriculum were developed by Septima Clark, Bernice Robinson, and Black Southerners who had been participants at previous Highlander workshops addressing civil rights, Jim Crow racism, and daily life problems in their local communities.

Similarly, several students from multiple semesters joined together to develop a conference for participants beyond their courses. They began developing the conference by (1) revising their workshop sessions for an audience of youth development professionals and (2) seeking faculty and community partners to take on technical support and chat moderation roles during the online conference sessions. Over 300 education, social work, and youthwork professionals from around the world attended and received continuing education credits.

Stage 4: Broader Movements

Highlander was masterful in joining with broader movements. It never attempted to "own" the Citizenship School Movement but instead offered ownership, leadership, and expansion to others, so that programs and ideas could grow beyond Highlander, creating an early form of open resource sharing (Horton et al., 1990). Those of us still working on this project finished with the conference and started to ask: What next? We decided to collaboratively write, talk, and reflect on what we had done, the impacts of our work, and where we could next take our new understandings.

As one community-oriented example, Angela facilitated a class on the movement by youth organizers to remove school resource officers from schools in the Twin Cities Metropolitan area (Reding, 2021). In our generative reflective writing, Angela noted:

> After facilitating the class, I grew more empowered in my facilitation skills. I took what I learned to support a cohort of youth organizers as co-teachers and learners from a local Anti-Racist Coalition. They wrote, facilitated, and participated in an 8-week Underground School program. They taught each other direct action tactics, political art-making, political theory, and movement history. I believe the most radical part of what our class did was not in our facilitations or teach-ins, but it was in the way we grew more empowered to know

ourselves and each other as teachers and learners and then felt moved to bring that empowerment back into community and justice work.

Collectively and individually we are taking our changed perspectives into other aspects of our work and practice, including presenting at conferences (Alexander, 2022; Pence et al., 2022).

GLIMPSES INTO "DISRUPTING HIERARCHIES"

In analyzing our collaborative writing, we identified five themes demonstrating disrupting hierarchies. We begin with an example of the instructor's invitation to co-create, and then student co-authors from YOST3032 elaborate on building relationships that matter. We use these glimpses to examine the unlearning we were called to engage and to acknowledge the work of making room for new relationships to learning. Invitations into co-creation also pushed us to confront the imposter syndrome phenomenon, and working through this led to us turning learning into public action. Each glimpse that follows is written by a co-author who is identified in the opening lines.

Glimpse 1: Invitation

Alex Fink

My most important concern in co-creating a learning space with 10–20 participants is establishing an ethos of invitation and participation oriented toward more just communities and politics. Based on notes across several class sessions, a typical first class starts with exchanges like this:

> *Alex (A):* "If the first 10 minutes of our gathering establishes a precedent for the way we will gather for the rest of the semester, and you were in my position, what would you do first?"
> *Student (S) 1:* "Go over the syllabus!"
> *A:* "Good idea. It's common for a first day. How would that impact our coming together?"
> *S1:* "We'd know what's coming and could decide if we wanted to stay in the class. I'd feel less nervous about the unknowns."
> *S2:* "Yeah, but every class does that and it's boring. We need to do something that creates a good environment for us."
> *S3:* "We should do a community-building activity."

We spend time exploring the impacts of these and other ideas, and then a student points out: "This *was* the first 10 minutes of our class—way longer. What we spent our time doing was establishing a culture of making decisions together about how we're going to do things in this class."

Students used to classes where instructors set the semester plans right away might worry that an instructor who deviates from this does not have a plan. It can take time to adjust to a new approach, as Kaiya (one of this chapter's authors) observed:

> When you told us you had thought of many directions we could go and had plans as a starting point for each direction, I relaxed a lot. Later, I realized I was trained by the education system to expect that the teacher always had a specific plan. It took time for me to accept that I could be part of shaping how our class would work.

Indeed, I (Alex) had plans for each class—multiple plans, in fact. However, I offered plans as options; I called them "invitations." An invitation could always be taken up but also could be adjusted, even rejected. For example, this might be a common exchange in class:

A: "I had an idea for us to work through what we read in small groups, and then come back as a large group and share our thinking. I had a couple questions in mind. . . ."

S1: "I think I'd rather talk in a large group today and hear what everyone thought. We've been working in small groups and I'm missing hearing everyone's voices."

S2: "Yeah, but in small groups we each get a chance to say more and actually talk with each other. I'd rather work in small groups."

S3: "OK, what if we work in small groups for a while, but we make room for questions beyond what Alex proposed, then come back to the big group?"

S1: "Yeah, I like that plan. But let's do different groups than last time."

Interacting in a feedback loop moved us into organizing learning in ways that were increasingly more effective for students as co-owners adopting, modifying, or completely changing a springboard plan I offered or one created by students.

Glimpse 2: Building an Us We Could Trust

Kaiya Woller

When we started class, I was apprehensive. Though I had experienced alternative, self-organized K–12 education, and was part of YOST classes that involved some negotiating with instructors about learning, Alex had me worried: "*We* were supposed to decide what we did in the course? I am paying you to organize the course!" I had anxiety about grading, assignments, and ways the class would unfold. When Alex said he had a plan for each class period that we could review online—it helped me calm down. There *was* a plan to fall back on, and he was really offering us decisions about how we wanted to proceed. I realized that I needed the push to think about how to create democratic and participatory spaces with young people—*and* that I also needed some sense of a rudder. Learning the intention behind how we approached the work made it possible for me to trust an unusual process.

The tension between the teacher providing a structure to start from *and* an invitation to change it together formed the basis for trust within our group. The follow-up relationship and community building put that trust to work when we started facilitating team-building for each other. Acting on the invitation to bring our own knowledge and experience into the room, we started recognizing that we had things to teach and learn from each other. We dove deeper into our own interests, giving ourselves time to sit with and listen to each other. In teaching each other, we deepened that trust. After the course, we continued to develop these relationships as we stepped into new roles to organize the AMPLIFY conference. For example, I decided to create a peer review and support group to help develop conference presentations from our course facilitations by organizing students and program faculty into practice and feedback sessions. Organizing faculty was intimidating! Here I was, an undergraduate, telling faculty what to do, facilitating meetings where *I* was leading *them*. But I was able to draw on the experiences we had together in class to pull this off—and this experience has made everything I have done since just a little less intimidating.

Glimpse 3: Unlearning

Angela Kunkel-Linares

> "We need to be taught to study rather than to believe, to inquire rather than to affirm"
>
> —Septima Clark

As students, we entered our classroom with academic identities and histories. What I know most about myself and the ways I show up has to do with the identities I claim. I am a first-generation "american" queer youth raised by a Brown immigrant mom from Peru and a White father from rural Minnesota. I am also a learner, sister, nieta, and community organizer.

I grew up with imagery of what it meant to be Latinx. They were caricatures of my tias, my mom, and of my community. Played by Sofia Vergara or Salma Hayek, these characters were objects of Americans' humor, their sexualization, and their exoticism. I heard their accents and found the voice of my mom's; I heard the comments made about their bodies and saw my own. In

13 years of public schooling, I never had a Latinx teacher; I was never taught about histories that uplifted success and excellence from my communities.

Our current, colonial school system forces students to find a spot in the binary of good or bad student, smart or dumb kid. While the world told me folks from my communities were not holders of knowledge, I knew from my own experiences that many of my teachers existed outside the borders of school as clever engineers, weavers, cooks, dancers, and stewards of our planet. If we change our definition of learning to be expansive and multidimensional, it would include learning from people like my mom. In experiencing the American public school system, I lost sight of my mom as a teacher, the many ways elders taught me how to be respectful and resourceful, or the way my father taught me how to fish and garden. In this realization, I noticed that in order to begin finding justice in education, I had to unlearn my beliefs around who owned knowledge and who was worthy of learning. Three lessons emerged for me to unlearn:

- White, cis-het, able-bodied, wealthy men are the holders of truth.
- To be worthy of learning is to be obedient.
- Learning is best done under the strict guidance of one, older teacher.

After we unlearn what it means to be worthy of learning and who holds knowledge, a door emerges for us to return home. To return to truth telling.

As bell hooks, my first teacher in this, noted: "The heart of justice is truth telling, seeing ourselves and the world the way it is rather than the way we want it to be" (1999, p. 78). In my work I have chosen to expand from just recognizing the oppression that exists around me to remembering what realities can be made possible. When we abandon our spiritual connection to truth, we abandon the path of justice. For me, that spiritual connection is felt anytime someone gives me knowledge that deeply resonates. It is in moments of resonance that my spirit is telling my body that it remembers—all the teachers, mothers, and grandmothers that planted those seeds of wisdom. Truth unveils space where seeds of love and care can be planted in our community. By reaching out to my community of organizers, elders, and youth to get feedback on my class presentation, I surrendered myself from dominating this hierarchy of knowledge. As a class, we put this in practice by seeing one another as holders of knowledge. The practice of learning in community must mean we give up the notion that we "own" our learnings. Releasing our power over knowledge is a loving practice. It is only when we unlearn the hierarchies associated with "student" and "teacher" that we can begin to develop new practices focused on us all as learners, as valued holders and cocreators of knowledge. In educational spaces, this is our path toward justice.

Glimpse 4: "Imposter Syndrome"

Morgan Pence

I am a daughter of two parents with college degrees: my mother, a second-generation Filipina-American, and my father, a White male. Growing up in Northern California where the public education system is often grossly underfunded, I was taught from an early age that education is valuable and important. I had the luxury of attending some of the best private schools in the area and therefore had high expectations for myself and my learning, and worked hard to meet those expectations. Even so, I often felt like I was an imposter, especially as I showed up as myself in college. Despite all of the hard work and preparation that got me to college, I still felt anxious presenting in front of large classes, nervous about networking with professionals, and scared when applying to jobs. I learned to understand the phrase "imposter syndrome" as feeling as though you are not as competent as others, that you are a fraud, or that despite all your successes you are not worthy.

Coming to this course, I was faced with the most intense versions of these fears: that I was not qualified to be presenting this information; that if I did not have all the answers, all my hard work and accomplishments over the past 3 years would not be enough. The focus of my presentation was on mental health and how we as youth workers could reduce the stigma while supporting young people with their mental and emotional well-being. I had interest and passion for the topic, and many psychology courses had prepared me for this conversation. Yet, when researching and presenting my own information, I felt scared and ill-prepared. When participants posed questions, those questions left me doubting my own expertise. Yet, in presenting my workshop three times (in this class, as a guest in a different class, and for the conference), I experienced serious engagement and felt included in a community of practice, as exemplified by anonymous comments from conference attendees that left me aware of the expertise and confidence I had gained:

- "That activity you led was really powerful. Do you have ideas for what I could do as an activity for this topic?"
- "I know someone working on your topic—do you want me to connect you?"

To achieve this, I, and we collectively, needed experiences of collaboration and co-creation, which required students and teacher alike to move from the teacher-as-expert to a notion of expertise that drew from the knowledge and experiences of students, the teacher, and community members.

Glimpse 5: Learning as a Public Act

Bemnet Habtamu

Somewhere trekking through the United States' education system, I lost my own intuition about how to learn. Learning became a terrible kind of acting: my teachers acting like they knew everything important and my peers and I acting to please them, pretending we cared. The world around us became a game where we would "fake it 'til we make it," and this game eventually became the only way we could understand learning and education.

As a result, I needed to be told by experts, professors, and other adults how to ensure that I could become the "best learner." So I left our first class with Alex confused and even flustered. Our collective agreed that we all initially felt that sense of vulnerability; that signing up for such a class was possibly a mistake; that creating our own rubric, crushing the idea of "teacher versus student," and gaining a sense of autonomy in the first class were intimidating.

One of the worst parts of the education system for me was that my teachers stopped seeing that as a learner, I had wants, aspirations, and needs. Students like me are rarely shown how education can be useful for our lives, work, and communities. Education, then, becomes preparation only for the future. As Nancy Lesko puts it in *Act Your Age*, we live in "expectant time"—frozen in waiting for a time *after* school is done to actually participate (Lesko, 2012, p. 122).

By asking us to help create and revise the course—to "make the road by walking"—our class became an invitation to start using my education as an opportunity to make my work better. When we started to teach each other about the work and practice *we* cared about, I realized that we each have something powerful to give to the world.

I am the daughter of two immigrants. They moved and dropped everything they knew for their kids to have access to quality education. I spent much of my time in the education system hyper-focused on fulfilling what I understood to be my parents' wishes, which I interpreted as valuing the highest grades and acting my part as the "good" student. I was lucky enough to have understood my life's passion for working with neurodivergent youth at a young age, thanks to my younger brother's diagnosis; I had a passion for working with young people with disabilities, with an emphasis on autism spectrum disorder. Years later, after touring a summer program with my parents for my brother to participate in, I asked on the car ride back, "Do we even know if the workers completed any education about the population they're working with?" My mother calmly responded, "That's not what matters to me. I'd rather they care for him and his quality of life." She continued, "You don't have a degree, Bemnet, but if they care about the kids as you do, that will leave me fulfilled."

As my experience in class took hold, I realized my mother's wisdom. I was surprised by her response when I told her about my experience in the course, about the way it was shifting my own expectations away from "good grades" and toward learning that was useful to my work. She told me that what mattered most was that my education was useful and that it mattered to me. I heard her words as "You don't need a degree or even good grades to gain fulfillment; you need to apply your learning to do meaningful work with the time you are given in the present."

CONTINUATIONS

We hope these brief glimpses coalesce for you into a picture of the ways we worked toward significantly shifting hierarchies of traditional education. To close here, we offer a few insights that we continue to explore, and summarize a way of beginning a course redesign based on what we've shared in this chapter:

- Trust and relationship-building made it possible for course participants to address the emotional labor required to transform students' collective relationship to education.
- For teachers and learners, it is hard to bring that energy to new contexts every semester, and classes with different (and differing numbers of) students, in different historical moments, may organize and take up the invitations of the class in varied ways.
- Making space for co-creation requires shifting traditional (implicit and explicit) institutionalized classroom structures and expectations.

And as a beginning for course redesign, we suggest that teachers use the principles set out in the course design framing and project outline Alex shared with students (Fink, 2020c; Learning4All, 2015), consider the learning contract approach to grading, and develop multiple pathways for students to practice co-creating and offering feedback through class sessions, activities, and assignments.

When teachers and students collectively push default assumptions aside, they are able to create a different kind of space; as dialogue partners, intergenerational conversation can emerge where teachers like Alex (and their teachers like Ilene) share knowledge and experience in authentic conversation. In dialogue, a teacher can hold a two-eyed view of students: where they are at presently and where they might go; and the students too can hold this view while interacting with themselves and their worlds, their teachers, and each other.

Finally, the work of creating change requires teachers' open invitations: How would you like to be part of this? What are your ideas? How would you like me to be part of those? It requires accepting that this work cannot be forced. Not every student will wish to join in doing something bigger, nor to commit to ongoing work; some students need to select ways they can be present and complete coursework to simply meet the basic requirements. Not every teacher will wish to take on this big commitment every semester, even for one course; co-creation requires tremendous emotional labor and relational effort. From our perspective, the work of "Institutionalizing Social Change" requires (1) course- and program-level engagement with pedagogical changes that foreground the kinds of course design and teaching/learning practices we highlight in this chapter; and (2) course interactions that nurture ongoing feedback conversations among learners, teachers, and community learning partners. Fostering changes at institutional levels requires cross-unit collaborations such as ours, where instructors collaborate with teaching centers *and* with students, engage in multidisciplinary professional development opportunities, and take up pedagogical leadership roles in faculty governance contexts.

As a closing, we offer this short mantra: Stay rooted in relationships and always work through invitation.

DISCUSSION QUESTIONS/ACTIVITIES

1. Select one passage from the chapter that challenged or inspired you. Reflect and write about why.
2. "We cannot know love if we remain unable to surrender our attachment to power. If any feeling of vulnerability strikes terror in our hearts, lovelessness torments."—bell hooks (2000, p. 253). How does shame (internalized or imposed directly in your class by grading, classroom atmosphere, etc.) impact space for vulnerability, (un)learning, and trying new and challenging activities?
3. "When we started to teach each other about the work and practice we cared about, I realized we each have something powerful to give to the world in the now"—Bemnet Habtamu. Consider your own learned expectations of the roles of teachers and students over the course of your education. Consider also the hierarchies that establish space (in-class or during-course/"outside" of class) and roles (teacher/student; expert/learner) in your class. How does your relationship with power figures in (non-)educational spaces reflect how you show up in a classroom?

REFERENCES

Alexander, I. D. (2021, July 8). *Creating transparent assignments*. Academic Integrity Resources for Teachers. Retrieved from https://docs.google.com/document/d/1d1OKItjyGSqSwtv_JhpapsClOlDEsjGIVmm4qeKi-CA/

Alexander, I. D. (2022, September 6). *Consulting and co-creating as a learning partner: A case study* [Conference presentation]. ALTC 2022 Convention, Manchester, UK. Retrieved from https://youtu.be/JfbcFaSr1Uc

Alexander, I. D., & Fink, A. (2018). Designing an inclusive intercultural online participatory seminar for higher education teachers and professionals. In N. B. Dohn, S. Cranmer, J. Sime, M. de Laat, & T. Ryberg (Eds.), *Networked Learning: Research in Networked Learning* (pp. 125–148). Springer International.

Clark, S. (1986). *Ready from within* (C. S. Brown, Ed.). Wild Trees Press.

Coffield, F., & Learning and Skills Network (Great Britain). (2008). *Just suppose teaching and learning became the first priority . . . .* Learning and Skills Network.

Fink, A. (2015). We don't want a teacher: Using the past to offer fresh eyes to contemporary practice. *Child & Youth Services, 36*(1), 56–78. Retrieved from https://doi.org/10.1080/0145935x.2015.1015886

Fink, A. (2020a, August 4). Transitioning to online teaching (Part 1)—Think-Out-Loud. *Public Fragments*. Retrieved from https://publicfragments.org/2020/08/04/transitioning-to-online-teaching-think-out-loud

Fink, A. (2020b, August 26). Transitioning to teaching online—Contemporary issues in youth development, OER Project. *Public Fragments*. Retrieved from https://publicfragments.org/2020/08/26/transitioning-to-teaching-online-contemporary-issues-in-youth-development-oer-project/

Fink, A. (2020c). *YOST3032—Project outline and student-generated rubric, course document*. Retrieved from https://docs.google.com/document/d/1gECZScTo3mPXgnxGeyqIQ_cGCc7J5PJOfntlEOma0oo

Fusco, D. (Ed.). (2012). *Advancing youth work: Current trends, critical questions*. Routledge.

hooks, b. (2000). *All about love: New visions*. William Morrow.

Horton, M., Freire, P., Bell, B., Gaventa, J., & Peters, J. (1990). *We make the road by walking: Conversation on education and social change*. Temple University Press.

Horton, M., Kohl, J., & Kohl, H. (1997). *The long haul: An autobiography*. Teachers College Press.

Learning4All. (2015, April). *The 4A's of course design* [Video]. YouTube. Retrieved from https://youtu.be/nqAFFYkm_qM

Lesko, N. (2012). *Act your age! A cultural construction of adolescence* (2nd ed.). Routledge.

Pence, M., Woller, K., Fink, A., & Alexander, I. D. (2022, March 16–18). *Co-creating educational resources with clients* [Recorded presentation]. Imagine Innovate Inspire/Minnesota Social Service Association, Minneapolis, MN. Retrieved from https://docs.google.com/document/d/1Nm2eEhtYAEMk590wS8wSM7VE65GBPlHAzCwVfGh8viI

Reding, K. (2021). *AMPLIFY workshops schedule*. Retrieved from https://docs.google.com/document/d/16rm—rPNkUd5TLSBoQRz3iIzy-3l9Aqsxzzn5Ynd88s/

Smith, B. L., & MacGregor, J. T. (1992). What is collaborative learning? In A. Goodsell, M. Maher, V. Tinto, B. L. Smith, & J. T. MacGregor (Eds.), *Collaborative learning: A sourcebook for higher education* (p. 11). National Center on Postsecondary Teaching, Learning, and Assessment.

CHAPTER 10

To Be "In and Not Of" the University, but Beyond

Estudios Rebeldes as Relational Disrupting for Change

*Agustin "Tino" Diaz, Hannah Filizola Ruiz, Leandra Hernandez,
Jose Coreas, Lydia Kerr, Jorge Garcia, Carlos Alarco,
and Mari Claudia Linares*

INTRODUCTION: OUR CONTEXT AND ASPIRATIONS

Within the last 10 years, the state of Utah in the United States has undergone vast demographic shifts. According to the 2019 annual report of the Utah System of Higher Education, increasing births and net migration to Utah, particularly from Latin American communities, will significantly increase its population size. The Kem C. Gardner Policy Institute produced a Race and Ethnicity report in 2016, stating that Utah County has the second-largest population of color increases in the state (Harris, 2016). However, despite an increase in the Black and Indigenous People of Color community within Utah County, 2019 census data demonstrates low educational attainment among these same communities (U.S. Census Bureau, 2019). As students, practitioners, and faculty from the Latin American diaspora at a university in North Central Utah, we live realities where our community continues to grow but is never truly heard nor recognized. In this setting, we offer a counter-story or a type of narrative that defies dominant and hegemonic discourse in our local university settings (Solorzano & Yosso, 2001). We do this through the form of *plática,* or storytelling, that demonstrates the relational praxis of educators and students confronting their socio-historic positioning. This takes place in a Latin American Studies program with a neoliberal agenda and at a university that upholds the teacher–student contradiction theorized by Freire (Margonis, 2007).

In the spring of 2021, several Latine educators and students formed an online reading group. It concluded with a roundtable discussion on community activism at our Latin American Studies conference that included three notable scholars and members of a local Brown Beret (Chicana/o activist organization) chapter. Here, relationships formed that challenged professional student–teacher dynamics by being vulnerable with personal information, sharing workloads equitably, having students take lead on projects, and even organizing and protesting together (Kezar, 2010). However, the reading group eventually distanced itself from the university's Latin American Studies program due to the program's failure to recognize the complex nature of Latinidad (Calderón & Urrietta, 2019). For example, certain faculty and staff refused to acknowledge members of the diaspora as a legitimate part of the community or did not bother to engage them on campus. In this chapter, we open with our thoughts on community and then discuss the cocreation of the *Estudios Rebeldes* (Rebel Studies) program. We further discuss our intent to nurture a space (and praxis) where our relationships as students and educators push against the transactional nature of neoliberalism and the colonial hierarchy of what Freire calls the teacher–student contradiction (Margonis, 2007).

Our title reflects Moten and Harney's (2004) theorization of the undercommons among universities, which states that radical change and abolition of the university are fostered by an ethic that resides in our university but is not grounded in the logic of higher education discourse that divides and creates distance between students and educators (Grande, 2018; Meyerhoff, 2019). To capture this ethic, our chapter demonstrates a virtual *plática* with four students and four educators from Latin American backgrounds who theorize and engage notions of community, relationality, identity, institutional politics, and hierarchy.

PLÁTICA AS METHODOLOGY

Pláticas allow researchers to engage with community ways of knowing through conversation and dialogue with various stakeholders. *Plática* directly translates to conversations but can also mean storytelling. In this sense, it becomes a way to connect via the stories within and among our community. While the term *plática* is sometimes considered a method, to suggest such is to label it as void of "theoretical or epistemological perspectives" (Fierros & Bernal, 2016, p. 106); it also provides a lens based in Chicana and Latina feminist scholarship. This perspective grounds the collection of data in lived experiences and knowledge from the body so that the words of Chicana feminists are valorized as "alternative sources of knowledge and the intellectual theorizing that takes place" (p. 107). Within the process of *pláticas* it becomes critical to affiliate these narratives not just as a means to collect data but also as a space to create theory and build knowledge—a methodology and not simply a method. In the following, we utilize this *plática* because it speaks to the relational nature of who we are among one another as students and educators and can best emphasize how we became learning partners seeking to *platicar* or tell our story.

PLÁTICANDO (STORYING) RELATIONALITY AND HIERARCHY

We start our *plática* in July 2022 by talking about Freire, the student–teacher contradiction, and begin to *platicar* about where we lived and our friendships. We had all just completed a research trip where everyone had a Latin American diasporic background with the exception of an educator and student. This experience, along with our Estudios Rebeldes activities that were basically a reading group of Latin American scholarship and literature that existed and was circulated outside of the Latin American academic program, informed the entirety of this *plática* as we came in contact with one another over and again to engage critical thought. These experiences also provided pathways for us to remain in contact with one another afterwards and for all of us to be engaged in local issues to some degree. Furthermore, every member has a story here that plays a role in how *plática* are unfolded.

First, there are the educators and practitioners: Leandra or Lea, Lydia, Carlos, and Tino. Lea and Lydia were faculty members. Lea works as a communication and media faculty member, and Lydia worked in the English department. Carlos was a program director in academic affairs, and Tino was a program director in student affairs. The students all knew of each other but came from different majors: Jose (Latin American studies), Hannah (English), Jorge (pre-med), and Mari (communications). Everyone has roots to Latin America but was raised here in the United States. This is why we also refer to ourselves as diaspora or a scattering of people whether by force or choice. This is the context of our online *plática* as we respond to the prompt: How has our sense of community developed from when the group started to now?

> *Tino:* So it's important to note that the Estudios Rebeldes started out of two things. First, the relationships that were already beginning with new Latine staff and faculty on campus and connecting these relationships with each other. Second, there was a frustration that the Latin American conference never engaged current Latine students nor staff and faculty who were from the Latin American diaspora in the U.S., and that from these beginnings of trauma, stress, and work, our community has grown and expanded, but also changed regarding its current members. We've lost members because of pushout and graduation, but we've also remained connected, so let's start from there.

Jose: I was thinking about what you [Tino] mean by we've lost people, because have we really? For example, you are not here and I am not on campus anymore either, but have we really lost each other? We stepped out of a physical place but we are still around each other so that makes me think we haven't lost each other. That being said, I think that there's a lot of solidarity within the Latine community, but there's a lot of alienation from local politics.

Hannah: I was thinking about the term community and how it can be a homogenizing term. I prefer to think of multiple overlapping communities, a network of relationships, instead of one big community. Because I do think that you know there's a lot of different ways to be Latine and there's a lot of different perspectives within that, so it's considerate to think of communities as being variable and complex in that way. Considering [the term] community in that way, as something that rotates and comes in and out of play based on the circumstances, helps me to understand the Latine community as something that's really flexible and fluid.

Leandra (Lea): I really appreciate Hannah's comments because I know several of us are on different ends of the spectrum with identity politics, not necessarily identifying with like Latina, Latinx, and Latine, and some of us not identifying with any, and then I got tripped up with the Utah County part because I live in Salt Lake County and I do most of my organizing there, so everything I really know about Utah County is through conversations I have with you all and our work on campus. With that context, I thought about how I understand community at the University and I started thinking about how all of this started: What was the genesis of all of these different projects [and] how we came to meet? The primary thing was the institutional barriers we encountered before we could all come together. These barriers either intentionally or unintentionally kept us from each other, such as programming based on rigid and institutional identity politics or the fact that none of our students even worked through our multicultural centers. There was really no place to connect.

Jorge: I've been wondering about that point, Lea. There's an argument to push departments to support us, but then there's this reality where we've done this on our own and there's power there for the community, but it's tough, it's difficult, which makes me wonder, how do you support something like what we've created? Something that is institutionally supportive, but on the flip side maybe we don't want the institution too involved.

Carlos: It's a valid question. What do we do when something becomes institutionalized? Because there's the threat that it becomes forced, but the fact that we created this organically means that even after we leave [graduate, transfer, pursue different employment] and wherever we go after this place, we're still connected because it began amongst ourselves. We're not doing this because we have to [formally] meet. Does that create solidarity or community?

Leandra: So, I was thinking back to our Latin American studies colloquium, about how on our end we were trying to find funding and navigate and negotiate the bureaucratic angle of bringing in our speakers, making sure we could compensate them, making sure we could sustain our research assistants and so on and so forth. But on the other hand, the fact that we didn't have a lot of funding meant we could do whatever we wanted because we had little to no oversight. What's at stake with more institutional recognition? What sorts of freedoms or power do we have if we don't necessarily have that institutional recognition and then by extension, who's getting hurt without it?

Jorge: I felt that answered a lot of questions for me in terms of like, how do we build our own spaces as a community? There is this complexity where there are benefits to both, something organic or formed grassroots outside of the institution that requires nurturing. However, realistically speaking, if you want to broaden the scope of this work for racialized and minoritized youth, that does require institutional resources. In some ways, that makes it seem very process-oriented, but some of those organic relational touch points have to happen first on their own, and then they spring out into programming. In a way, that's how all this unfolded with separate projects that eventually coalesced into this relational web with educators and students.

Carlos: There were a lot of these projects that were just happening individually, but people were already connected. We were connected to each other in one way, shape, or form, whether it be socially, through a program, or something else, and it just naturally coalesced and people just came together.

Mari: Going back to what Tino said with regard to building our own spaces and about how touch points have to occur before natural programming in systems can happen, that phrase can be used in reference to just about anything because touch points are the foundation. And with whatever one does, the foundation always needs to be made first. I agree with Carlos, people do interconnect with each other while working on separate projects, but I think that is also because everything in life is so interconnected. If we decide, for example, to focus on the health disparities among the Latine community, then we will also have to analyze the income disparities that affect these families as well. Hence why many people started networking and sharing their ideas.

Leandra: I feel like there was a lot of intentionality on behalf of other people, right? I always like to call my good friend, one of the faculty members in our department, like our cultural whistleblower. She was the one who said, "Hey Lea, you should meet Tino. He's an incredible human, and you both have a lot in common and will get along really well," and then she also introduced me to Jorge because he was a student in one of her classes. I started talking with Tino and it evolved organically from there, but if I never met him through my good friend, I don't know how long it would have taken for me to meet him or anyone else.

Hannah: I think it's a mixture of both intentionality and serendipity. It can start with finding people who share a common experience with you, but can also be about holding space for difference because I think we can be stripped of our specificity as Latines in Utah. That's why I love interacting with those from my community who embody difference, because I'm Mexican and Brazilian and I think that it's really cool to see how those different communities hold space for difference and individuality.

Tino: I wanted to unpack what Hannah mentioned [earlier]. How do we understand community? How do we understand our relationships to each other? Especially coming from a Latin American diasporic context where people blanket our relationships as smooth or harmonious because we identify as a similar ethnic group, but that isn't always the case. Within our community, there's a lot of factors that play into identity and belonging, like how well you speak Spanish, [or how we refer to the community] or colorism and sexual orientation. At times, it's been messy, but also very beautiful and powerful and so I try not to sterilize it by saying we all get along without problems.

Lydia: Here's a personal example of the messiness you're talking about, Tino: Except for when I'm around my Puerto Rican and Mexican American family members, I haven't always felt "authentically" Latina. Because I don't speak Spanish fluently, I sometimes feel like an imposter among those who do, especially around my colleagues in the Latin American studies program. But in this group, our community, linguistic identity is one of the messy things I feel we can actually talk about instead of just allowing it to define us and our relationships. That's one of the biggest ways that our project has disrupted hierarchy for me. With you all I feel less like a professor with knowledge and authority and credentials and more like a student learning from your perspectives and comfortable adding my own such as pushing the boundaries of language and identity by including x's and e's or seeing your aspirations inform my own questions of community relationships.

Carlos: Let me say something to that because I get where you're coming from. I'm looking at community in a different way. I'm Peruvian by way of Australia so I don't actually consider myself part of the larger Peruvian community. I was sort of part of a number of communities and many times I meet people who are part of the Peruvian community and they drop names and ask if I know so-and-so. This makes me feel like I'm supposed to act a certain way, but I never grew up in that community. I don't feel like I fit one particular community, I look for a wider community net and that's how I interpret community.

Leandra: I was thinking a lot about this question of community in relation to hierarchy, because when other faculty members find out about our group and our relationships, I am met with equal parts bewilderment and just like straight up confusion where they say, "What do you mean you have a book club with students, where y'all talk about culture and gender and race? Sometimes y'all get emotional? Isn't that weird for you? Aren't you worried that they're going to think you're a little less professional?" My response is always, "Why? Because they're able to see me being human in the same way that they're human and we're able to talk about all of the amazing parts and the worst parts of our culture together?" and they're like, "Yeah, when I mentor students, I want to be in a lab, I want us to follow a procedure. They write up something for a conference paper, and we call it a day" and I think what I love so much about our time together, like the relationality of our community, is the number one thing that scares other people away. It's complicated, because you know it blurs hierarchy for other faculty members and staff members in the way that we're socialized to think about our relationships with students.

Lydia: I really relate to this point, Lea, because our lived experiences inform relational praxis. I've gotten similar reactions from some of my colleagues in the English Department: "You're facilitating a reading group? In the summertime? And you're not getting paid for it?" So in addition to all of those dehumanizing aspects of our (or any) institution—those academic settings and procedures and power relations that Lea mentions—I think another thing that gets in the way of community is the transactional nature of higher education. We're socialized to think about our relationships in economic terms. We tend to think "what will be my return on investment?" before taking on work. And this project has been so liberating for me precisely because we're not concerned with things like compensation and grading. We do it because we want to.

Hannah: This reminds me of a thought we had about how we disrupt the structures that inform our interactions as educators and students. I think that relationships like the ones we've built here can disturb others by disrupting their worldview. Our work around Estudios Rebeldes is a type of relational praxis like when we took the lead on asking questions at the conference or facilitated discussions in our study group. We held leadership roles in those spaces, even directing conversation for staff and faculty. Systematically speaking, how students perceive education informs their roles and how they think about them. Nevertheless, the unique reality of relationships is not without messiness. It doesn't completely erase hierarchy. There is still a hierarchy and I consider my relationship with each one of you differently depending on your role. I do think hierarchy is kind of like a misnomer here because . . . it's a bit more based on the experiences that I have had with each of you individually. In other words, . . . my understanding of hierarchy is . . . rooted in my respect for each of you as individuals and it's definitely not based on imaginary conceptions about who carries the higher worth as an individual, but more the extra validity of your opinions.

Carlos: That brings up a great question. How do our ethics change as time passes? Obviously, there are a number of factors at play in terms of age and the depth to our unique relationships amongst each other. For me, I feel that as time passes and I get to know some of you better, I also become aware of other things. Such as specific lines or boundaries I don't want to cross for the sake of our relationships, particularly with respect to educator and student ethics like personal matters with family or having conflicting feelings on social issues. When I think of hierarchy, I think of engaging the messiness of boundaries and ethics, but that thought did come to mind as we continue to *platicar*.

Jose: Now that you mention it, Carlos, I kind of have thought about that as well. I'm thinking about Leandra when she was my professor. That tripped me up a little bit because I remember the first few days where another Latina student in our relational group and I were in class and we're like, "what do we call her? Do we call her Leandra? Do we call her Professor Hernandez?" I also thought about what can I say to her in the classroom, whereas I had to change my lens when speaking to her about other things outside the classroom. Even though I met her first as a professor, her involvement in this group made me think of her as family versus professor, like in a hierarchical manner. In the classroom

I had to think of her as someone with authority over me. Not sure why that shift would happen. It just did.

Jorge: There is a comment that Hannah made that I also vibe with, that not all hierarchy is bad. Because I think if you're looking at one specific mode of hierarchy, like Western and colonial, like that's something that dominates the globe, but what does it mean when you set up your own hierarchical standards with each other or from an agreed upon cultural base? It's complex. It reminds me of when your *abuela* [grandmother] becomes a key source of knowledge while also realizing that these ethics are entangled with violence toward women, queer, and trans folks in Latin America or within our community. I just feel like not all hierarchy is bad, especially if it's coming from an ethical place.

Hannah: I don't want to use the word hierarchy, because I feel like it just has that connotation every time, but I think that you can respect someone and value them above others because of a familiarity that is rooted in history between you and that person. You can be really introspective and rigorous about why you're going to validate that ethic and still be critical about other structures that put people in unjustified hierarchies. So, I think that there are hierarchies that you can decide to participate in and there are hierarchies that are imposed on you. I think that when I talk about the hierarchies that I experience in this group I feel generally positive. I think it's really about consent. What you are willing to participate in and not.

Jorge: I think it also contests this idea that we have to belong to the same dynamics within a racialized group. Think about how diverse Latin America and its U.S. diaspora are. I haven't seen an example of engaging that from the institution. All I've seen are more top-down relational modes that adhere to professionalism and keep mentorship within the range of academia, versus life and experiences. The relational ethics we seek, we have developed ourselves.

Lydia: I love these points, Jorge. It's almost as if relational praxis resist institutionalization inherently. There's something about the messiness of life and experiences like these that can't be categorized, monetized, or quantified. This group and the relationships we're building are special. Like, I can't imagine trying to grade or assess the work we do. There's no rubric! And that's a good thing.

Carlos: I wonder about what would happen if it was made official, like a type of program. The [college] president would want something that they could measure, crunch numbers, make charts, and show off to the legislature to get more money for the athletics team. That being said, it can help to have these types of things funded and institutionally supported, like if the president went through Diversity and Inclusion and gave us X amount of budget for outside events.

Jose: Because there's also that reality that events just end up being another way to measure success. At the center where I did my fellowship, even though our events were for social impact there was always an attempt to measure it and it ended up just being a metric. If the president did sponsor those lunches or events it would just eventually turn into a metric. So I don't think that institutions generally, being the way they are and seeing them being run like a business, would ever disrupt those structures. In the end, I think it would just end up being another way to gauge metrics for the sake of success.

Leandra: I keep going back to this question of assessment and metrics and all of those buzzwords that keep fluttering around academia and all of our committees and all of our meetings. And I was going back to this idea of the events—my primary question for all of this is "What's the main goal?" If we have to work within the system somehow, if our events will be metrics or assessments in some form or fashion, so be it. But I go back to thinking even about our Hispanic Heritage Month "Pizza and Politics" event that was organized by the campus where there were mostly White folks in the crowd. Sure, was it an opportunity to spotlight Latine student voices and a few faculty members and staff who got roped into it? Yes. But we were able to build more relationships and get more folks together, who eventually came to our book club.

Hannah: I completely agree, it is something you have to be critical of. However, I do think that it's not all negative. You can still participate in these kinds of programs or efforts and perform xyz assessment, especially if you can predict the ways in which you're going to be forced to participate in these structures and institutions. That way you can account for that and still leave room for yourself to be creative and innovative. I have a lot of examples of things that I've participated in with everyone here where it starts as strictly programmatic and then it becomes something more organic and relational. Things like our alternative break or the center for social impact, because look at all of us right now. I think that speaks volumes to what is possible.

CONCLUSION

Hannah's closing comments suggest that structured and institutionally based programming does not always have to end as metrics for a department's report. Rather it can be a liberatory space where relationships flourish and university hierarchies are disrupted to form a more liberating and grounded ethic. According to Margonis (2007), formal education systems operate under a specific logic of relational ethics that are linear and powered by inherently divisive Western colonial power dynamics. Despite these systemic characteristics of our educational institutions, students and educators in numerous spaces have sought and continue to explore various ways in which Western colonial hierarchies are disrupted and ruptured to discover new forms of relationality. In this chapter, several students and educators from diasporic Latin American backgrounds attending a college campus in North Central Utah facilitated a *plática* where they discuss their own theorizations of community, hierarchy, relationality, and highlight how these ideas unfold as praxis among learning partners.

Freire (2005) frames praxis as "human activity" that "consists of action and reflection" (p. 125). Our activity came out of various relational moments and a willingness to connect with each other in a place where that was not fostered or encouraged through the methodology of *plática*, which we have come to understand as a way of being that resonates with us because it comes from the cultural wealth of our community. In other words, not everyone can just use *plática* as a method. One must put in the work to understand *plática* as a relational and culturally relevant tool to generate the stories needed for alternative praxes (D. D. Bernal, 2019, as cited in ASHE, 2019). This is embodied in how we acted and reflected throughout the entirety of the process by studying together, collaborating with our local Brown Beret chapter, and then reflecting on the Beret's call to pursue our own relational resistance or praxis. There are a number of questions introduced in our *plática*, which sometimes do not have a universal answer because *plática* as a methodology is not meant to answer questions as a science but rather become a means to co-create knowledge and to do so in relationship with other humans. Instead, we share what this meant personally for us, and that was building and organizing community outside of institutional bounds and confronting the racist and Eurocentric violence of our own university. This means not pursuing institutional reform but seeking liberation among ourselves as the ultimate disruption of hierarchy within and outside the university.

Recommended Practices

We would like to offer the following as recommended practices in disrupting hierarchy as a form of praxis:

- Sandy Grande (2018) writes a piece called "Refusing the University," and her work stresses relationality as a means to contest the colonial makings of the college. Center the relationships you form within the university that they may also be a wealth of community resilience outside of the institution.
- Educators need to be aware of power dynamics among relationships with students. They will always be present. Not all hierarchies

are a form of unhealthy ethics. Build your own relational ethic, something agreed on collectively, not institutionally, and this will open pathways toward liberation.

- Create a unique experience by which to build on relational foundations. An off-campus experience organized by educators and students collectively, while engaged in a form of study, is a type of praxis.

DISCUSSION QUESTIONS/ACTIVITIES

1. What culturally relevant methodology informs your work, and in what ways does it disrupt and/or perhaps reinforce hierarchy?
2. How would (or have) you as students and educators reflect on and theorize the powered relations that exist in your current relationships, and from what theoretical or experiential traditions do you draw?
3. Do you work/study in an environment where neoliberal or transactional relationality treat particular groups to which you belong as monolithic? What can you do (or have you done) to disrupt this?

REFERENCES

ASHE. (2019, November 16). *Reimagining inquiry: Reflections on feminista methodological interventions* | Dolores Delgado Bernal [Video]. YouTube. Retrieved from https://www.youtube.com/watch?v=89pzgS5nTVQ&list=PLAZfC99ubVj JVGLNOCpSPi63gOtQzNKJX&index=8

Calderón, D., & Urrieta, L. (2019). Studying in relation: Critical Latinx indigeneities and education. *Equity & Excellence in Education*, *52*(2–3), 219–238. Retrieved from https://doi.org/10.1080/10665684.2019.1672591

Fierros, C. O., & Bernal, D. D. (2016). VAMOS A PLÁTICAR: The contours of Pláticas as Chicana/Latina feminist methodology. *Chicana/Latina Studies*, *15*(2), 98–121. Retrieved from http://www.jstor.org/stable/43941617

Freire, P. (2005). *Pedagogy of the oppressed*. Continuum.

Grande, S. (2018). Refusing the university. In E. Tuck & K. W. Yang (Eds.), *Toward what justice? Describing diverse dreams of justice in education* (p. 19). Routledge.

Harris, E. (2016, December). *State and county population estimates for Utah: 2016*. Policy Brief. Retrieved from https://gardner.utah.edu/wp-content/uploads /20161207_2016-DUPC-Estimates-Summary-Final.pdf

Kezar, A. (2010). Faculty and staff partnering with student activists: Unexplored terrains of interaction and development. *Journal of College Student Development*, *51*(5), 451–480. Retrieved from https://doi.org/10.1353/csd.2010.0001

Margonis, F. (2007). A relational ethic of solidarity? *Philosophy of Education*, *63*, 62–70. Retrieved from https://doi.org/10.47925/2007.062

Meyerhoff, E. (2019). *Beyond education: Radical studying for another world*. University of Minnesota Press.

Moten, F., & Harney, S. (2004). The university and the undercommons. *Social Text*, 22(2), 101–115. Retrieved from https://doi.org/10.1215/01642472-22-2_79–101

Solorzano, D. G., & Yosso, T. J. (2001). Critical race and LatCrit theory and method: Counter-storytelling. *International Journal of Qualitative Studies in Education*, 14(4), 471–495. Retrieved from https://doi.org/10.1080/09518390110063365

U.S. Census Bureau. (2019). *Annual estimates of the resident population: April 1, 2010 to July 1, 2019*. Retrieved from https://data.census.gov/table?q=utah&y=2019

Utah System of Higher Education. (2019). *Utah system of higher education 2019 annual report*. Retrieved from https://ushe.edu/wp-content/uploads/pdf/reports/2019_USHE%20Annual%20Report_final.pdf

Part III

REFLEXIVITY AND CONSCIENTIZATION FOR SOCIAL CHANGE

CHAPTER 11

"Uncertaining" the Teacher and Student

Reflections Between a Professor and a Medical Doctor

Nyna Amin and Laura Campbell

INTRODUCTION

This chapter explores the supervisory relationship between a PhD candidate (Laura) and the supervisor of the study (Nyna), from 2009 to 2011. At that time, Laura, a medical doctor and specialist in the field of palliative care, worked in an institution of higher education. Laura was involved in a project to train and prepare qualified nurses and unqualified volunteer caregivers to provide homecare for patients facing life-limiting illnesses. It was also the area in which she wanted to conduct qualitative research for a doctoral study. She was unsuccessful in finding a supervisor in the School of Health Sciences as the expertise of the faculty there lay in quantitative research.

In 2009, Nyna was appointed as a lecturer at the same institution of higher education. Although she had only graduated the previous year with a doctorate in teacher education, she had multi- and interdisciplinary research proficiencies nurtured through her involvement in an innovative doctoral support program, first as a student and then a supervisor. The doctoral program comprised doctoral candidates and supervisors from various disciplinary, methodological, theoretical, and philosophical backgrounds. Its innovativeness was in the shift from the master–apprenticeship approach to supervision (Bitzer & Albertyn, 2011; Herman, 2009). Role reversal became a feature of the cohort approach, and at times, the "master" became the learner and the apprentice became the teacher. This shift reflects Freire's (1970/2005, p. 72) ideal of avoiding the "banking concept" in education.

Additionally, the doctoral program was designed to improve the completion rate of PhD studies, compensate for inadequate supervision experience, and, more importantly, promote deeper and wider learning beyond the focus of a study (e.g., De Lange et al., 2011; Samuel & Vithal, 2011). After learning about the doctoral program Nyna was a part of, Laura asked her to supervise her study.

This chapter documents the dynamics of our supervision relationship. In it, we reflect on our decisions, choices, and responses regarding Laura's study, and we describe the disruptions, tensions, and complexities of engaging, neutralizing, and transforming the opposing binaries embedded in our relationship (student–teacher, candidate–supervisor, apprentice–master, and novice–expert).

As a medical doctor, Laura was preoccupied with quantitative approaches to research, having no experience in and little knowledge about qualitative research. For Laura, working in an unfamiliar research terrain resulted in an uncertainty that will be discussed in the following sections. Nyna's aim was to guide Laura to become a researcher and a knowledge-generator, rather than a clone of the supervisor (Blackburn et al., 1981; Nelson et al., 2009). In higher education, pedagogical practices can reproduce sameness in training that leads students to think like the mentor or supervisor (Essed, 2004), stifling independence of thought.

In the context of higher education, "pedagogies operate on assumptions based on decades of teaching rituals and experiences: the teacher is the knower, the student is the learner; teachers are the knowledge producers and students, the consumers" (Amin et al., 2021, p. 14). Higher education is saturated with hierarchies that generate disproportionate and unproductive oppositional binaries that reduce the possibilities for alternative interpretations of received knowledge. According to Western convention and logocentric rationality, usually one in the hyphen-ated binary represents the subservient position to the authority of the second-mentioned (Rorty, 1979), and in some instances, a negation of the second-mentioned. In the case of the teacher–medical doctor binary, the "importance" and "esteem" of the medical field, we believe, surpasses that accorded to the teaching profession. On one occasion Nyna was asked, "Dr. Amin, where is your medical practice?" When she explained that she was a social scientist, the response was, "So, you're not a real doctor."

Nevertheless, in higher education and the student–supervisor arrangement, the power differential, it appears, favored Nyna as Laura was beholden to Nyna's knowledge and authority. In this instance, however, power was not possessed solely by the knower (Nyna); instead, it moved back and forth between us, and was challenged and dispelled by Laura, giving credence to Foucault's notion that "power is everywhere" and "comes from everywhere" (1998, p. 63). Indeed, we disrupted and transcended the supervisor–student hierarchy, "uncertaining" the sense of self-importance.

Uncertainty by definition refers to a state of not knowing what to think, believe, or do (Cambridge Dictionary, 2023). By affixing the suffix "ing" to uncertain, we attempt to capture the fluidity and vulnerabilities of veering between certainty and uncertainty, and the feelings of doubt and undecidability that characterized our relationship.

DISRUPTING HIERARCHY: STUDENT AND SUPERVISOR PERSPECTIVES

Laura: I am a White, Irish-born physician living in post-apartheid South Africa. Born in the 1960s in Belfast, Northern Ireland, I qualified in medicine at the University of Aberdeen. During my final year in 1986, my mother died from cancer in a care facility. In 1994, I moved to South Africa, my husband's domicile, and over time, became interested in palliative care and completed a diploma through the University of Cardiff and a master's at the University of Cape Town in South Africa. In my experience, research generated objective and standardized knowledge.

In 2009, a new curriculum for hospice caregivers was introduced by an organization involved in palliative care training in South Africa. In my opinion, the curriculum was imported from the United Kingdom without consideration of African contexts, local cultural practices, and values. As an example, the new curriculum emphasized the use of morphine to control pain, yet the caregivers I worked with had little or no access to morphine for patient use. Naively, at that time, I thought it was my professional duty (and right) to speak on behalf of the "voiceless" people of South Africa. I had been marginalized and voiceless as a Catholic growing up in Protestant-dominated Belfast during the era of the Troubles in Northern Ireland. I felt that a PhD would be a platform to explore the shortcomings of an imposed curriculum that was silent about offering palliative care in contexts of deprivation.

At that time, the only person with a PhD in palliative care was a nurse at a local university, and she agreed to supervise my study. However, the Health Sciences' ethics committee would not permit an academic with a nursing background to supervise a medical doctor even though the nurse with a PhD was indeed qualified to supervise me.

Though frustrated, I was still determined to pursue a PhD, to improve palliative care training. I went to a workshop hosted by the Faculty of Education and heard Nyna speak. I was impressed by her enthusiasm and openness; I explained my study idea to her and my dilemma of finding a supervisor. I shared with her deeply personal experiences of power imbalances between Catholics and Protestants during the Troubles in Northern Ireland, and how important it was for me to recognize oppression and marginalization in other contexts; I was excited that this desire was going to be realized through doing a PhD. The School of Education valued philosophy over content, and, fortunately for me, multidisciplinary studies were not only acceptable but encouraged. I was finally on my way as I had now found a supervisor.

Nyna: I am of Indian origin, born in South Africa, and a qualified teacher. Disillusioned with the unresolved challenges of the basic schooling system, I resigned when the gifted child program in which I worked was discontinued. I returned to university to study for a master's degree in education followed by a doctorate. The next year, I started working full time as a lecturer at a research-intensive university, and Laura was the first student I was privileged to supervise.

When Laura and I met at a presentation to prospective doctoral candidates without backgrounds in education, I had no supervision experience except in my role as supervisor in the cohort program. My presentation focused on the value of qualitative approaches. Laura liked what she heard and told me that it resonated with her goals for a study she was keen to pursue. Laura broke with tradition and disrupted the disciplinary hierarchy by registering in the School of Education. We were sure that we could work together.

At our first supervision session, Laura surprised me with ideas of developing an instrument to measure palliative care. Caring for persons, I argued, could not be counted, measured, or ranked. "What would be the criteria that could be measured?" I asked. She had no idea and agreed that it was not feasible.

However, when she shared her ideas during discussions in subsequent supervision sessions, I realized that she had not grasped the necessity of embracing the conceptual and methodological shifts that were required. To embark on a qualitative study would require unpacking the philosophy, practices, and notions of palliative care. She needed to grasp curriculum theory and the ways in which it is researched.

Furthermore, in most social science research, the goal is neither the pursuit of forensic truth nor the description of actual reality (Vasilachis de Gialdino, 2011). Would she, I wondered, accept her role as analyst, not adjudicator, of her participants' constructions of the world? She referred to Paulo Freire's *Pedagogy of the Oppressed* without understanding its implications for curriculum design or teaching.

Her vision was to introduce cultural elements to the palliative care curriculum from her own understanding, not from those who lived the culture and practiced it. She was trapped in positivist thinking—prediction and control, objectivity, discovering reality, and finding truth. In my opinion, Laura did not perceive curriculum as "currere," that is, lived experience, autobiographical in essence (Pinar, 1994; 2019). Curriculum, from her perspective, was about content, a text used for teaching. Unknowingly, we were already treading an uncertain path: the novice supervisor and the expert palliative caregiver.

CONFUSIONS, COMPLICATIONS, AND CRYSTALLIZATION

Nyna: Laura was a passionate student. She read widely but was driven and excited by ideas of creative expression exemplified by integrating images, poems, and metaphors, and by writing a novel rather a thesis. These ideas were fed to Laura in her first year of PhD studies during sessions on innovative writings, for example, Feyerabend's *Against Method* (1975) and *Troubling the Angels* by Lather and Smithies (1997). I pushed for rigor, but she believed that qualitative research operated without rules and that she could do as she pleased.

Within 6 months, I realized that she needed to experiment with her ideas. As a supervisor, I was on my own as I could not rely on the collective wisdom of my colleagues to enrich the feedback I was providing as Laura had abandoned the cohort program. She felt the comments and critique she received were not useful to her. I believed that she knew how to research palliative care. In contrast, I felt "uncertained." The process of uncertaining chipped away at my beliefs and supervision competencies.

Nevertheless, in the 3 years she was registered as a student, Laura wrote three drafts of about 80,000 words each. Her prodigious output was simultaneously impressive and oppressive. How could I reject her drafts when she produced so much work? There was so much to read, and much of it had strayed from the focus of the study. This meant that I had to spend an enormous amount of time reading and making comments—it felt sometimes that I too was writing a thesis when providing written feedback. I knew about the structure, rigors, and technical demands of a thesis. But Laura's resolve to be creative and to generate an entire draft within a short period tested my expertise and made me doubt my ability to guide Laura as a doctoral student. Uncertaining and disrupting hierarchy were at play, and it was uncomfortable.

Laura: I was in my first supervision session with Nyna, distressed and thinking about how to convince her about my intention to develop an instrument to measure palliative care. I had no experience of anything other than quantitative research with its focus on standardization and control of confounding variables.

"Nyna will never understand me," I thought. I was trying to explain palliative care and about health care practitioners' care for patients who face imminent death from incurable illnesses such as cancer or HIV/AIDS. I described who "qualifies" for palliative care and the troubling aspects of its narrow interpretation in South Africa. The practice was heavily influenced by the World Health Organization's definition that a clear diagnosis of life-limiting illness has to be made by a doctor (see Randall & Downie, 2006). But my work with communities, especially in rural areas, was a sad revelation; there was a shortage of doctors, so palliative care, provided by unqualified volunteers, was done without knowing whether a person had a disease or was dying because of undernourishment.

It was clear to me what I was trying to say. But Nyna kept asking questions: What about patients who are dying from diseases such as diabetes and dementia, do they not qualify for palliative care? I shook my head, no, according to the definition, these patients are not offered palliative care. She asked, what is different about palliative care? How is it different from other medical specializations? I grew exasperated and explained to her that all I wanted to do was show that the new curriculum was irrelevant, so I would have to develop an instrument to measure it. We were trapped by our stances: She was a critical thinker who questioned all my ideas, and I was adamant that my passion and experiences mattered and were important for what I wanted to achieve.

Her questions about palliative care did not shake my beliefs and intentions about the study. However, I was so uncertained by her seeming inability to grasp notions of palliative care that I thought about finding another supervisor with a medical understanding of my proposed study. But after the second meeting with Nyna, I let go of the idea of developing a measuring instrument when I realized that it was inconsistent with the qualitative-only approach I was interested in.

I therefore did the research proposal as she advised and collected data from nurses and caregivers. I wanted to analyze the data independently and write it in a way I felt highlighted the marginalization and oppression I thought I recognized from my troubled upbringing in Belfast. I wanted to save Nyna time by preparing as much as possible before our meetings.

Nyna: During the early sessions, I often did not look forward to meeting with Laura to discuss her written submissions, which I felt were presented as final versions rather than works-in-progress. We spent a lot of time debating each other's positions. She could not seem to wrap her head around qualitative approaches. She appeared not to appreciate the critical comments I made, perhaps because I was not a medical doctor, an example of the hierarchy that existed between us. Based on my experience in the doctoral cohort program, I knew that the breakthrough would come at a later stage. In the meantime, I had to just be patient, although trying to be understanding was arduous.

She had conceptualized her study exclusively on her personal experience; and it also lacked philosophical and theoretical justification. She wrote chapters for the thesis before the research proposal had even been approved by the higher degrees committee. I recommended readings, and asked her to attend the master's module I taught on "Research Discourses and Methodologies in Education." She obliged. I was getting somewhere.

I had to let her write with her heart: descriptions about her feelings, the context of her work, and the emotional aspects of palliative care. It helped to smoothen our relationship when we both gave in to each other's ideas occasionally—the importance of which was realized in hindsight.

Laura: After Nyna critiqued my first proposal for the study, I took her advice and read widely about qualitative research, ethnographic studies in particular, and became excited by what I read. Slowly I began to understand my position in the study.

For example, it took 6 months for me to begin to understand the conceptual differences between my dual role of the palliative practitioner and teacher of palliative care. I also became aware that context was not synonymous with culture. In particular, I began to separate my own voice from my research participants' voices. As an example, participants noted that patients did not challenge doctors' diagnoses nor complain when they had to wait to be attended to. This got me thinking about the status quo that existed in the clinical setting. Patients accepted their marginal status even in the presence of palliative care staff. Patients and palliative caregivers could not and would not voice their displeasure or ask questions either because they were unaware that they could challenge the status quo or because they had simply accepted it. It slowly dawned on me that I was not hearing the participants' "voices" because I was so focused on my role in social justice. I realized that my voice was not the voice of the research participants.

Qualitative research thus uncertained my voice. What right did I actually have to speak on behalf of others? Additionally, why was I ignoring all that Nyna was trying to tell me about scientific rigor or qualitative research? I realized I had been arrogant and stubborn and following my own ideas of how to carry out qualitative research.

As a specific example of my lack of clarity about qualitative research, I had read Alan Paton's (1948) book *Cry the Beloved Country*. I admired Paton's ability to describe the themes of racism, colonization, and consequent suffering. I wrote my thesis based on his book and presented it to Nyna. I was confident in my role as the "savior" of the "oppressed."

Nyna: I was appalled when I read Laura's first thesis. The thesis was descriptive. It lacked critical engagement with the literature and the theoretical framework, and the voices of the participants were absent. I had to be honest and hoped she would trust my advice. I asked Laura why a White man's perspective (Paton, 1948) dominated the thesis about Black caregivers' experiences of providing care in the rural areas of our province. I asked, "Where are the voices of the research participants?"

Laura told me she was stunned by my comments. She explained that she had no idea who Alan Paton was; she thought he was a Black man. As an immigrant, she was unaware of the nuances of the context she worked in. I did gather, however, that she was genuinely concerned for the palliative care patients and the challenges faced by the caregivers she trained.

Laura: Although it was hard to hear, I realized that Nyna's feedback was honest and open, and I was disturbed by my lack of insight around South African literature and grew equally disturbed by my lack of understanding of qualitative research.

Under Nyna's guidance, I realized that I could not base my work on Paton's book. Nyna pointed out to me that I had "cherry-picked" the respondents' data from the study to support my thesis (participants were oppressed and voiceless and the new curriculum was hegemonic). She said, "I am more interested in the data that does not support your theory," and warned me about the "vicious cycle of righteousness." I took her advice and identified data that directly contradicted my beliefs. She suggested a narrative analysis, and to my surprise, the data analysis became much more interesting and reflected the complexity and nuance that the participants in the study had experienced.

My first engagement with narrative analysis guided me to find contradictions in the data, which was very different from my previous method of reducing data to dominant themes. I was excited and became more inclined to listen more carefully to what Nyna had to say. I did not mind being uncertained because I came to understand that asking for Nyna's advice did not mean giving up my independence. I grew to trust her more and grew more confident through learning from her.

However, nothing in life is simple. I thought I understood what Nyna was telling me, and I rewrote the thesis using images and stories of elephants as a cohesive device to convey my data analysis in what I thought was an interesting, novel, and "African" way. For example, "the elephant in the room" captured the idea of unheard voices, and the parable of the blind men touching different parts of the elephant to guess what was being examined conveyed notions of multiple realities and truths. I had put in much effort and was certain that this creative thesis would be received as unique, transdisciplinary, and of universal value.

I did not want to bother Nyna too much as I knew she was busy and wrote a draft without consulting her. I had done this in my master's quantitative work, as supervisors in medicine usually only wanted to see a completed version of a study. I did not realize that the supervisor was more involved along the entire research process in the School of Education.

Nyna: The use of the elephant metaphor was interesting, to a point. In trying to extend it throughout the thesis, Laura was forcing interpretations based on the notion of "the elephant in the room." Like the first thesis, Laura chose to work independently and did not consult me. The issues avoided in the analysis were not obvious to Laura. In some interviews she had done with participants, they did not hint nor allude to issues of culture and belief systems; rather they were explicitly voicing their opinions. Furthermore, Laura was contradicting her intentions to "give voice." In fact, the elephant metaphor dominated chapters in the thesis. The audience, I explained, would not understand the arguments she was making as they were quite disconnected. I was afraid that her study would provide confirmation to individuals in the medical field that qualitative research was just "fluff" without substance. The critique I offered uncertained our relationship because what I believed to be honest feedback was perceived as harsh critique by Laura.

The second version differed from the first in that it contained the motivation for Laura's study—the trauma of witnessing her mother's suffering in her final months. This study, I learned, was more than a qualification; it was vital to her psychological well-being and healing. The work was a memorial to her mother.

It was necessary to harmonize our differences and to work together on structure, argument, thesis, rigor, coherence, and our relationship. I had to take the initiative to change the nature of our relationship, as the student–teacher one was not serving us.

Now in the 3rd year of study, we shifted into friendship mode and gave up coercion and one-upmanship; we began the process of disrupting hierarchy. We listened to each other. We met informally, in my home or at a coffee shop. We discussed our roles, the nature of a PhD, and the audience for her study. We exchanged ideas and acknowledged each other's strengths—her knowledge of palliative care and my knowledge of PhD expectations. We acknowledged the joint nature of the doctoral journey. Reflecting on and disrupting the student–teacher hierarchy were the gateways to a deeper friendship.

Laura: By now, Nyna and I were engaging more like friends than student and supervisor. Her comments made more sense to me as I had begun working in the Department of Family Medicine at a local university and was assisting doctors in publishing clinical data. I began to understand the importance of critique in improving the quality of published research leading to an increasing number of publications. Out of the fog, I began to clearly see the differences between quantitative and qualitative research.

As I embarked on the third version of my thesis, Nyna asked me, "who are you writing your PhD for?" I realized I wanted it to be read by healthcare workers, and suddenly "the penny dropped": The third version was aimed at a medical readership. From my perspective as a medical doctor, I explained qualitative research with its attendant concepts of theoretical and conceptual frameworks, paradigms, epistemology, ontology, axiology, validity, ethics, and thematic analysis. The jargon was foreign but I knew it was important to explain it within a medical framework as my work would be read by health care professionals. I was also keenly aware of how the validity of qualitative research was often questioned in a field dominated by quantitative research, but with Nyna's help, I was able to disrupt the qualitative–quantitative divide between my field and my study.

Fully trusting Nyna's help and appreciating her input had taken me more than 2 years. Key to this was seeing her not just as a supervisor but as a friend and colleague.

Nyna: Laura and I reviewed the data in depth and determined that we needed to turn to post-structuralism to do the data justice, and this crucial turn led to the final version. Three iterations later (description, critical theory, post-structuralism), the work was done. The results were original, and the study was praised by both international and national reviewers. By working together and changing the nature of the relationship, we became friends.

Toward the end of the study, we began to write scientific papers based on the results of the study, and this collaborative writing solidified our relationship (see, e.g., Amin & Campbell, 2014; Campbell & Amin, 2012, 2013, 2014). The order of authorship of publications was uncontroversial; whoever came up with the idea for a paper became first author. We even became traveling companions and conference attendees and copresenters.

NOVICES AND EXPERTS

In the beginning, our relationship was characterized by hierarchy, misunderstanding, contested worldviews, and divergent research approaches. Laura approached research with a positivist mindset, while Nyna analyzed data through the lens of deconstruction, pulling us in opposite directions. Each of us was an expert in our field, and each was a novice in the other's field, which challenged the hierarchy from the start and uncertained the dynamic between the medical doctor and the education doctor. Because expert and novice were categories at the same time, a situation of undecidability emerged (Derrida, 1981). Undecidability shatters binary oppositions; neither of us could dominate a conversation because both areas of expertise, curriculum and palliative care, were central to the study. Fortunately, the need for success became the glue that prevented complete fragmentation of the relationship.

READING THE WORLD, READING EACH OTHER

Freire's well-known mantra "Read the Word to read the world" seemed quite apt for our situation (Freire, 1983). It may seem far-fetched to imagine that reading for a doctorate has the same intent as "reading the world," and it may well be that academic education is not a sufficient prerequisite for looking at the world from the perspective of others or for changing oneself. However, reading the world is relevant in this case because we had different and fixed worldviews about research. In practice, we used our knowledge to change our relationships by reflecting and investing our newfound understanding to reread the context of the study participants' experiences and the nature of our own interactions. It was only through teaching and learning from each other that we became "literate" in the inequities and inequalities faced by palliative care workers. Reading the world meant shifting our gaze from self to other and being wary of self-centeredness and selfishness.

Nyna: Despite the above simplified account of the way we traversed the path of supervision, it was not easy to break through the various hierarchies, as our relationship challenged Bill Green's assertion that supervision must be understood as a pedagogical practice that produces "subjects who are directly and actively engaged in the socio-symbolic work of subject formation" (2005, p. 152).

In retrospect, I can no longer fully support Green's assertion. Supervision pedagogy is not only subject formation. It is also subject reformation and transformation of supervisor and supervisee.

REFLECTIONS ON HIERARCHY

On reflection, we finally understood that hierarchies are about status based on knowledge–power differences (Mattern & Zarakol, 2016). A hierarchy exists when one person rules over another, whether economically, intellectually, or politically, to force them to think or act. In a higher education institution, professors and doctors have a higher status than students. Academics are assumed to have knowledge, and candidates are there to learn and be guided. Since we were both doctors, and experts in our fields, feelings of supremacy were balanced. Laura was able to make her case, but her savior complex was interrupted by Nyna's questioning of the gaps and silences in her research. Similarly, Laura's insights and experience in palliative care allowed her to take the lead in discussions. Over a 3-year period, the relationship transformed from one of misunderstanding to one of recognition of each other's strengths and the value of complementary worldviews and collaborations.

MOVING FORWARD

Remarkably, we were able to successfully mediate the path of doctoral supervision by accepting that both academic and social relationships are necessary and indeed complementary (Kaur et al., 2022). Our supervisory relationship was complex due to the multiple emotional, cultural, linguistic, and personal differences as well as working in a multidisciplinary environment. It also involved interdependence, shared learning, and reflexivity. Consequently, the end of the study was the beginning of a lasting relationship that continues to this day.

Laura will soon embark on a second PhD in creative writing in Ireland. She has asked Nyna to be her co-supervisor. Nyna continues to supervise studies that attract candidates from a variety of fields: mathematics education, teacher education, electrical engineering, drama and intimacy, language policy, social media behavior, and disability. Nyna is now aware that every student is different and a universal approach to supervision must be avoided. More importantly, Laura is now a resource and support for the challenges Nyna faces in mentoring.

It took more than 2 years to break through the hierarchy; uncertainty accompanied the journey, but the uncertaining of the teacher and the student (or the novice and the expert) were key to a lasting relationship.

DISCUSSION QUESTIONS/ACTIVITIES

1. Is uncertaining a useful concept? Why or why not?
2. In what ways can you disrupt hierarchy between academic disciplinary siloes and knowledge production (e.g., between natural and social sciences)?
3. In *Pedagogy of the Oppressed*, Freire argues that the "oppressor" is not capable of liberating the "oppressed" or themselves. In relationships of stark imbalances, what does disrupting hierarchy look like, without saddling those who are oppressed with the responsibility for liberation?
4. Discuss how the concept of uncertaining could be:
   • promoted in relationships that involve some kind of supervision
   • applicable in other domains of life.

REFERENCES

Amin, N., & Campbell, L. (2014). Imagining a post-structural curriculum for palliative care. *Alternation, 12*(2014), 150–170.

Amin, N., Dhunpath, R., & Devroop, C. (2021). Uncertainties and ambiguities of re(learning) to teach in the context of crises. In N. Amin & R. Dhunpath (Eds.), *(Re)learning to teach in the context of crises* (pp. 1–25). CSSALL.

Bitzer, E. M., & Albertyn, R. M. (2011). Alternative models of doctoral supervision. *South African Journal of Higher Education, 25*(5), 874–888.

Blackburn, R. T., Chapman, D. W., & Cameron, S. M. (1981). "Cloning" in academe: Mentorship and academic careers. *Research in Higher Education, 15*(4), 315–327.

Cambridge Dictionary. (2023). *Uncertainty*. Cambridge University Press. Retrieved from https://dictionary.cambridge.org/dictionary/english/uncertain

Campbell, L., & Amin, N. (2012). A poststructural glimpse at the World Health Organization's palliative care discourse in rural South Africa. *Journal of Rural and Remote Health*, *12*, 2059 (online).

Campbell, L., & Amin, N. (2013). Dilemmas of telling bad news: Children's palliative care providers' experiences in rural KwaZulu-Natal, South Africa. *South African Journal of Child Health*, *7*(3), 113–116.

Campbell, L., & Amin, N. (2014). A qualitative study: Potential benefits and challenges of traditional healers in providing aspects of palliative care in rural South Africa. *Journal of Rural and Remote Health*, *14*, 2378 (online).

De Lange, N., Pillay, G., & Chikoko, V. (2011). Doctoral learning: A case for a cohort model of supervision and support. *South African Journal of Education*, *31*(1), 15–30.

Derrida, J. (1981). Plato's pharmacy. In *Dissemination*. (B. Johnson, Trans.). University of Chicago Press.

Essed, P. (2004). Cloning amongst professors: Normativities and imagined homogeneities. *NORA—Nordic Journal of Feminist and Gender Research*, *12*(2), 113–122. https://doi.org/10.1080/08038740410004588

Feyerabend, P. K. (1975). *Against method: Outline of an anarchistic theory of knowledge*. New Left Books.

Foucault, M. (1998). *The history of sexuality: The will to knowledge*. Penguin.

Freire, P. (1970/2005). *Pedagogy of the oppressed* Continuum.

Freire, P. (1983). The importance of the act of reading. *Journal of Education*, *165*(1), 5–11.

Green, B. (2005). Unfinished business: Subjectivity and supervision. *Higher Education Research & Development*, *24*(2), 151–163. Retrieved from https://doi.org/10.1080/07294360500062953

Herman, C. (2009). *Exemplary PhD programmes in South Africa: A qualitative report of constraints and possibilities*. Academy of Science of South Africa.

Kaur, A., Kumar, V., & Norman, M. (2022). Partnering with doctoral students in research supervision: Opportunities and challenges. *Higher Education Research & Development*, *41*(3), 789–803. Retrieved from https://doi.org/10.1080/07294360.2020.1871326

Lather, P., & Smithies, C. (1997). *Troubling the angels: Women living with HIV/AIDS*. Westview/HarperCollins.

Mattern, J. B., & Zarakol, A. (2016). Hierarchies in world politics. *International Organization*, *70*, 623–654. Retrieved from https://doi.org/10.1017/S0020818316000126

Nelson, J., Robison, D. F., Bell, J. D., & Bradshaw, W. S. (2009). Cloning the professor, an alternative to ineffective teaching in a large course. *CBE Life Sciences Education*, *8*(3), 252–63. Retrieved from https://doi.org/10.1187/cbe.09-01-0006

Paton, A. (1948). *Cry, the beloved country*. Jonathan Cape.

Pinar, W. F. (1994). The method of "Currere" (1975). *Counterpoints*, *2*, 19–27.

Pinar, W. F. (2019). Currere. In *Key concepts in curriculum studies* (pp. 50–52). Routledge.

Randall, F., & Downie, R. S. (2006). *The philosophy of palliative care: Critique and reconstruction*. Oxford University Press.

Rorty, R. (1979). *Philosophy and the mirror of nature*. Princeton University Press. https://doi.org/10.2307/j.ctvc77b6z

Samuel, M., & Vithal, R. (2011). Emergent frameworks of research teaching and learning in a cohort-based doctoral programme. *Perspectives in Education*, *29*(1), 76–87.

Vasilachis de Gialdino, I. (2011). Ontological and epistemological foundations of qualitative research. *Forum: Qualitative Social Research*, *10*(2), Art. 30. Retrieved from http://nbn-resolving.de/urn:nbn:de:0114-fqs0902307

CHAPTER 12

Working Toward Trauma-Informed Praxis

Reflections on a Shared Learning Process

Juleus Ghunta and Ute Kelly

The work of disrupting hierarchies and transforming oppressive structures is both intellectual and deeply embodied, an engagement with the world around us and the worlds within us. Attending to the causes and impacts of trauma is one important way of bridging these dimensions. This chapter reflects on our learning from conversations and collaborations that began in 2017 when Juleus was a student in the Peace Studies MA program at the University of Bradford (UK) and Ute was his dissertation supervisor. Our collaboration has been a process of conscientization and deepening reflexivity, a back-and-forth between lived experiences and academic insights. Our reflection takes a collaborative autoethnographic approach (Chang et al., 2012) and is written in separate voices to make differences in our experiences and perspectives more visible.

We begin with brief overviews of our journeys into peace studies at Bradford. We then reflect on how we connected and collaborated there during Juleus's dissertation and the questions it raised around making sense of difficult personal stories in academic contexts and beyond. We continued exchanging ideas and questions after Juleus left Bradford, and over time, this led to an awareness of the need for trauma-informed practice (SAMHSA, 2014) in education and other areas of society (Ghunta & Kelly, 2019). Principles for trauma-informed practice include safety; trustworthiness and transparency; collaboration and mutuality; and engagement with cultural, historical, and gender issues, and inequalities (SAMHSA, 2014). Our reflections suggest that these principles are important and that their realization in practice can be challenging because they demand significant personal, interpersonal, and structural work.

The final part of the chapter describes how we have taken this learning into our separate contexts and explores some of the questions that are central to trauma-informed pedagogy and praxis in light of the hierarchies and inequalities that characterize much of the world in which we live and work.

Juleus: In 2010, I attended a peacebuilding conference in Rwanda. Much of my time there was spent visiting genocide memorials such as the Mbyo Reconciliation Village near Kigali. In Mbyo, victims and perpetrators of the 1994 genocide lived together (Tumwebaze, 2010). Prison Fellowship Rwanda, an NGO, built Mbyo and similar villages as part of the reconstruction efforts (Durr, 2014). I listened to the apologies of a man who had killed 13 members of one family. The family's only survivor sobbed quietly as she spoke of her grief. The perpetrator stood beside her, shoulders slumped, head hung in penitence. She said forgiveness was her contribution to Rwanda's reconciliatory work. I wondered whether it was possible to heal and move on from such a devastating tragedy.

I had carried "memories of terror" (van der Kolk, 2014, p. 2) from my childhood to Rwanda and had hoped to deepen my understanding of their effects on my adult life. I grew up in the 1990s in rural Jamaica, initially with my mother and three siblings. My mother struggled to take care of us, and my father's lack of support made life extremely difficult. Some days, she compared me to him and beat me until I was unable to breathe. These and other challenges made learning difficult. I repeated grade 6 and learned to read at age 12. At 14, my family forced me to live on my own. During this period, I was afflicted with many illnesses, including chronic depression, auditory hallucinations, and blackouts. I sought respite in education—in high school and later at the University of the West Indies (UWI) in Kingston—but felt unseen and isolated because my classes did not provide any meaningful opportunity for me to engage in critical self-reflection and my academic success was determined by the extent to which I "consented to existing arrangements" (Mayo, 1995, p. 366).

Years later, standing in Mbyo, my illnesses felt insurmountable. I thought about what this meant in the context of peacebuilding and education, and about the dangers of reconciliatory and pedagogical approaches that widen psychological wounds instead of closing them (Durr, 2014; Kee & Carr-Chellman, 2019).

Almost a decade later at Bradford, I wrote my dissertation on the impacts of my adverse childhood experiences (ACEs). My work examined a significant body of research on the nexus between ACEs such as poverty, physical, emotional, and sexual abuse, and toxic stress response. Toxic stress increases risks for maladaptive outcomes across various developmental domains (Boullier & Blair, 2018). I learned that children with four or more ACEs have high odds of nonengagement in schools (Crouch et al., 2019), and that those with two or more are likely to repeat a grade (Blodgett & Lanigan, 2018). My dissertation deepened my understanding of the complexities and intergenerational dynamics of adversity and trauma and opened the way for me to attain a measure of healing (Ghunta, 2018).

Ute: In contrast to Juleus, I have not lived through any ACEs. I grew up in West Germany in the 1970s and '80s, a place and time that permitted, even encouraged, certain forms of critical engagement. My influences included parents and teachers who were open to critical questioning, political and left-leaning songs and stories, engagement with national socialism and the Holocaust and the distrust of national pride associated with this, feminism, liberation theology, and some of the solidarity movements of the 1980s. This collection of influences gave me conceptual tools and the confidence to question hierarchical structures and ways of thinking. It also gave me some consciousness of struggles for justice around the world (e.g., the anti-apartheid struggle and resistance movements in Latin America). Some of these formative influences, though, came with a tendency to romanticize "the oppressed," to idealize victims, to regard "the poor" as "blessed." In my childhood, "the oppressed" felt a long way away, in place and/or in time—present in some of the discourses I heard, read, and participated in, but absent as embodied and complex human beings in our relationships, interactions, and shared spaces.

I first came to Peace Studies at Bradford as an undergraduate student in the 1990s. A key part of that experience was the opportunity to look critically at the construction of social realities and to imagine their reconstruction. I felt inspired by lecturers who treated students as participants in shared conversations in which they, too, were developing their ideas.

Later, my experience of teaching in a university setting made me more conscious of what others (e.g., in Brantmeier & McKenna, 2020) have also observed and experienced: that the question of power between teachers and students is complex. It is often easier for teachers who are more secure, more privileged, and more established to move toward dialogical, less obviously hierarchical ways of teaching than for those who are struggling for recognition from students or colleagues; it takes confidence, experience, and a degree of security to hold space for conversations that might go to unpredictable or challenging places or to experiment with creative ways of teaching.

In unintended but noticeable ways, the spaces and forms of learning I invite students into have tended to come most naturally to students who look and sound similar to me: often women from privileged backgrounds, mostly people who come to their studies with some ambivalence about their own positionalities. For some of my other students, my approach does not easily fit with their ideas of what a university education looks like because they are used to education systems that are more hierarchical, closer to what Freire (2005) calls "the banking model of education." One of the reasons my exchanges with Juleus have felt significant is that they have broken these molds.

Juleus: At Bradford, I struggled in classes where others did not think that revelations about my ACEs could add meaningful insight to complex conversations in development and conflict studies. In one of Ute's classes, while students were engaged in a spirited debate about definitions of peace, I insisted that conventional definitions were insufficient because of the overwhelming focus on the appearance of political stability at the expense of equally important considerations such as the psychological trauma that results from prolonged stress and violence. I argued that any liberatory definition of peace must consider the psychological ramifications of various forms of violence (Galtung, 1969). This realization concretized my desire to spend my time at Bradford examining trauma and emotions in conflict and the notion that inner peace is a crucial facet of conflict transformation (Ghunta, 2018).

Ute: I have asked many students, before and since, to make their assumptions about the meanings of peace, violence, and conflict visible to themselves and each other, and to locate them within the wider field of scholarly discussion. Many of the themes repeat from one year to the next, though each group brings a particular flavor to these discussions. To me, Juleus's proposed definition of "peace" (quoted below) raised issues that have also been present in discussions with other students—mental health, inner peace, structural and cultural violence—but expressed them in a way that felt deeply rooted in lived experiences:

> Peace is the absence of chronic internal or mental conflict (such as trauma), absence of physical violence, equilibrium, opportunities to be seen, to be heard, to heal and to be able to love, opportunities for vertical mobility. Seeing extraordinary possibilities in ordinary people. It is to be able to live without having to perform.

I think it was this desire "to be seen, to be heard, to heal and to be able to love . . . to be able to live without having to perform" and the vulnerability this generates that opened up the possibility of dialogue and mutual learning.

Early in this process, Juleus invited me to witness some disturbing experiences from his childhood that he had analyzed in an autoethnographic essay on constructions of masculinity in Jamaica and their links to direct, structural, and cultural forms of violence (Galtung, 1990; Ghunta, 2018). The essay also discussed some of the connections between these experiences and Juleus's struggles with (il)literacy. Reading it had a strong emotional impact on me. In part, this was to do with its content; at the same time, it demonstrated the potential of bringing traumatic personal experiences into conversation with theoretical concepts, not only for academic purposes but also as part of personal healing processes. Engaging with Juleus's work heightened my awareness of the ways in which traumatic experiences can be present in our classrooms, whether or not we make space for them to be seen and heard. I felt challenged to think more consciously about how to respond.

The explicit inclusion of "vertical mobility" in Juleus's definition of "peace" also challenged me, though in other ways. My experiences of working in a hierarchical institution had made me suspicious of vertical structures, ambition, and the pursuit of status. A period of bullying and division had left me feeling alienated and demoralized, and I am still exploring whether or not naming these experiences and their impacts as traumatic is accurate or helpful. I know they left me with what Lederach (2005) calls "the gift of pessimism"—a suspicion of superficial promises of change. They also left me with a longing for spaces and interactions to "model and exhibit the fairer and more mutually sympathetic world that is sought" (Thompson, 2015, p. 439).

In some of our early exchanges, my habitual attempts to push back against hierarchy or the pursuit of power and status came up against Juleus's knowledge of what it takes to survive, to claim humanity and dignity against a backdrop of trauma, violence, and inequalities: engaging in performances of success or status, for instance; working harder than everyone else; looking for ways to escape from contexts in which violence and trauma are so deeply embedded that talk of change can feel meaningless; knowing the value of money; hearing, or telling, inspirational stories of triumph against the odds.

Freire talks of how "the oppressed, as divided, unauthentic beings" can end up hosting "the oppressor"—living "in the duality in which *to be* is *to be like*" (2005, p. 48). Against this background, conscientization encourages people to reframe the pursuit of status within hierarchical structures as part of the problem, not as the solution. My initial responses to Juleus's interest in vertical mobility took a similar stance. It has become clearer to me through our conversations, though, that critical consciousness and the need to make compromises can and often must coexist, particularly in times and places that are far from revolutionary. My narratives and longings for horizontal, dialogic relationships and structures started to feel more problematic, differently positioned: a stance that could be read not only as resistance to hierarchy but also as a function of my privilege. In this context, it is important to acknowledge and honor the fact that our ability to engage as equal learning partners was built on Juleus's efforts to pursue vertical mobility. I have some sense now of how much it took for him to get to a "here" that had been a more or less taken-for-granted place in my own trajectory.

What we have done with this and other themes might be described as a form of decoding (Freire, 2005): noticing the reactions they provoke in us not just at an intellectual but also at an emotional level, and unpacking their origins and implications. This has taken time and effort. There is a sense in which this work could be described as the development of literacy—the ability to read the stories each of us tells with a deeper understanding of their meanings.

Juleus: When Ute accepted my request for her to supervise my dissertation, I gave her a copy of Bessel van der Kolk's (2014) book *The Body Keeps the Score: Brain, Mind, and Body in the Healing of Trauma* to widen her understanding of trauma science, including the challenges many survivors face while pursuing emotional clarity and post-traumatic growth. I felt the book would help us engage in deeper discussion and appreciated her admission that I had invited her into a reality that was far from her own.

Many of my peers at Bradford who had escaped difficult situations in their countries failed to access similar support. For instance, one colleague from Japan, who quit her job to care for her sick parents for 20 years, argued that the courses did not provide opportunities for self-examination in ways that could mitigate psychological distress. Often, students' personal experiences, especially those underpinned by familial trauma, are not considered useful material for serious academic engagement about complex issues in peace education. Evidence of this can be seen in the resistance to autoethnography and similar approaches that see this kind of liberatory reflection as key to empowering students to interrogate the causes of their reality (Kee & Carr-Chellman, 2019).

In my autoethnographic dissertation, I analyzed the ways in which poverty, trauma, and toxic stress had affected my capacity to engage fully in education, and how telling my story was not only therapeutic but also an act of rebellion against people who accused me of valorizing despair (Ghunta, 2018). I explored the notion of "the performance of wellness"—the ways in which trauma survivors and marginalized groups often hide their suffering behind a veneer of contentment and confidence. I saw this as a kind of false consciousness and wanted Ute to understand how such performances often make teacher–student interactions inauthentic and shallow. We needed to embrace a kind of sociological and moral imagination (Lederach, 2005; Mills, 1959) to enable us to enter each other's worlds with humility and open-mindedness.

Ute: Juleus's exploration raised important questions that connected with my evolving educational practice. The experience he named as "the performance of wellness" resonated with other students who did not easily feel at home within the university. These conversations strengthened my belief that in peace and conflict studies, higher education is not a separate sphere but part of "the field"; they prompted me to consider more consciously how to respond to the fact that my classrooms include students who have lived through violence, discrimination, and poverty, alongside those from more privileged backgrounds who are motivated by desires to "help others" and to "make a difference" that often need deeper, more critical reflection.

Our initial attempts to unpack and respond to these realities included extracurricular workshops on personal storytelling and the exploration of otherness with students at Bradford. These workshops made space for explorations that went beyond the main curriculum. They opened up questions around what it might mean to listen to ourselves and each other more carefully, how to understand personal stories within wider structures, and how to negotiate the challenges of otherness and inequality (Kelly, 2019).

Juleus: Our collaborative process of exploring personal experiences and their relevance to peace studies has been challenging. At different points, we have had moments of tension in which we both felt misunderstood and in which I rejected theoretical conceptions of contentious issues that did not reflect my reality.

Growing up in marginalized communities in Jamaica, my reality included being subjected to and witnessing sexual and other forms of violence perpetrated by women and men against men and boys. Some of my most challenging exchanges with Ute have been about the harmful impacts of entrenched mainstream pro-feminist policies and practices that sustain such violence (Sivakumaran, 2007; Verlaan, 2018). I noted, for instance, the deliberate efforts of some intergovernmental organizations and NGOs to suppress research and undermine policy imperatives on sexual violence against males, thus leaving survivors with no funding, judicial recourse, or psychological support (Chynoweth et al., 2017; Sivakumaran, 2007; Verlaan, 2018). I shared observations of these challenges from my work with prominent feminists and NGOs in Jamaica and felt Ute's responses failed to do justice to the experiences and needs of boys and men while overemphasizing those of women, including women with significant privilege.

These difficult conversations have forced us to examine the embodied experiences and intense emotions that undergird our particular frames and have widened our perspectives and deepened our understanding. However, I still wonder whether it is possible for Ute, who has lived a very different life, to truly understand the nature and effects of the marginality that has characterized much of my experience.

Ute: What does it mean to "truly understand" experiences that are very different from our own? I think that because "the body keeps the score" of traumatic experiences and because our bodies themselves position us in the world in different ways, there are real limits to what can be understood from the outside. I think that those limits—the not-knowing, the challenges of empathy, the dynamics of power and resistance that are at play (Diaz, 2020; Jones, 2004)—need to be acknowledged and negotiated with care. At the same time, we also need to resist the potential for othering that comes with regarding the differences between us as so vast that they cannot be bridged. I think it is helpful to name and explore these tensions, even when that process is painful and challenging.

When I reflect on the exchanges Juleus and I have engaged in, I can see both the importance of mutual care and the learning that has come from challenges and confrontations. My experience of these exchanges confirms that when we come to them from positions of relative privilege, one of the hardest but also one of the most important elements is being challenged for "critical" thinking that becomes overly confident, comfortable, or disconnected from complicated lived realities (Freire, 1994).

Juleus: As part of my efforts to discuss these complicated lived realities with wider audiences, I wrote *Rohan Bullkin and the Shadows* (Ghunta & Moss, 2021), a picture book that explores the notion of "shadows" as a metaphor for the negative impacts of ACEs and toxic stress on academic achievement. With Ute's support, the manuscript went through numerous drafts over a 4-year period, an arduous but fulfilling process during which the story evolved into more challenging and accurate depictions of the links between survivors' ability to read and think critically and trauma recovery. Ute's questions and suggestions, and our conversations and arguments over major themes and minor changes, were important to the book's success (Kelly, 2021).

Soon after the book's release, I received an invitation from Jamaica's Ministry of Education to join the newly formed National Task Force on Character Education. The Force's principal objective is to create and spearhead the implementation of a comprehensive character education program in primary and secondary schools. As a member of the Research and Psychosocial Committee, I contributed to a diagnostic study (Gayle et al., 2022) that revealed extremely high levels of ACEs among Jamaican students. This finding fortified calls from several members for a comprehensive plan that would address the causes and effects of toxic stress in schools. Despite the evidence (Gayle et al., 2022), the Ministry ignored much of the advice, opting instead for a model similar to previous programs that have failed to stem the tide of violence and normlessness.

Behind the scenes, Ute and I engaged in critical reflection, questioning the Ministry's rationale for choosing a failed model over one that might lead to an emergence of consciousness and more effective ways of assessing and addressing deep-rooted dysfunctions. We discussed the difficulties in creating effective programs for far-reaching systemic change and how these challenges play out in our respective contexts.

I experienced the scale of these demands when I returned to Jamaica and worked within the formal education system as a facilitator of workshops on ACE awareness and as a teacher at a high school. Funded by the British High Commission, the workshops guided teachers in assessing how ACEs science might help them to address students' academic underperformance and disruptive behavior and engendered discussions about the links between ACEs and social dysfunctions in the wider society.

As a teacher in one of the most marginalized high schools in Kingston, I engaged my colleagues in reflections on their ACEs, including how they impact approaches in the classroom. With almost daily schoolwide disruptions and violence, it was clear that meaningful change would require strategic intervention from the Ministry of Education. Despite decades-long pleas for help, no government had offered the school any meaningful support.

Taken seriously, trauma-informed practices demand fundamental shifts in how we craft, fund, and sustain systems, policies, and relationships, as well as constant tailoring for different situations and contexts over long periods. Reflecting on my journey, I can understand why many organizations are reluctant to adopt these practices despite the research that supports them.

Ute: My attempts to take these explorations and insights into my personal pedagogical praxis and the wider context of the university increased my awareness of both the potential and the challenges of this work. At the small scale of my classrooms and in one-to-one interactions, this includes making space to explore personal experiences and intersecting identities: sharing our stories of "how we got here," reflecting on how we tell these stories, unpacking positionality and its implications for our scholarship and teaching, and engaging in collaborative and creative autoethnographic work (Kelly, 2023).

I try to imbue this work with what James Thompson (2015, 2022) calls an "aesthetics of care": an approach that attends to the sensory qualities of our interactions—their sound, their feel, the nature of the spaces and relationships within which they take place. Such attention, Thompson argues, is "a necessary counter to the dislocations and disruptions already faced by many in our contemporary over-individualistic world" (2022, p. 8). Inspired by these and similar arguments (Lederach, 2005; Ó Tuama, 2021), I invite my students into a shared effort to make our classrooms hospitable to each other. This includes attempts to make imperfect physical spaces look and feel more welcoming, acknowledging that the challenging work we do requires patience and care with/for ourselves and others, and trying to find a balance between celebration and critical engagement when students share work that is meaningful to them and that comes with a degree of vulnerability. It also includes giving ourselves and each other permission to choose silence when speech, or the desire of others to know, feels too painful, unsafe, or intrusive (see e.g., Jones, 2004; Li Li, 2004). Taking a "careful" (Thompson, 2022), trauma-informed approach to education (and to peacebuilding) involves the recognition that "people need to be able to disclose, then keep covered, then disclose, and keep covered with their own consent to themselves" (Ó Tuama, 2021).

I am still reflecting on how to position this work vis-a-vis other approaches to working with trauma in pedagogic contexts, particularly those that foreground its potential to disrupt and disturb as part of attempts to challenge oppressive realities (Berlak, 2004; Erickson, 2004; Halabi, 2004; Matias, 2013). I have argued for more confrontational and discomforting approaches myself, both in writing (Kelly, 2004) and in my teaching. Similarly, I am left with questions about how this work aligns with Freire's pedagogy. How does my effort to hold space for exploration, complexity, ambivalence, curiosity, and vulnerability (Kelly, 2022) relate to the idea of education taking a stance against oppression? Can we do both simultaneously?

Where possible, I invite students to be part of these explorations and reflections. As in my exchanges with Juleus, I have found the back and forth between personal experiences and academic perspectives particularly fertile in working with students, and this has generated valuable mutual learning.

The need to negotiate possibilities and imperfect responses is also apparent in my additional role as associate dean for equality, diversity, and inclusion. While this is an opportunity to work at a more strategic level, it also quickly runs up against a series of constraints built into a globalized, marketized, and hierarchical higher education system. How far can we move toward genuine equality, inclusion, or trauma-informed practice within a system that was designed for other ends and purposes? How do we negotiate tensions between our reliance on a business model sustained by increasing numbers of international students and our declared commitment to decolonization?

These questions do not come with easy answers, and perhaps our praxis as students and educators will always be located in the space of questions and tensions that remain unresolved. My exchanges with Juleus and my work with other students since have made me more conscious of some of the contradictions and ironies involved in the work of "disrupting hierarchy"; for some of us, the impulse to do so is in itself a function of privilege and is sustained by hierarchical structures. I have found, for example, that students from more privileged backgrounds often find it easier to write reflective essays on decolonization or critical pedagogy than those who have lived with the legacies of being colonized. The question of what it truly means to "disrupt hierarchy" in higher education, then, remains complex. Some of the most important learning is difficult to capture. Written down, much of it looks like things I already knew. The difference, I think, is what "knowing" might mean. I would describe this as a movement toward greater vulnerability and more embodied, deeper ways of knowing. It seems to me that building trust and engaging in dialogue across difference/otherness have a particular potential to unsettle and loosen, but also to expand and enrich what or how we know, to help it sink in and resonate. Some of the learning that matters most is not linear but circular—to be returned to, relearned, deepened, and absorbed over time (Lederach & Lederach, 2010). If this is true, the work of conscientization, developing reflexivity, and working toward meaningful change is less an event than work-in-progress—open-ended and never quite finished.

Juleus & Ute: As the shared exploration we have documented here illustrates, we feel there is value in trying to do meaningful work in the messy, compromised settings in which we find ourselves. In this spirit and in lieu of conclusions, we end by posing questions for further reflection.

DISCUSSION QUESTIONS/ACTIVITIES

1. The work of mutual learning in becoming trauma-informed practitioners is small-scale, inter- and intrapersonal, but we also recognize the need for much larger, systemic changes. It can be difficult to engage meaningfully in both at the same time. Where do we put the emphasis and energy in our work, and why? Does—and should—this shift over time?
2. In working with groups of students who come from very different backgrounds but are in the same classroom, how do we negotiate the different needs that are present—the tension between affirmation and critical interrogation, the need for healing and the need for disturbance, respect for silence and the importance of voice?
3. In contexts that are shaped by intersecting and longstanding hierarchies and by academic cultures that encourage and expect performances of knowledge and intellect more than personal exchanges, it can be difficult to overcome deep-rooted and embodied patterns of relating to each other. What can we do to disrupt hierarchies and to enter into a space of vulnerability and authentic exchange while also acknowledging the limits of what is possible and appropriate within formal education systems and the realities of power dynamics that remain?

REFERENCES

Berlak, A. C. (2004). Confrontation and pedagogy: Cultural secrets, trauma, and emotion in antioppressive pedagogies. In M. Boler (Ed.), *Democratic dialogue in education* (pp. 123–144). Peter Lang.

Blodgett, C., & Lanigan, J. D. (2018). The association between adverse childhood experience (ACE) and school success in elementary school children. *School Psychology, 33*(1), 137–146.

Boullier, M., & Blair, M. (2018). Adverse childhood experiences. *Paediatrics and Child Health, 28*(3), 132–137.

Brantmeier, E. J., & McKenna, M. K. (Eds.). (2020). *Pedagogy of vulnerability.* Information Age Publishing.

Chang, H., Ngunjiri, F., & Hernandez, K.-A. C. (2012). *Collaborative autoethnography.* Taylor & Francis.

Chynoweth, S. K., Freccero, J., & Touquet, H. (2017). Sexual violence against men and boys in conflict and forced displacement: Implications for the health sector. *Reproductive Health Matters, 25*(51), 90–94.

Crouch, E., Radcliff, E., Hung, P., & Bennett, K. (2019). Challenges to school success and the role of adverse childhood experiences. *Academic Pediatrics, 19*(8), 899–907.

Diaz, N. (2020). *Postcolonial love poem: Part one. Between the covers podcast with David Naimon.* Retrieved from https://tinhouse.com/transcript/between-the-covers-natalie-diaz-interview/

Durr, B. (2014). *Rwanda genocide survivors back reconciliation.* Aljazeera. Retrieved from https://www.aljazeera.com/features/2014/4/5/rwanda-genocide-survivors-back-reconciliation

Erickson, I. M. (2004). Fighting fire with fire: Jane Elliott's antiracist pedagogy. In M. Boler (Ed.), *Democratic dialogue in education* (pp. 145–157). Peter Lang.

Freire, P. (1994). *Pedagogy of hope: Reliving pedagogy of the oppressed* (R. R. Barr, Trans.). Continuum.

Freire, P. (2005/1970). *Pedagogy of the oppressed* (M. B. Ramos, Trans.). Continuum.

Galtung, J. (1969). Violence, peace, and peace research. *Journal of Peace Research, 6*(3), 167–191.

Galtung, J. (1990). Cultural violence. *Journal of Peace Research, 27*(3), 291–305.

Gayle, H., Ghunta, J., & Amen-Ra, M. (2022). *Character education in Jamaica: A diagnostic study.* [Unpublished Manuscript]. Ministry of Education, Youth and Information, Jamaica.

Ghunta, J. (2018). *Adverse Childhood Experiences, the performance of wellness, and storytelling as victimisation, therapy, and defiance.* [Unpublished MA dissertation]. University of Bradford, UK.

Ghunta, J., & Kelly, U. (2019). *ACEs in higher education: Lived realities, academic insights and raising awareness.* Retrieved from https://www.pacesconnection.com/g/aces-in-higher-education/blog/aces-in-higher-education-lived-realities-academic-insights-and-raising-awareness

Ghunta, J., & Moss, R. (2021). *Rohan Bullkin and the Shadows: A story about ACEs and hope.* CaribbeanReads.

Halabi, R. (Ed.). (2004). *Israeli and Palestinian identities in dialogue: The school for peace approach.* Rutgers University Press.

Jones, A. (2004). Talking cure: The desire for dialogue. In M. Boler (Ed.), *Democratic dialogue in education* (pp. 57–67). Peter Lang.

Kee, C. J., & Carr-Chellman, D. J. (2019). Paulo Freire, critical literacy, and Indigenous resistance. *Educational Studies, 55*(2), 89–103.

Kelly, U. (2004). Confrontations with power: Moving beyond "the tyranny of safety" in participation. In S. Hickey & G. Mohan (Eds.), *Participation: From tyranny to transformation? Exploring new approaches to participation in development.* Zed Books.

Kelly, U. (2019). Explorations of otherness and the politics of (self)representation. *The Politics of Representation Collective.* Retrieved from https://medium

.com/the-politics-of-representation/explorations-of-otherness-and-the-politics
-of-self-representation-eede32f971d5

Kelly, U. (2021). *What Rohan Bullkin taught me about reading*. PREE. Retrieved from https://preelit.com/2021/11/28/5330/

Kelly, U. (2022). Peace/walls: A century of observations in [the]north[ern] [of] ireland. *From the Honesty box* [blog]. Retrieved from https://fromthehonestybox.home .blog/2022/06/14/peace-walls-a-century-of-observations-in-the-northern-of -ireland/

Kelly, U. (2023). Towards post/critical peace education? A meditation-in-progress. In T. Archer, B. Hajir, & W. McInerney (Eds.), *Innovations in peace and educa- tion praxis*. Routledge.

Lederach, J. P. (2005). *The moral imagination: The art and soul of building peace*. Oxford University Press.

Lederach, J. P., & Lederach, A. J. (2010). *When blood & bones cry out: Journeys through the soundscape of healing & reconciliation*. Oxford University Press.

Li Li, H. (2004). Rethinking silencing silences. In M. Boler (Ed.), *Democratic dialogue in education* (pp. 69–86). Peter Lang.

Matias, C. E. (2013). On the "Flip" side: A teacher educator of color unveiling the dangerous minds of White teacher candidates. *Teacher Education Quarterly*, *40*(2), 53–73.

Mayo, P. (1995). Critical literacy and emancipatory politics: The work of Paulo Freire. *International Journal of Educational Development*, *15*(4), 363–379.

Mills, C. W. (1959). *The sociological imagination*. Oxford University Press.

Ó Tuama, P. (2021). *In the shelter & borders and belonging*. Between the Covers podcast with David Naimon. Retrieved from https://tinhouse.com/transcript /between-the-covers-padraig-o-tuama-interview/

SAMHSA. (2014). *SAMHSA's concept of trauma and guidance for a trauma- informed approach*. HHS Publication No. (SMA) 14–4884. Substance Abuse and Mental Health Services Administration.

Sivakumaran, S. (2007). Sexual violence against men in armed conflict. *European Journal of International Law*, *18*(2), 253–276.

Thompson, J. (2015). Towards an aesthetics of care. *Research in Drama Education: The Journal of Applied Theatre and Performance*, *20*(4), 430–441.

Thompson, J. (2022). *Care aesthetics: For artful care and careful art*. Routledge.

Tumwebaze, P. (2010). A visit to a reconciliation village. *New Times*. Retrieved from http://www.newtimes.co.rw/section/read/81622

van der Kolk, B. (2014). *The body keeps the score: Brain, mind, and body in the healing of trauma*. Penguin.

Verlaan, S. (2018). Male victims of wartime sexual violence: An ignored phenom- enon. An analysis of implications. *Staat, Recht und Politik—Forschungs- und Diskussionspapiere: 6*. Universitätsverlag Potsdam.

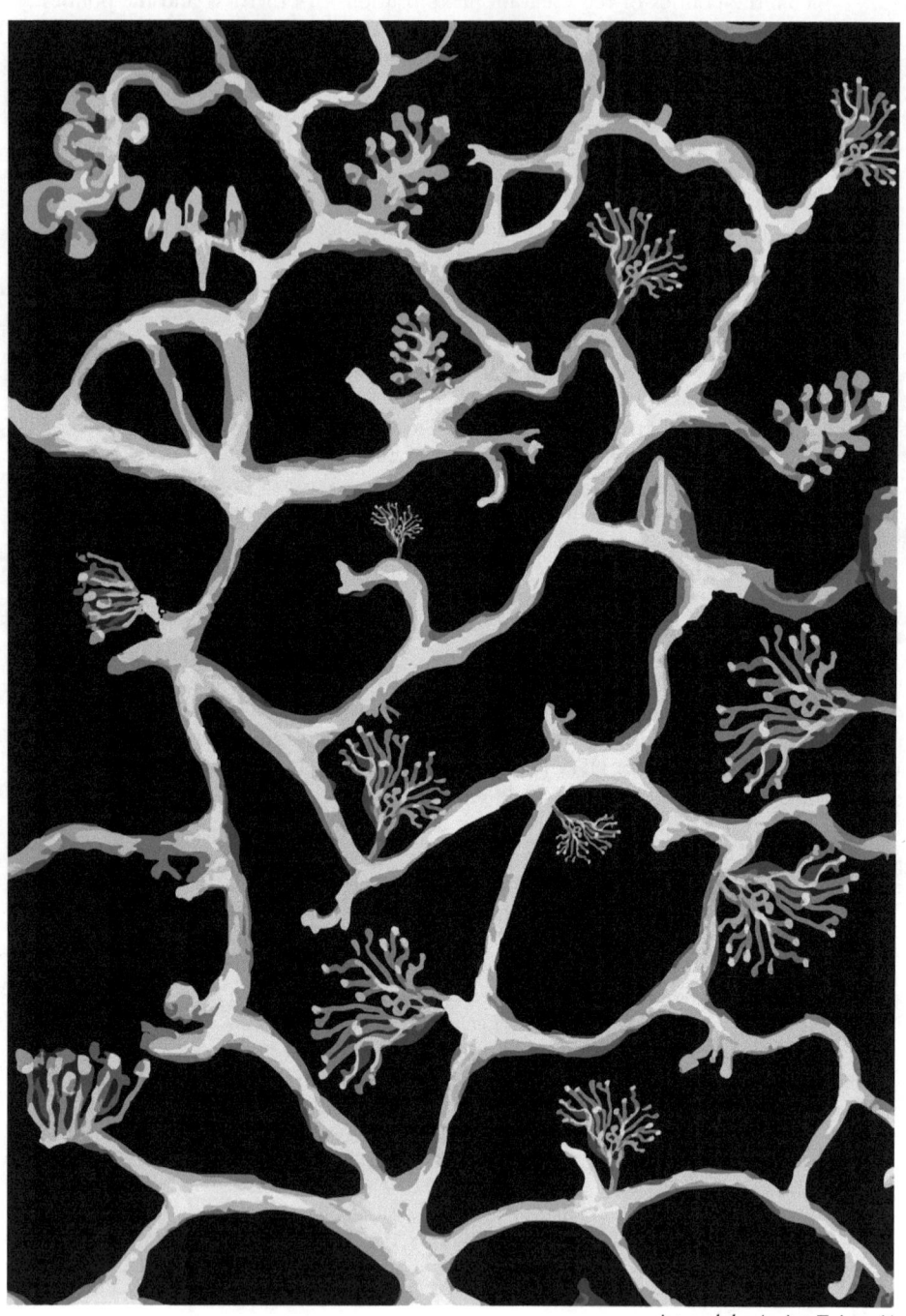

Artwork by Amina Zaimović

We Are the Ones We've Been Waiting For

Justice-Grounded Leadership

*Hana Huskić, Christina M. Noto,
and Hakim Mohandas Amani Williams*

"Eliminating things that harm us is not the same as creating things that heal us . . ."

"We spend all of our time resisting . . . fighting . . . confronting . . . deconstructing . . . challenging . . . and very little time creating belonging, cultivating healing, inventing new systems, designing our future. . . . Trust, vision, wholeness, humane relationships, and hope are the real lifeline of movement building."

—Ginwright, 2022, pp. 7–8

This final segment of our book is not a conclusion per se, but a reflection on justice-grounded leadership, which is rooted in rhizomatic relationalities and radical solidarities, both of which are about intentionally harnessing non-hierarchical interconnectedness and interdependencies. We also reflect on the intimate and vulnerable journey the three of us embarked on with this project.

The origins of the phrase "we are the ones we have been waiting for" are a bit obscure, but we interpret it as an ethical, communal, and spiritual call to the leader in all of us, guided by (and toward) justice and healing. "Spirit" here refers to the dynamic and creative energy that emerges from connectivity and grounding (across time and space). In turn, we refer to the terms justice and healing as action words. Justice is about equity and reparations for the systematic abuse of peoples and the planet, accompanied by the upholding of rights of all beings on Earth. Healing, then, is a culturally mediated, nonlinear movement toward, and practice of, wholeness (mind–body–spirit equilibrium). It is about facing wounds, traumas, unhealthy patterns (for individuals and communities) and addressing them with care, compassion, and the necessary resources for well-being.

Justice-grounded leadership is not a self-centered, boastful vision but a transgressive pivot away from our conditioned investment in hierarchical co-nceptions of the singular, charismatic leader to whom we often look for responses to or resolutions of injustice. Nondominant forms of wisdom, talent, and agency are abundant but are often devalued or not cultivated. We look therefore to the reinvigorated beloved community for a "grassroot-ed" collective leadership where we all are empowered and responsible for co-crafting a world in which all beings can thrive. To actualize more just and sustainable futures, we need more sustainable praxes that invite, reflect, and shape justice-grounded leadership.

We interpret justice-grounded leadership as another action phrase that requires the constant practice of disrupting hierarchy (see Center for Economic & Social Justice, 2018, for their definition of justice-based leadership). Justice-grounded leadership decenters the obsession with individual leaders and instead centers justice, healing, community, and praxis (critical reflection + action). If we do not heal ourselves and the Earth from centuries of plunder, violence, and trauma, then it is difficult to think outside of toxic orthodoxies and to birth just tomorrows.

Individual and community "obstruction spots" prevent us from discerning how the violences we perpetuate become normalized: "because we have an obstructed view, we sometimes can't see how we show up in our relationships, how we work with others, and even how we relate to ourselves" (Ginwright, 2022, p. 42). Rhizomatic relationalities and radical solidarities stand in contrast to toxic relationalities that hinder attempts at disrupting hierarchy and facilitating healing.

A rhizome is a stem structure that grows horizontally underground and generates different stems in unpredictable directions. Deleuze and Guattari (1987) use this concept to critique vertical, hierarchical aspects of Western rationality and linearity, and to argue for a multiplicity of ways of knowing and being in the world. Rhizomatic relationalities are then the very antithesis of the colonial, hierarchical, disembodied, atomized ways of relating to each other and the planet. In "resist[ing] taxonomies and creat[ing] interconnected networks with multiple entry points" (Irwin et al., 2006, p. 4), rhizomatic relationalities are about making human–nature–planet interdependencies and interconnectedness the basis for sustainability-oriented justice work.

We view radical solidarities as an iterative redistributing and reconceptualizing of power, privilege, and resources to foster and sustain mutually symbiotic systems so that all beings can thrive. Cultivating radical solidarities is therefore the practice of mutual symbiosis as revolutionary relationality. Narro (2022), in writing about radical solidarity, states that there is a spiritual core of activism that is a wellspring of sustenance for justice work. Together, rhizomatic relationalities and radical solidarities are fueled in part by constant reflexivity: having the courage to face the mirror

(Ginwright, 2022) and understand (and accept) our responsibilities to self, others, and the planet, and how our actions (or lack thereof) impact many ecosystems.

MIRROR WORK

As coeditors, we had to navigate (and try to deconstruct) multiple hierarchies. We consciously interrogated our subjectivities, aware of power imbalances in editing and academic publishing. In the diverse projects of disrupting hierarchy in this book, we marveled at the coauthors' ability to foster and model rhizomatic relationalities and radical solidarities. We contend that community-anchored iterativity, as a value and practice, can help prevent such critical projects from being easily co-opted or dissolved. Fusing constant reflection and action rooted in our varied communities, community-anchored iterativity is praxis based in rhizomatic relationalities and radical solidarities. We ought to build not in siloes but in an intricately diverse network of communities, always asking: How are my/our actions impacting you? How can we help each other to heal and thrive?

Justice-grounded leadership and disrupting hierarchy beckon constant curiosity about the communities' members' hopes, fears, victories, and setbacks (Gatto, 2017, p. 52). The three of us started as teacher and (former) students, with a comradeship of shared interests, but only after vulnerably attempting to practice rhizomatic relationality and radical solidarity did we start noticing how our project with the coauthors represented richly textured webs of community-anchored iterativity. That is where our own collaboration started unfolding, with curiosity about the possibilities of this intellectual–spiritual journey, an intentional deconstruction of our own initial teacher–student hierarchy, and an ethical care for each other. In an attempt to explore these possibilities, we had to conduct our own mirror work.

Assembling our book required confronting and working through our insecurities despite their persistence. We were all taught in school and by society to refrain from speaking up if we were not entirely certain of our arguments. How often do great ideas get unexplored because they start in uncertainty, we wondered. Schooling almost successfully trained us to be swayed by false binaries and to believe what holds more value: facts over emotions, present-day realism over visions of equitable futures, and academic theorization over life experience.

Hana and Christina are still at the beginning of unlearning these ideas. It is often difficult to acknowledge that getting discouraged is a part of this process. Even though we found refuge in practicing our agency in the Education for Social Change class when we were in college, critical consciousness would sometimes feel more like a burden when we would walk through other spaces in the college and beyond, where the same rigidly traditional ideas would trump our curiosities, and radical hopes and dreams.

Even when we started working on this book, during which we intentionally enacted our agency, we were often consumed by doubts. For example, we pondered if we are hypocrites to coedit a book about disrupting hierarchy if we had to consciously battle through the instinct to double-check everything with Hakim because he was our teacher. We asked our coauthors to refer to each other by their first names (vs. titles such as Dr.), but we had to make an effort to stop calling Hakim "Professor Williams" in the first place. Believing that disrupting hierarchy is a fluctuating, ongoing ethic and practice through which we untangle some remnant hierarchy (or even new ones that emerge in its place) is one thing, but giving yourself grace to truly engage in this process with patience and kindness for yourself and all of your collaborators is another.

As we made sense of the hierarchy among the three of us, we were at times daunted by the fear of this project and its postulates and ethics. Hana often doubted the validity and clarity of their input; their native language is Bosnian, and many coauthors are established academics whose native language is English. At times, offering editorial suggestions seemed like "talking back" and talking back seemed like—disrespect. Christina also doubted her understanding of Freirean pedagogy and her ability to edit and provide input. She also struggled with wondering if she was "pulling her weight" and contributing enough. Hakim was concerned about taking up too much space as their former professor driving this process. We often reflected on these doubts (personally and to each other in conversation), and it helped that we purposefully kept creating space to support each other as the project unfolded. We were mindful that much of our work was completed through email and WhatsApp across several time zones and significant life events such as Christina moving across the United States and switching careers, Hana graduating from college and moving back to Bosnia, and Hakim doing research on sabbatical in four countries. We learned to be vulnerable with each other and laugh together, which would then create even more productive reflection and dialogue: praxis in motion.

One particular anecdote comes to mind. The email containing the first draft of our contract from Teachers College Press started with the cordial "Dear Prof. Williams, Prof. Huskic, and Prof. Noto." We shared a good laugh that that was perhaps a manifestation for Hana and Christina! Yet this benevolent mistake signals the existing hierarchies within academic publishing. Telling stories through credible platforms is far too often reserved for those who hold titles and certain kinds of experiences.

Additionally, we had several conversations about the order of editors and the order of chapter authorship. While we wanted to exist outside of the first-author hierarchy and use a different system such as alphabetization, we also recognized that we, as well as our coauthors, exist within a system where author order matters for hierarchical systems such as academic tenure and promotion. We as coeditors decided that we did not want our idealism to create additional barriers or hierarchies for coauthors.

Although it was liberating that we (the coeditors and coauthors) entered this space as students, artists, workers, non-English speakers, and many of us non-academics, participation in the very system that often rejects us at times felt dishonest; but we persisted, because we realized that fear (in our case, doubts that come with being a part of a project of this scale) and revolutionary dreams are linked. Fostering rhizomatic relationality, radical solidarity, and community-anchored iterativity helped us recognize our fear as a signal that we were engaging in "critical opposition to the status quo and in transformative work toward the manifestation of our revolutionary dreams" (Darder, 2017, p. 42). For us, this meant engaging with what we sensed as a visceral yearning for the potential of education where we are free to practice our agency.

As Freire did, we wondered "how to wrestle with the yearning without allowing it to turn into nostalgia" (2021, p. 39). Nostalgia, in some Romance languages, derives from the Latin word *ignorare* (to be unaware of, not know, not experience) (Kundera, 2002). Looking back on the early stages of our schooling, we recognized a deep need for justice-grounded leadership and healing, despite at the time not knowing what that meant, despite never experiencing healing in the classroom. Nostalgia, as we interpret it here, turned into continuous efforts of (re)inventing new ways of living. Alternative collaborations inside and outside of the classroom challenge and balance longing and the unknown, foster healing and hope, and are the driving force of the action-based projects that make our book.

REFLECTING ON THE "EDITORELATIONSHIP"

Hana: I left home (Kakanj, Bosnia and Herzegovina, BH) at 17 to complete high school in Mostar, BH, and have been living away from home since. Education has been my conduit for finding confidence and agency. Yet for most of my schooling, I felt like a bad student. I had passion, but I would often find myself stuck, unable to transform my thinking into action, afraid that I would not meet my expectations. At times, I felt like the only way to compensate for my homesickness would be to excel at school, but that would often just result in overthinking and procrastination. I was creative, intuitive, and confident, but I lacked what teachers called discipline to see things through. My growth, though fluctuating, directly relates to my luck of meeting and working with teachers and mentors who responded to my anxieties not with punishment but with kindness, patience, and vulnerability. This approach, which is at the heart of all of the collaborations in this book, made me a more accountable person who has built up strength to practice open communication. I felt seen, appreciated, and secure to ask for help while working with Hakim, Christina, and our coauthors. For me, this kind of support is what I needed to start unlearning shame and guilt for often finding it difficult to move through the traditional educational system. Leaning onto each other requires timely self-reflection to recognize that you could use help. It sounds logical, and even easy in theory, but to start practicing it, I needed a lot more confidence and security, which I found working with Christina and Hakim.

Christina: In high school and college, I hated group work mainly because we focused on getting right to work, instead of learning the needs, working styles, and strengths of each group member. This was not the case with Hakim and Hana. Although we cared about this final product, we also cared about each other as people, and this reinforced the need to implement praxis into our work. For example, I was very comfortable taking the lead in meetings, setting up our system for obtaining coauthor copyright forms, and proofreading. While I was able to read and provide comments on our book contract, addressing the legal questions was not my strength. For us, to coedit a book does not mean everything needs to be split evenly. We had to balance our strengths and areas of growth, when to use our strengths, when to ask for help, and when to struggle. Through reflection and conversation, I came to feel like an equal learning partner. It takes practice to disrupt hierarchy, and sometimes I felt the hierarchy more than other times. For example, as a White person, because I am in the "dominant group" (in the USA), I feel racial dynamics differently and sometimes less aware of them. I also generally think about gendered dynamics as a woman and feel those at times. Meanwhile, I am often aware of the academic hierarchy because I do not have a master's/PhD. Our identities were important to reflect on but also to talk about as we worked together.

Hakim: I was not given the nonviolent tools as a child to process trauma and insecurities. I internalized colonialism, colorism, and homophobia, and it almost destroyed me from the inside out. Growing up poor in a colonial educational system made me into a fighter (e.g., for equity, justice, etc.) but not so much a facilitator of healing. Through this book project, I have realized that power sharing is not easy when you are acclimated to an academic/educational system of hierarchy and competition, and where power is conceptualized as zero-sum. I had to relinquish the need to approve everything, or even have the chapters all read the same way (re: Western academic cadences). I trusted Hana's and Christina's brilliance (and care for me and this work), and by leading with that, I learned how key trust is to rhizomatic relationality and radical solidarity. We also created an internal peer review process among all the authors to foster some comradeship (and community-anchored iterativity) in the project so that it was not only the editors' voices that shaped this final product.

These lessons and praxes are not automatic; I am still engaged in considerable unlearning, part of which is to trust vulnerability as a potent way of being and connecting. Despite having practiced being vulnerable for a while now, it does not mean that it is always easy. There is still a fear of it being weaponized against me and used to undercut my ideas and my identities. There is a fear that once you let people in, they will take advantage of you and diminish their respect for you. I know it is irrational, but this is how deeply embedded these toxic notions of relationality go.

Reflecting on the Chapters

We view our book as a rhizome and invite readers to explore different ideas and questions presented in it, however they see fit, making personal and community connections with varied testimonies and praxes.

We divided the chapters into three domains: engaging diverse publics, institutionalization via skills and program development, and reflexivity and conscientization. Surely, these are not exhaustive domains as regards social change (and neither is there a hierarchy of importance among them), but we do believe that concurrent work in multiple domains is necessary. These are not siloed domains; for example, one can be engaging diverse publics but also involved in skills development, or one can be tending to oft-neglected reflexivity while creating new programs and structures to nurture social change work.

The chapters reflect this overlap and intersectionality. What crisscrosses all of them is a demonstration of how disrupting hierarchy among learning partners fosters counterhegemonic practices (i.e., dismantling status quo oppressions), dispositions, skills, programs, norms, and structures. There is always a risk of co-option whether you are engaging with diverse publics or based at an institution. It is why we stress community-anchored iterativity, which has intrapersonal, interpersonal, and community reflexivity built into it. We see how counterhegemony—emergent from disrupting hierarchy— can create fissures and major disruptions; to us this is necessary because a decolonial enterprise must involve dismantling and disruption, but also regeneration. The last part is important: creating anew; and these projects in this book show us how these learning partners did just that, despite lingering hierarchies and/or new barriers.

There is not any perfect way to disrupt hierarchy between learning partners. In these chapters, the modalities are diverse: radically retooling a class/ course; creating new programs or organizations; conducting research; spotting the imbalanced teacher–student relationship in other spheres (e.g., curators and artists); or interrogating how, why, and who are engaged in this challenging but rewarding work. These projects, in different ways, explored the necessity of learning partners harnessing the power of intergenerational, coalitional, and intersectional work, so that we prefiguratively foster intra-/ interpersonal, communal, and institutional habits of entrenching praxis. While both learning partners and those who are impacted by the disruption of hierarchy will sometimes feel fear, anxiety, and disorientation from actual or perceived loss of power, disrupting hierarchy is not for its own sake; it is meant to shake up the status quo, for the better. We confronted and even reframed this fear and anxiety, because they have been mightily generative.

Healing as an Ongoing Praxis

The coauthors and learning partners have shown how rewarding it can be to reject putting people into rigid categories, instead leaving space for the flourishing of our most liberatory values. Like the rhizome, direction and form of social change efforts are almost limitless, but we call for a "scaling out" of revolutionary values: infusing the value of disrupting hierarchy into government, state-to-state interactions, and eventually to the dissolution of physical and symbolic borders.

The various praxes from our communities, in this book, demonstrate how to alter the symbolic and sometimes institutionalized divides between students and teachers into something empowering and ever-growing. Therefore, as much as this book is about learning partners working together to disrupt hierarchy, it is also a nod to the healing power of community storytelling, and community-anchored enactments of justice-grounded leadership. Through the coauthors' co-balancing of theorization, reflexivity, and challenges (within their projects and in the overall editorial process), and their narratives of power sharing, liberation, and healing, we have witnessed how to splinter the idea of a singular and authoritative point of view for knowledge production and leadership. Students (and former students), through this collaboration, affirmed their right to tell their stories with their own voices and asserted themselves into larger conversations about social change. They continue to unlearn much of what banking education has taught them and to *live* a problem-posing education as a praxis of healing.

We are thankful for the trust that the coauthors have put in us over all the (what must have felt like endless) rounds of edits. They voiced their concerns at times, be it to push back on some of our own (or external) editing or expressing emotions that come from a project about disrupting hierarchy, while still engaging in publisher–editor–author hierarchy. We found that it was not only necessary to reflect on the difficulty of balancing the process of disrupting hierarchy and abiding by our contract with the press, but also making dialogic space for some of the coauthors' ideas to generate some unexpected rhizomatic turns.

A rhizome "may be broken, shattered at a given spot, but it will start up again on one of its old lines, or on new lines" (Deleuze & Guattari, 1987, p. 9).

Our praxes of vulnerability and honest and robust analysis were fertile soil for deeper relationalities and radical solidarities, because we must disrupt this arid and sterile status quo if we are to create the conditions for regeneration and healing. As Subar (2021) states, "there is a time to plant and there is a time to uproot" (p. 16); the stories that make our book do both: They disrupt *and* they plant anew. We hope these projects will inspire the justice-grounded leader in you to pursue your own disruption of hierarchies. Harness the vibrancy of community for this work. Dare to dream boldly and to relate to and care for each other and the planet in radically egalitarian ways. May our shared visions for revolutionary futures take root!

REFERENCES

Darder, A. (2017). The passion of Paulo Freire: Reflections and remembrances. In A. Darder (Ed.), *Reinventing Paulo Freire: A pedagogy of love* (pp. 39–52). Routledge.

Deleuze, G., & Guattari, F. (1987). *A thousand plateaus: Capitalism and schizophrenia*. University of Minnesota Press.

Freire, P. (2021). *Pedagogy of hope: Reliving pedagogy of the oppressed*. Bloomsbury.

Gatto, J. T. (2017). *Dumbing us down: The hidden curriculum of compulsory schooling*. New Society Publishers.

Ginwright, S. (2022). *The four pivots: Reimagining justice, reimagining ourselves*. North Atlantic Books.

Center for Economic & Social Justice. (2018, October 15). *Justice-based leadership*. Center for Economic & Social Justice. Retrieved September 16, 2023, from https://www.cesj.org/justice-based-leadership/

Irwin, R. L., Beer, R., Springgay, S., Grauer, K., Xiong, G., & Bickel, B. (2006). The rhizomatic relations of a/r/tography. *Studies in Art Education, 48*(1), 70–88. Retrieved from https://doi.org/10.1080/00393541.2006.11650500

Kundera, M. (2002). *Ignorance*. Gallimard.

Narro, V. (2022). *The activist spirit: Toward a radical solidarity*. Labor's Bookstore.

Subar, R. (2021). *When to talk and when to fight: The strategic choice between dialogue and resistance*. PM Press.

Note: Find out more about our book project, stories featured in it, and others that are in the making at http://disruptinghierarchy.com/

Afterword

Monisha Bajaj

In the preceding chapters, the editors and contributing authors of this book have "disrupted hierarchies" between the academy and the community, between the Global North and the Global South, and between historical and contemporary movements for justice and futures-oriented "freedom dreaming" (Kelley, 2003) through "prefigurative decolonial praxis" (Chapter 5). We have traversed the globe with examples and engagements from the United States, Canada, Mexico, Jamaica, Brazil, the United Kingdom, South Africa, and elsewhere.[1]

The authors have exemplified Gramsci's concept of "organic intellectuals," those who develop a social and political consciousness "organically" in opposition to an unequal and unjust dominant culture (Gramsci, 2000). These organic and public intellectuals have shown us how they have catalyzed their individual and collective transformative agency (Bajaj, 2018; Freire, 1970) to take their resistance outward in order to reimagine classrooms and communities. Throughout the pages of this book, radical educators and philosophers—such as bell hooks, Paulo Freire, Myles Horton, and Septima Clark—are cited and their ideas brought to life through vivid, rich, and engaging examples of initiatives for social change.

The three domains offered by the editors of this volume to situate the chapters are a groundbreaking contribution to our understanding of the necessary components of community-engaged praxis, namely, (1) Engaging Different Publics for Social Change, (2) Institutionalizing Social Change, and (3) Reflexivity and Conscientization for Social Change. The tools we learn about in the chapters vary as do the contexts in which they are utilized. In the K–12 schooling and community context, we learn about op-ed writing in South Africa (Chapter 1); the development of community radio in New York City and Sao Paulo (Chapters 2 and 4); and the application of Johnston's (2014) concept of slow curating in an artists' wellness space in Brooklyn (Chapter 8). Many of the examples come from higher education where we learn about collective action to address climate change (Chapter 3); the formation of a network of multicultural scholars amidst racialized state violence in the United States (Chapter 6); the reorientation of higher education classrooms to be practice based (Chapter 7); the use of co-teaching and learning circles inspired by the Highlander Folk School (Chapter 9); virtual spaces to develop "rebel studies" for Latinx university students, faculty, and staff in Utah (Chapter 10); and the shifting of hierarchies between graduate students and their supervisors through the "uncertaining" of relationships in South Africa (Chapter 11) and the use of trauma-informed autoethnographic approaches in the U.K. (Chapter 12).

The editors have mapped Freire's cycle of praxis in useful ways onto a schema for understanding how initiatives that draw from Freire can be analyzed and extended. One critique of Freire's work has been that his writings are dense and inaccessible to those seeking to take his ideas into practice (Ayers, 1987); this book, however, applies Freire's ideas and texts and puts them into meaningful dialogue with on-the-ground work across the globe at multiple levels that seeks to implement his (and others') liberatory ideas of education for social change. This work of translation is essential and urgent to face the crises of our times. Taken together, the chapters of this book bring to life bell hooks's envisioning of education—in and outside of the classroom—as a site of possibility and transgression (or disrupting as this edited collection aptly titles it) in our collective practice of freedom (hooks, 1994).

This book is a handbook for educators in K–12, community, and university settings for how to use education as a tool for liberation in pursuit of what the editors have so beautifully identified as the "rhizomatic relationalities" (Irwin et al., 2006) and radical solidarities that are needed for upending hierarchies and advancing social transformation. This book is an invocation, an inspiration, and an invitation to all who believe, as Arundhati Roy has stated, that "another world is not only possible; she is," indeed, "on her way" (2003, p. 75).

NOTE

1. Thank you to University of San Francisco School of Education graduate student Isabel Hallock for her assistance with preparing this afterword.

REFERENCES

Ayers, W. C. (1987). Review of *A pedagogy for liberation: Dialogues on transforming education* by Ira Shor and Paulo Freire. *Teachers College Record, 89*(1), 162–163.

Bajaj, M. (2018). Conceptualizing transformative agency in education for peace, human rights, and social justice. *International Journal of Human Rights Education, 2*(1), 22. Retrieved from https://repository.usfca.edu/ijhre/vol2/iss1/13

Freire, P. (1970). *Pedagogy of the oppressed* (M. B. Ramos, Trans.). Continuum, 2007.

Gramsci, A (2000). *The Gramsci reader: Selected writings 1916–1935.* New York University Press.

hooks, b. (1994). *Teaching to transgress: Education as the practice of freedom.* Routledge.

Johnston, M. (2014). Slow curating: Re-thinking and extending socially engaged art in the context of Northern Ireland. *Oncurating.org, 24,* 23–33.

Kelley, R. (2003). *Freedom dreams: The Black radical imagination.* Beacon Press.

Roy, A. (2003). *War Talk.* South End Press.

About the Editors and Contributors

Imaan Adams is currently in her first year studying human resources management at the University of Stellenbosch. She enjoys topics of critical engagement, debating, and philosophy. Being a part of this journey through writing this chapter has been an honor.

Carlos Alarco has been at Utah Valley University since 2005 and has worked at distance education, Fulton Library, and is currently an associate director at the Office for Global Engagement. He holds a bachelor's degree in digital media from Utah Valley University and a master of education from the University of Missouri.

Ilene Dawn (Ida) Alexander is a teaching-learning consultant focusing on inclusive, accessible, social justice, and feminist pedagogies; and a Preparing Future Faculty graduate program instructor. She works with University of Minnesota system instructors across disciplines in designing learning-centered courses and syllabuses for a broad range of learners and learning spaces.

Katie Allison is a student in the Harvard Graduate School of Education's Teaching and Teacher Leadership program and Identity, Power, and Justice in Education concentration. She taught for 3 years and looks forward to returning to the classroom to read the word and the world with young people on graduation.

Krista Ambats is a Germany-based artist and designer. At the time this project was initiated, she was a student of Matt Meyer's and a Harlem-based community activist. She went on to study at the Université de Paris 8 and City College of New York and has worked for several international art galleries.

Nyna Amin is full professor in curriculum studies, university distinguished teacher, and a National Research Foundation–rated researcher at the University of KwaZulu-Natal. She is cofounder and subeditor of the journal *African Perspectives of Research in Teaching and Learning* and has coedited two books on higher education curriculum.

Monisha Bajaj is professor of international and multicultural education at the University of San Francisco. She is the editor and author of several books and numerous articles on international development and education policy; peace and human rights education; migration and education; gender; race and xenophobia; and environmental justice and education. See https://www .monishabajaj.net/.

Laura Campbell qualified as a physician through the University of Aberdeen in 1987. During the early HIV epidemic, she developed an interest in palliative medicine for people dying from AIDS. Her PhD thesis theorized the relationship between the palliative care curriculum and the context of care as an uncertain one.

Mariana Casellato has an MA in international education development from Teachers College, Columbia University. Her background is in nationwide projects in environmental and citizenship education with youth in Brazil. Her research interests include decolonization in education, environmental and media education, and youth participation.

Chief Baba Neil Clarke is internationally acclaimed as a percussionist, involved with African drumming and the percussive arts for more than half a century. He has made it his mission to continue the pioneering work of his mentors and collaborators who include Randy Weston, Harry Belafonte, and many more.

Jason Cloete is a 2nd-year law student. He is involved in several programs with Bottomup as well as with student leadership programs in high schools. He is part of a continual and developing library project that provides a space for critical engagement and pedagogy.

Jose Coreas is completing his master of arts in Latin American studies at the University of Utah. He enjoys learning and researching Central American migration and hopes to then complete a PhD program and stay in academia.

Antonia Darder is an internationally recognized Freirean scholar and professor emerita at Loyola Marymount University, where she held the Leavey Presidential Endowed Chair of Ethics and Moral Leadership. Through her decolonizing scholarship on the body, ethics, and methodology, she has contributed to rethinking questions of empowerment and liberation in the lives of oppressed populations.

Agustin Tino Diaz or Tino teaches on education, culture & society at the University of Utah as an adjunct professor while also working in social impact. He continues to do research on critical university studies while organizing locally around educational access and building community among Latin American peoples.

Jorge Garcia is a 1st-generation undergraduate student studying biology and molecular biology. He hopes to one day provide affordable health care to marginalized women as a physician scientist specializing in OB/GYN. He has a lot of female mentors that he respects and would love to have the privilege of giving back.

Roberto Garcia, a counseling psychology doctoral student at the University of Wisconsin-Milwaukee, researches the relationship between identity, sociopolitical context, work fulfillment, and well-being. As the network's inaugural fellow, he established a safe haven for BIPOC graduate students to connect genuinely on campus.

Juleus Ghunta is a Chevening Scholar and member of Jamaica's National Taskforce on Character Education. He holds an MA in peace studies from the University of Bradford. Juleus's work explores the links between toxic stress and academic underachievement. He is the author of *Rohan Bullkin and the Shadows.*

Vickie Godfrey is an assistant professor of literacy education in teaching, learning, and educational leadership at Eastern Kentucky University. Her research explores critical perspectives of literacy, adaptive practices in reading instruction, and preservice teacher education.

Daniela Fifi, EdD, is a doctoral graduate in art and art education at Teachers College, Columbia University, and has a master of arts in art gallery and museum studies from the University of Manchester, UK. She is currently the cultural researcher and community liaison consultant at Brooklyn Arts Council.

Alex Fink is an assistant professor in social work at Augsburg University. His main area of practice is transitioning leadership, utilizing participatory and youth-led program design, evaluation, and research to support transitions to youth leadership in youth-serving organizations. He sees teaching as an opportunity to train practitioners as change leaders.

Jessica Fisher is a primary-grade educator located in central Texas. She graduated from the University of Texas at Austin.

Virginia Gomes is a PhD student at University of Maryland, College Park. Her interests are in youth empowerment through cooperative and solidary learning for social transformation in the Latin American context. Her life-long goal is to improve education in Brazil to narrow its stark social and economic inequalities.

Desiree Gordon received a Smithsonian Institute fellowship for her work in the cultural field and is a graduate of Yale University. She curated and produced community engagement initiatives at organizations like the Brooklyn Museums, the Caribbean Cultural Center African Diaspora Institute, the Schomburg Center, and the Studio Museum in Harlem.

Anna Grigoryeva (Higher School of Economics—Moscow alumna in cultural studies) holds an MA in sociology from the European University at St. Petersburg. She is a PhD student at the International Education Policy program at the University of Maryland. Her research interests include the academic profession, young scholars, and diversity and inclusion in education.

David Gumbs is an award-winning interdisciplinary artist from the Caribbean island of Saint-Martin. He is a faculty member at the California College of the Arts (CCA) visual arts school, where he has taught interactive media, motion design, and mixed-media design since 2009.

Joey Haavik is in his 2nd year of pursuing a master's degree in international education policy and serves as UMD's graduate student government president. His research interests include global climate change education; diversity, equity, and inclusion in international student exchange; and education in emergencies.

Bemnet Habtamu understands how little society listens to youth, especially youth with disabilities, and hopes to create a more accommodating world. She currently works alongside youth in order to guide them through emotions, continuing work as an occupational therapist supporting them through how to navigate the world physically.

Jasmine Hashemi is a pre-kindergarten–4 teacher who uses research-based practices to foster a literacy-rich learning environment in her classroom. She is also a graduate student in the Mentorship, Teacher Leadership, and Professional Development program at the University of Texas at Austin.

Leandra Hernandez (PhD, Texas A&M University) is an assistant professor in the Department of Communication at the University of Utah. She enjoys teaching journalism, media, and health communication courses. She utilizes Chicana feminist approaches to inform her research, gender violence on reproductive justice, and critical communication pedagogies.

James Hoffman is a professor of language and literacy at the University of North Texas and the Meadows Chair for Excellence in Education. The primary focus of his research has been on teaching and teacher preparation. Dr. Hoffman has published more than 150 articles, books, and chapters on literacy-related topics.

Taahirah Hoosain lives in Grassy Park, Cape Town. She's a Muslim woman interested in radical change that prioritizes love, dignity, justice, and respect. She studies photography at the Cape Peninsula University of Technology. In 2021, she was chosen to be part of a youth research board for Changing the Story.

Hana Huskić holds a BA in anthropology with minors in peace & justice studies, and women, gender & sexuality studies from Gettysburg College. They are currently completing a master's degree in democracy and human rights in South East Europe in Sarajevo, Bosnia and Herzegovina.

Daniel Jones is an MA graduate from the Committee on International Relations at the University of Chicago. He holds BAs in both public policy and religious studies. His dream is to anchor himself in community and remind his generation that we are the ones *we* have been waiting for.

Lydia Kerr is a first-generation academic from a Nuyorican family in Queens (New York) and Miami (Florida). At Utah Valley University, she teaches and studies 20th- and 21st-century American literature, Latine(x) Literature, African American literature, U.S. cinema, and literary and critical theory.

Milena Klinke, a psychologist and therapeutic companion, graduated from Mackenzie Presbyterian University in São Paulo. She works with mental health therapeutic processes with youth and young adults. She specializes in group and educational activities.

Angela Kunkel-Linares is passionate about working alongside young people to create liberatory learning spaces that are centered on radically loving and reciprocal relationships. She is specifically working to create popular education opportunities where young people can engage with strategies that disrupt the embodiment of White supremacy and capitalism.

Beatrice Kyle is a primary educator in North Texas. She graduated from the University of Texas at Austin.

Catherine Lammert is an assistant professor in the Department of Teacher Education and anchor faculty in literacy teacher education in the College of Education at Texas Tech University. Her research focuses on translating learning theory into practice-based teacher preparation.

Paulina S. Lim is a doctoral student in the Clinical Psychology Program at the University of Wisconsin-Milwaukee. Paulina's research focuses on pediatric psychology and the impact of child health on parental and familial well-being. As a network founding member, she established a fellowship in which graduate students received payment for their anti-racist work.

Grácia Lopes Lima is a teacher and PhD in education from the University of São Paulo. She is the founder of Projeto Cala-Boca Já Morreu—porque nós também temos o que dizer! and currently works with consulting in educommunication.

Jing Lin is professor of international education policy at University of Maryland, College Park. She has done extensive research and published 16 books and numerous articles on education in East Asia and Africa; peace and environmental education; religion, spirituality, and education; and contemplative and holistic education.

Maria Linares or Mari is currently a student at Utah Valley University studying social media and digital outreach. She is also the Communication fellow for the UVU Center for Social Impact.

Maha Malik holds a master of arts degree in international education from George Washington University and a bachelor of science in public health. Her research interests include education for sustainable development, global environmental dispositions, and the impact of climate change on education.

Julie Mazur is a 4th-grade reading and writing teacher in Miami Beach, FL. She works with an academically and culturally diverse group of learners.

Thea Mennas is 20 years old and currently a youth organizer of the Student Assembly within *Bottomup*. Also a 2nd-year law student, she enjoys research and, in her quiet time, a slice of cake and tea with a book.

Matt Meyer, currently secretary general of the International Peace Research Association, was a New York City–based high school social studies teacher and Alternative High School's multicultural coordinator.

Shue-kei Joanna Mok is a doctoral student in international education policy at University of Maryland, College Park. Her research critically explores the concept of citizenships (from legal to planetary) through arts. Some current projects include visual representations of nature and climate change, and (re)connecting with nature through creative writing.

Jacqueline Nguyen, PhD, is an associate professor in educational psychology at the University of Wisconsin-Milwaukee. Her research is on cultural and contextual factors in adolescent/emerging adult development, cultural identity development, and sense of belonging as individuals adapt to various sociocultural environments. She is lead co-convener for the network.

Theresa Nguyen graduated from the University of Texas at Austin with high honors in 2019. She graduated with a bachelor of science in applied learning and development with a specialization in literacy and a focus on intervention and vulnerable children. She has been an elementary teacher for more than 2 years.

Christina M. Noto grew up in Cooperstown, NY, and graduated from Gettysburg College in 2019 with a BA in history and minors in women, gender & sexuality studies, and peace & justice studies. After graduation, Christina completed an alternative teacher certification program and taught for 3 years in Washington DC. She now lives in Denver with her dog, Quincy.

Morgan Pence is a student and passionate youth worker interested in understanding young people's lived experiences through psychological, societal, and cultural lenses. She is a strong advocate for mental health, is certified in youth mental health first aid, and is driven to create change within the educational system.

Griselda Rodriguez-Solomon, PhD, is a Black-Dominican mother, wife, and professor at the City College of New York. She earned her PhD in sociology from Syracuse University. Griselda has conducted extensive research on anti-Black racism among Dominicans. Along with her twin sister, Miguelina Rodriguez, PhD, they are the Brujas of Brooklyn.

Miguelina Rodriguez, PhD, has many years of experience teaching urban studies as a professor. She holds a PhD in public policy from Rutgers University; her dissertation was a critical ethnographic study on the gentrification in Washington Heights (NYC) and its effects on second-generation Dominicans.

Zane Rodulfo completed his graduate study in jazz studies at New York University and holds bachelor of music degrees in both jazz performance and ethnomusicology from the Oberlin Conservatory of Music. He has performed at illustrious venues such as Jazz at Lincoln Center.

Helene Rousseau is a cofounder of Bottomup and has an interest in dialogical learning and the implementation of culturally responsive teaching. She loves curating resources and materials that are relevant to youth that can mediate between grasping difficult sociological concepts and furthering their knowledge to promote a better world.

Hannah Filizola Ruiz is a queer Latine of Brazilian and Mexican descent. They are the Community Engaged Learning & Research Fellow at the UVU Center for Social Impact and graduated from Utah Valley University in spring 2023. Hannah also hosts the Critical Mass podcast for their fellowship.

Jordan Scanlon is a practitioner in the field of education in emergencies and protracted crises, with a focus on gender equality. She earned her MA in international education policy from the University of Maryland, College Park, and dual BA degrees in English and communication arts from Salisbury University.

Natalie M. Schneider is a management science PhD candidate at the University of Wisconsin-Milwaukee whose research addresses diversity issues in the workplace. She served as the head librarian in developing the database of anti-racism resources.

Ashley Visagie is a Canon Collins scholar and a cofounder of Bottomup. Ashley has a deep concern for youth in South Africa who suffer because of the unjust education system and seeks to contest deficit narratives. He is optimistic that a fairer and more just world is possible through collective action.

Emmanuel Wanjala is a doctoral student in the International Education Policy program at the University of Maryland. His research interests include the internationalization of higher education, youth empowerment, climate change mitigation, and sustainable development.

Hakim Mohandas Amani Williams, proud son of Laventille, Trinidad, is the Daria L. & Eric J. Wallach Professor of Peace and Justice Studies, and associate professor of Africana studies at Gettysburg College. He completed his doctorate in international educational development and peace education at Teachers College, Columbia University. For more info, see www.hakimwilliams.com.

Kaiya Woller studied youth studies and family social sciences at the University of Minnesota Twin Cities. Her current work focuses on disrupting school push-out rates by engaging with young people's passions and joys. She centers her work around pride in learning while challenging detrimental effects of the Western educational systems.

Index